The
Caravan
Handbook

Dedication

This book is dedicated to my late father, John Wickersham, who lived and breathed the outdoor life. Widely accepted in the Industry as the caravanning guru (having written many notable publications, including the *Caravan Manual*, *Motorcaravan Manual* and *Build Your Own Motorcaravan*), what he didn't know about caravanning wasn't worth knowing. However, for me, dad was the catalyst that inspired my passion for travel and adventure, building a multitude of ever-lasting memories. It is a privilege to share that journey and impart this finely-honed knowledge with other like-minded caravanners.

ISBN 978-1-8384043-0-7

Printed in Malta

Front cover photo: Courtesy of the Caravan & Motorhome Club.
Rear cover photo: Courtesy of Bailey of Bristol.

The Caravan Handbook

Sammy Faircloth

ALL YOU NEED TO KNOW IN ONE CONCISE HANDBOOK

Contents

Chapter One

Purchasing a caravan

▲ Whether you buy new or second-hand, there are many points to consider when buying a caravan.

If you decide to buy a second-hand caravan, what precautionary measures should be taken? For example, how can you establish that a caravan being offered for sale privately is owned by the vendor and not subject to a hire-purchase agreement?

Alternatively, if you're in the fortunate position of being able to buy a brand-new model, what points should one bear in mind? Issues like these are discussed in this chapter.

Buying a caravan

Not surprisingly, buying a caravan is not the same as buying a car. For instance, a caravan doesn't have a mandatory registration document. This means that if you're looking at a second-hand model, its date of manufacture is often hard to establish. Moreover, there is no official MoT test to confirm the integrity of a caravan. You must also be absolutely sure that a pre-owned 'van is being offered for sale by its rightful owner.

These issues don't arise, of course, if you intend to purchase a brand-new caravan from a dealer. However, choosing a dealer isn't quite as simple a task as you might imagine. For example, an impressive discount from a caravan specialist whose headquarters are a long way from your home carries a problem that doesn't arise when you're buying a car. If a warranty repair is needed at a later date, you will usually have to take the caravan all the way back to its original supplier. It's not the same with a car, where warranty work can be done at any franchise dealership. Also be aware that factory warranties differ from one manufacturer to another.

Matters like these are discussed in this chapter. In addition, the purchase of a new or a pre-owned model is considered in detail.

Which caravan?

Before even venturing out and looking at caravans, sit down and write a list of what you want from the caravan. Are you looking at using it all-year-round or just for the summer; are you yearning to get back to basics and go off-grid*? These are all questions that you need to ask yourself.

Establish how many people you intend to accommodate as this will help decide on which berth to purchase – 2 berth, 4 berth and so on. Single axle or twin axle? Twin axles tend to be the larger berth caravans, but some couples just like the extra space that they offer. Wider caravans are becoming more popular with 8-foot-wide models available on the market. These are great for long stay holidays, but could be quite challenging towing down some country lanes in counties like Devon and Cornwall.

Always check that your tow vehicle is compatible to tow a single/twin axle or 8-foot-wide caravan *(see Chapter 3)*.

Awnings can offer much needed additional sleeping space and are discussed in more detail in Chapter 5.

* Off-grid means to camp without a hook-up supply and other luxuries like washroom facilities.

▶ *8-foot-wide caravans offer increased internal space, but might be a challenge for a novice to tow down narrow lanes.*

▲ It is important to test the comfort and size of the beds.

Layouts

Consider the ideal layout for your requirements - this is a very personal thing and there is no right or wrong. It maybe that a fixed bed is a priority, avoiding the need to make up a bed every evening and dismantling it in the morning. Young families tend to like bunk beds, but these may not be ideal for growing teenagers. Test the beds for comfort and size as the last thing you want is your feet dangling over the end.

Washroom facilities can be located at the rear of a caravan, as a central room separating the sleeping area from the living area or as a central side washroom, which is more traditional. Always make a point of sitting on the toilet or standing in the shower as size and space may be an issue.

Kitchen layouts may be important for those that like to cook, particularly worktop space, cooking equipment and refrigerators. Young families may wish to avoid having the hob near the entrance door for safety reasons.

Upholstery can sometimes sway a person's decision. There are some great companies out there that can re-upholster the cushions and curtains if you don't like

the pattern or the cushions are damaged. If you like to take your pet away with you or you have children, then you may want to steer clear of lighter fabrics or leather.

Lightweight caravans

Lightweight caravans or compact caravans have been around for a while, but there is an increasing resurgence for these styles of caravans. Being lightweight is a definite advantage for those with a driving licence issued from 1st January 1997 as this allows you to tow a trailer up to 750kg Maximum Authorised Mass *(MAM – this is discussed in more detail in Chapter 3).*

These tiny caravans can lessen fuel consumption and don't require as much storage space, meaning that some may fit in a garage. Also, you do not need a huge car to tow a lightweight caravan, but always check the tow car and caravan relationship before purchasing *(see Chapter 3 for more detail).*

Here are some examples of lightweight caravans:

Pop-top caravans

As the title implies, it is quite simply a caravan with a roof that pops up, allowing standing room/headroom inside the caravan. Some popular examples of pop-tops are the Eriba and Silver Evasion.

▶ The pop-up roof on the Eriba offers increased standing room inside this small caravan.

▲ *Micro caravans are compact and lightweight making them ideal for small tow cars.*

Folding caravans

On the road they look like a trailer, but once erected they become a caravan with solid walls. The roof is lifted using the end panels to support it, then the side panels are lifted into place. Examples of folding caravans are Gobur Carousel, Rapido and Esterel to name a few.

Micro caravans

These are more traditional style caravans, but on a much smaller scale and lightweight. Companies, like Freedom, have been making lightweight caravans for over 30 years. The larger manufacturers are now starting to produce similar small caravans to meet the demand.

Teardrop caravans

The name for this caravan is derived from its unique shape. They certainly have a following and can be quite funky looking, like the T@B Mexican Sunset. These compact caravans can have limited room inside and can be quite minimalist.

▶ *The T@B Mexican Sunset has a funky design with its teardrop shape, porthole windows and bright decals.*

▲ *Fifth Wheelers are ideal for those that own a truck.*

Heavyweight caravans

For that home-from-home feel, then some of the heavyweight caravans will tick your box, but you will need deep pockets and the right vehicle to tow them. With slide-out sides, it can feel like you are in an apartment on wheels. Not really the weekend away vehicle, but ideal for long stays, seasonal pitches or those that spend a lot of time at the racetracks.

▼ *Look out for the Surveyor that is often displayed at The National Motorhome & Campervan Show in Peterborough.*

Fifth Wheelers

These are an American style recreational vehicle built for the British market and use a fifth wheel hitch that is built into the bed of a truck.

American style caravans

The big daddies in the caravan world, sitting high up from the ground and with slide out sides, they simply dwarf most British caravans. Definitely suited to the large American Freeways, you would have to plan your route carefully. They really are a luxury weekend retreat and would be ideal on a seasonal pitch *(see Chapter 2)*.

Buying new

Choosing a dealer
Most dealers specialise in a particular brand
of caravan, although this often extends
to include products from two or three
manufacturers or importers. In other words,
if you merely call at your nearest supplier,
you're only going to see a small selection of
caravans currently on the market.

▼ *Most dealers tend to specialise in a particular
marque – although some retail new caravans from
two or three manufacturers.*

Models held in stock

Occasionally a dealer might have an
example of the model you want back
at their base. However, in reality that
is often unlikely because to stock
every model with all the different
permutations of internal layout and
equipment would take up a large
amount of space on a dealer's
forecourt.

If you look at a 'Buyer's Guide' in one of
the monthly caravan magazines you'll see
there are around 18 different marques made
in Britain and nearly ten imported brands.
To be strictly accurate, it's true that in recent
years the Swift Group has manufactured
caravans bearing the brand names of Abbey,
Ace, Bessacarr, Sterling and Swift (Abbey and
Ace are no longer manufactured); just as the
Erwin Hymer Group Ltd (formerly the Explorer
Group) has been manufacturing models
under the brand names Buccaneer, Compass,

Crown and Elddis. However, there's plenty of
choice even if there are less manufacturers
today than 20 years ago.

Moreover, these two major
manufacturing groups retain individuality
in different models, just as Volkswagen
did when major takeovers brought cars
like Skoda, Seat, and Porsche into a major
conglomerate. Notice, too, that if a caravan
dealer is franchised to sell Swift Group
Caravans, this doesn't mean the dealership
will retail all the 'badged models' coming

from this North-Eastern manufacturer. So, to see what's on offer, a good way to gain a broad picture is to purchase several of the major monthly magazines. For instance, *Caravan Magazine* and *Practical Caravan* all publish monthly test reports and there are back-issue departments so that you can catch-up on reviews that you've missed.

In other words, if you're prepared to get hold of sales literature and to read test reports in magazines, a 'phone call to the manufacturers or importers will reveal where different dealers are located.

Alternatively, this information is normally given on manufacturers' websites. This enables you to see a product 'for real'. However, there's another approach to consider, namely a visit to one of the major indoor exhibitions or outdoor shows.

Getting model details and the addresses of manufacturers

Most monthly magazines include 'Buyers' Guides' in which key information is laid out in tabular form. This allows you to single out models which meet your particular needs using criteria such as weight, size, bed accommodation and so on. These magazines also include the addresses of manufacturers, thereby enabling you to send away for brochures. In addition, the majority of manufacturers run websites giving details of models as well.

▼ *A large selection of caravans are on show at indoor exhibitions such as the Motorhome & Caravan Show held at the NEC, Birmingham in October.*

Buying at an exhibition

The two largest caravan exhibitions are currently:

1. **The Motorhome & Caravan Show**, which is held at the National Exhibition Centre (NEC), Birmingham, in October.

2. **The Caravan, Camping & Motorhome Show**, which is held at the National Exhibition Centre, Birmingham, in February.

In addition, there are regional shows held in cities like Glasgow and Manchester, although these are organised on a smaller scale. There are also several outdoor shows where caravans are on sale and details of venues and dates are given in caravan magazines. Typically, these are held at agricultural show grounds or racecourses so there's plenty of room to show the exhibits.

By visiting a large event you can look closely at products and make your assessments. You'll also find that on caravan manufacturers' stands there are sales people from several approved dealers, together with staff from the factory as well.

You can also place an order at a caravan show, which is different from arrangements at motor shows where dealer representatives are seldom in attendance.

▶ *Sometimes there are special prices or 'add-on' accessories when orders are taken for caravans at an exhibition.*

Sales strategies

Not surprisingly, if you appear to be interested in a caravan displayed on a stand, a dealer is likely to approach and strike up a conversation. They will often enquire if you are already a caravan owner, and for anyone visiting a show as a potential purchaser, here is a good opportunity to conduct business. There may also be 'show discounts', either in the form of a price reduction or the inclusion of additional accessories as a buying incentive. Overall, it's a good way to compare prices and products.

Dealer location

First, you should establish where a sales person's base is located, because that is usually where you'll have to visit in order to collect the 'van you've ordered. Equally, you will usually have to return to the dealer conducting the sale if warranty work is needed at a later date. So, if you get the best-selling price from a dealer situated 200 miles from your home, the cost of travel to and from the base can quickly eliminate the apparent benefit of an attractive price.

Delivery

Secondly, you should appreciate that when purchases are 'signed and sealed' it is often many months before a caravan is built; supplied to the dealer; given its pre-delivery inspection (PDI) and made ready for collection. Orders taken at shows held early in the New Year are not always ready for use in time for Easter. Delivery is certainly a point to discuss with the dealer.

Technical issues

Lastly, you should check all the technical points raised in the accompanying chapters before placing an order. Some sales specialists are well-versed in details about their products and a few might own a caravan themselves. On the other hand, there are others whose understanding of technical detail is woefully limited. At a show, this need not be a serious handicap because there's usually a technical member of staff in attendance from the factory. So, don't be reticent to pose important questions; a less-knowledgeable salesperson should be able to provide answers by consulting the manufacturer's representative.

▼ *Dealers and members of the Caravanning Press are shown the following year's models in July.*

Delivery calendar

The fact that most new caravans are ordered rather than purchased directly from a dealer's forecourt inevitably means there is usually a waiting period.

Furthermore, the caravan industry calendar means that new models are usually launched every year. As it often turns out, changes might be cosmetic rather than radical but there are yearly changes nonetheless.

Many manufacturers finish making the prototypes of models to appear the following year as early as June or July. These are then unveiled to members of the caravan Press in July.

After this, one of the first trade shows falls in September; public exhibitions follow in late autumn.

Without doubt, the annual late autumn exhibition held at the NEC, Birmingham, in October is one of the best times to order a new caravan if you want to ensure delivery early next spring. Orders placed here set the manufacturing pattern over the winter period, even though many caravan factories have a traditional extended shut-down at Christmas/New Year.

Then there are the spring shows accompanied by spells of frenetic energy on the production lines. Some deliveries can get delayed quite considerably – partly because many manufacturers produce caravans in batches according to model. Hence all the twin-axle models might occupy the production line for a week, thereby putting on 'hold' the manufacture of single-axle models.

Spring is always busy both at the factories and dealerships. Even caravan workshops are stretched to the limits as customers arrange annual pre-season servicing.

Annual post-season sales

With the advent of new models not far away, there are typically late autumn sales where dealers make strenuous efforts to clear stock in readiness for new models. Some of the mark-down prices are notable, although for most people the summer has passed and the idea of caravanning with winter approaching acts as a purchasing disincentive. However, there are usually bargains at the close of each season.

Buyer's Tip
Timing a purchase

When planning to purchase a new model, be mindful of the caravan industry's annual roundabout. Arrange the dates with care so that your intended purchase will arrive well before your first planned trip. Unexpected delivery delays are not unusual.

Dealer 'specials'

As a way of boosting sales, several large retailers make arrangements with a manufacturer to produce a model specific to their dealership. Typically, this is a model already in the line-up, albeit with the addition of a new name; different external decals; a package of extras like a gas barbecue point on the side; an additional chest of drawers inside, and so on.

Similar techniques are employed, of course, by car dealers – particularly with high-volume hatchback models. The offer of something 'special' which includes 'complimentary' accessory items acts as a buying incentive.

How this strategy affects a resale at a later date is a little less clear. In truth, the benefits bestowed by a few 'add-ons' is unlikely to enhance a trade-in price. Moreover, a model associated with a particular dealer might not be so favourably viewed when offered as a trade-in to a rival supplier. Apart from that, there's little against buying a dealer special, especially if you like some of the extra items being thrown-in as part of the package.

Warranty terms and conditions

When considering new models for a shortlist, don't forget to compare manufacturers' warranties too. These differ in various ways, especially with regard to the period over which the external fabric of a caravan is covered against leaks arising from faults in construction. This particular affliction is often referred to as 'water ingress'.

Over the years, some workmanship has been disappointing, especially if it has led to damage caused by water ingress. When a survey undertaken in 1999 by the Caravan & Motorhome Club produced disturbing

Warranty conditions

You should take note what has to be done in order for a warranty to remain valid. As a rule, there's a stipulation that the 'van has to have a full service at regular calendar intervals at an approved workshop. Overlook this at your peril. Equally, you should establish what is deemed to be an 'approved workshop' in the eyes of the manufacturer.

findings, manufacturers responded and standards improved. Moreover, the confidence of some constructors led to warranties against water ingress through manufacturing faults being extended from three to six years. One manufacturer, Swift, is now offering a 25-year water ingress warranty on some of its models, but be sure to read the small print to make sure you are covered.

Buying second-hand

Private purchases

Specialist magazines and local newspapers usually contain a classified advertisement section devoted to caravans. Purchasing via the internet is becoming more popular too. There are certainly some very good caravans on sale privately – as well as plenty of poorer products. The term *caveat emptor*, or buyer beware, is particularly relevant here.

In truth, every transaction has to be evaluated individually and it is quite impossible to give more than a few guidelines. Suggestions include these points:

» Establish when a caravan was last serviced and ask to see the signed service schedule to ascertain the extent of the work undertaken.

» Ask to see approval certificates that the gas and electrical systems have been checked and deemed safe.

» Ask when the last professional damp check was carried out using an electrically operated damp meter and ask to see the certificate.

» Where possible, follow up the CRiS registration check described on pages 23 and 24.

Checking a caravan's credentials

A particular worry is establishing whether a caravan being offered for sale is wholly owned by its vendor. On the one hand it might still be the subject of a hire purchase or loan agreement; on the other, it might be a 'van that has been stolen. This is where the CRiS scheme is helpful, for an explanation of which see pages 23 and 24.

In practice these recommendations are easy to list but you'll soon find that many caravans are never serviced professionally. Others have been given a cursory service but the 'van is returned without any documentation outlining the extent of the work carried out. Equally, there are thousands of caravans that have never been damp-checked with a meter. Nor, for that matter, are many pre-owned models sold with certificates from appropriately qualified gas and electrical engineers to verify that their supply systems are in safe working order.

In acknowledgement of this, a cautionary purchaser might wisely decide to avoid anything not supported by this kind of documentation. On the other hand, if the price is attractive and you are prepared to get this work done as soon as you take ownership,

◀ When purchasing a pre-owned caravan, ask to see the results of its last damp check conducted at a service centre.

you might decide to proceed. There are certainly some cared-for caravans on sale that have been lovingly cherished and kept immaculately clean by fastidious owners. Many pre-owned examples like this have also brought much pleasure to their subsequent owners. Conversely, there are also appalling purchases that have proved to be disastrous. So, all I can add is: look closely, compare critically – and *caveat emptor*.

Dealer pre-owned models

Obviously, there are inherent risks when purchasing privately, whereas buying a pre-owned caravan from a dealer generally provides some post-purchase support if a subsequent problem arises. Admittedly, the degree of cover offered by a warranty on a second-hand caravan varies from dealer to dealer but there's far more likelihood of after-sale support. Needless to say, that's

Inclusion of accessories

Most dealers sell their pre-owned stock without accessories. Not surprisingly, a dealer will willingly direct you towards the accessory shop when you realise you need cutlery, crockery, a leisure battery, water containers and costly items like an awning. In contrast, private sellers often include these accessories as part of the sale. Admittedly some items might not be included where the private seller is purchasing another caravan in its place, but things like awnings might not fit the new model, so they tend to be included in the transaction.

one reason why the asking price is usually higher than it is on private transactions.

A further benefit of purchasing from a dealer is the fact that a caravan offered for sale is likely to have been serviced and fully checked over. In addition, a post-1992 CRiS registration transfer of ownership would normally be carried out on your behalf – a topic dealt with in the CRiS section later in this chapter. However, don't expect to find accessory equipment like an awning or water containers included in the package. They might be included in private sales, but at a dealers you normally get directed to the on-site accessory shop.

◀ *There's usually some form of after-sales warranty accompanying pre-owned caravans sold by a dealer.*

▲ *Dealer prices might be higher than private sales, but you can insist that the caravan is sold fully serviced before collection.*

All in all, many purchasers prefer the support that accompanies a dealer sale; it's just that you normally have to pay slightly more to secure the additional peace of mind.

Caravan auctions

Broadly speaking, caravan auctions are on two levels. On the one hand there are small-town affairs conducted by a local auctioneer and estate agent. Though comparatively unusual, these are sometimes staged at a caravan storage centre, near a factory or a dealership that has gone into liquidation. Also, there are the online auction sites like eBay.

Sales are also conducted by a specialist like British Car Auctions (BCA). This company's occasional 'Leisure and Caravan' auctions have taken place at several of the 20 or so BCA centres around the country but nowadays most are held online. BCA's online-only caravan and motorhome sales allow customers to bid and buy safely and remotely via the BCA Buyer app or BCA Online from wherever they may be located.

While the popular image of auctions depicts a situation where there's little purchaser protection, this is not necessarily accurate. Legislation affords more support than is often appreciated. Occasionally there are even brand-new caravans included in the sale as a result of company liquidations. Not surprisingly, purchase prices are often attractive.

Models no longer in production

There are many familiar names among the caravans that are no longer in production. These include the following, although there are many more lesser-known brands: ABI, A-Line, Astral, Auto-Sleeper, Avondale,

Berkeley, Bluebird, Caravan International, Carlight, Castleton, Cavalier, Cheltenham, Churchill, Coronet, Cosalt, Cotswold, Craftsman, Cygnet, Deanline, Eterniti, Europa, Farlander, Fisher, Fleetwood, Forest, Knowsley, Lynton, Mardon, Mustang, Panther, Pemberton, Robin, Royale, Safari, Silverline, Sprite, Sovereign, Stealth, Sunseeker, Thomson, Trophy, Vanroyce, Viking Fibreline, Viscount and Windrush.

Imported models

With caravans being built in several European countries, some potential owners enquire whether they can import a model independently. While this is certainly possible there are a number of disadvantages to bear in mind.

Firstly, the caravan door is normally situated on the opposite side to suit left-hand driving. When parked by the roadside in Britain, this presents a possible danger when you step from the 'van. However, there are exceptions, as the photo below reveals.

In addition, an imported caravan might not comply with British Standards. For instance, all UK-manufactured caravans now have to comply with the Furniture and Furnishings Fire (Safety) Regulations 1988 – which means that any foam in mattresses has to be fire-retardant. This requirement is not obligatory in all European countries.

As regards the gas supply system, some foreign models used to be fitted with different gas jets in appliances. That was because these caravans operated on a different operating pressure and were fitted with a gas regulator to achieve that setting. However, since 2003 there has been greater standardisation in respect of European gas systems, as described in Chapter Twelve.

In practice, Continental caravans imported into the UK by specialist companies are often fitted with items

▼ *This imported Knaus caravan has been purpose-built for the UK market, as the position of its door confirms.*

Imported caravans

Whereas some imported caravans have much to commend them, they are seldom fitted with a grill. Our friends from overseas seem not to have discovered the pleasure of toast. Equally, many imported models lack carpet, and while a vinyl floor covering is distinctly practical many British caravanners prefer a carpeted floor. And not surprisingly, a mains installation will have different switches, sockets and control units, unless the importing dealer has arranged for these to be replaced to suit British owners.

On the other hand, some caravans, especially Scandinavian models, are fitted with a greater level of thermal insulation to suit lower winter temperatures.

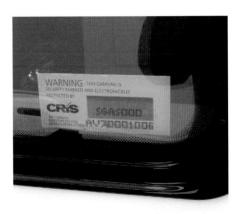

▲ Since its inception, the CRiS registration scheme has involved etching an identification number on a caravan's windows.

that British caravanners usually want. So, whereas the door position is unlikely to be changed, if you like a particular model built abroad it is better to buy through a specialist who carries out modifications, such as changing a cooker and altering mains electricity fittings.

Caravan Registration Identification Scheme (CRiS)

Unlike cars and other motor-driven vehicles, caravans had no registration document until the CRiS initiative was launched in 1992. This scheme was created by HPI Ltd working in partnership with the National Caravan Council (NCC). There is no mandatory registration but all new caravans launched with National Caravan Council badge accreditation were included from 1992 onwards.

The visible evidence of CRiS registration is given on each window, where the caravan's identification number is etched. Other features which developed later were:

1997
from July of that year, all new caravans from NCC member-manufacturers were fitted with a hidden electronic tag that carries the VIN (Vehicle Identification Number).

1999
from October of that year, owners of pre-1992 caravans and owners of imported models could also register them on the scheme. Points about this are as follows:

>> There is a small registration fee.

» A VIN is allocated.

» A DIY etching kit is supplied for marking the 17-digit code on the windows.

» At the time of initial registration, a DIY electronic tag can be supplied for an additional charge.

The benefits of CRiS are especially evident to anyone purchasing a pre-owned caravan; these are explained in the panel to the right.

Finally, when purchasing a CRiS-registered caravan, change of ownership procedures are as follows:

1. A private seller has to complete the Notification of Sale or Transfer (CVR7) section on the registration document and send it to CRiS.

2. The private seller should pass the rest of the document (CVR6) to the purchaser.

3. You, as purchaser, must then fill out the Notification of Changes section (CVR8) on the document and send it to CRiS. A small charge is payable.

Customer Handover

Before a caravan is driven away by its new owner(s), there's an important routine called the 'customer handover'. This is not to be confused with a 'Pre-delivery Inspection', which is a thorough inspection of a caravan by the dealer, to include a deep clean before handing over to the customer. In addition to the 'purchasing paperwork', this session includes a detailed explanation showing how everything works. For a first-time

CRiS benefits for buyers and owners

Through the CRiS scheme, caravan keepers have 'access to a vital register that can help protect the security of their caravans and help the police in returning stolen caravans to their rightful owners'.

Alternatively, if you want to purchase a second-hand model, you can verify that it hasn't been stolen, or can find out if any hire purchase payments are still outstanding. As a potential purchaser you can pay a small fee for a history check. All you have to do is to submit the caravan's 17-digit VIN code, a description of the 'van, and the name and address of the seller. This will then be checked with the database to see that everything matches.

But note: CRiS won't give away confidential information about the owner – merely whether your information and theirs matches.

You will also be able to establish if the caravan is:

» Currently recorded as stolen.

» Officially written-off by an insurance company.

» Still the subject of a loan from a finance house.

◀ *The customer handover is an important routine explaining how everything works and signing the purchasing paperwork.*

Additional Costs

Owning a caravan does come with additional costs. Here is a checklist of additional costs of which most will be covered in more detail later on in the book:

✓ Tow bar fitting *(see Chapter 3)*

✓ Number plate for rear of caravan

✓ Towing mirrors *(see Chapter 6)*

✓ Storage costs – at home, at a commercial storage unit, on a farm or campsite storage *(see Chapter 2)*

✓ Insurance and breakdown cover

✓ Annual Habitation Service *(see Chapter 14)*

✓ Gas cylinder, Leisure battery, water pump and fresh/waste water containers, 25m hook-up cable *(see Chapter 4)*

✓ Security – hitch locks, wheel locks *(see Chapter 4)*

✓ Alarms/Trackers *(see Chapter 4)*

owner this usually takes at least an hour. Sometimes it's longer, especially if the customer needs help when coupling-up their new caravan prior to departure.

Some dealerships, like Salop Leisure, offer the customer the loan of a video camera in order to record the whole handover process, allowing for them to listen and not be distracted writing things down. At a later date, a video link(s) is sent to them to peruse at their leisure.

The all-important handover may not be offered through a private sale; however, some might be lucky to get a diligent seller.

Chapter Two

Storing your caravan

▲ *There are many commercial compounds all over Britain offering a secure place to store your caravan all-year round.*

A point that often worries potential purchasers is where to keep their caravan. In practice this isn't the problem that many people imagine and seven suggestions are proposed in this chapter. There's certainly more scope than you might have thought.

A caravan usually takes up more space than the car that tows it, so storing it between holiday trips is a matter that needs some thought. Here are a few ideas you might like to consider:

>> On hard standing alongside your house.

>> In a commercial compound specifically designed for caravan storage.

>> At an indoor facility intended for storing caravans.

>> In a storage compound at a privately owned caravan site or a club site.

>> On a short-term seasonal pitch on a club or privately owned site.

>> On a farm, either inside a barn or outdoors.

>> At a storage facility abroad near a venue you return to on a regular basis.

▼ *Motorised movers like this Truma model are indispensable for some owners.*

Don't let storage put you off buying a caravan. There are caravanners who live in high-rise flats, in split-level houses on the side of a steep hill, or in properties where there's a dreadfully tight chicane in the driveway. Some own a house that offers sufficient parking space but they cannot contemplate reversing a caravan into the allotted position. A number of caravanners solve this by purchasing a battery-driven pulling device or have an electrically driven motorised mover fitted. Where there's a will there's a way.

So, let's look at the plus and minus points about different storage solutions.

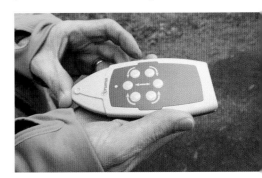

▲ *Most 12V motorised movers are operated using a cord-free hand control.*

Alongside your house

Of the seven alternative storage possibilities, parking a caravan alongside your house is the only one that doesn't involve a fee. On the other hand, this isn't always permissible. For instance, there's sometimes a covenant that a property developer imposed when your house was originally built. Covenants occasionally forbid the storage of a caravan, and these restrictions are often established on open-plan estates where front gardens are unfenced to give an overall impression of space.

Notwithstanding the existence of covenants, there are instances where stored caravans are screened from sight alongside a house, and when this is done discreetly neighbours seldom raise an objection. Common sense usually prevails, although there's no doubt that a conspicuously parked caravan can occasionally spoil the views of other residents.

In addition to covenant restrictions, it is equally likely that a Local Authority's permission will be required to park a caravan on Council-owned property. And be aware that in both these examples of possible restrictions, the references relate to an empty caravan; it stands to reason that using a caravan for additional permanent accommodation would not meet with approval.

With these points in mind, it should also be pointed out that several Acts of Parliament do permit a homeowner to store a caravan on their driveway in certain circumstances. The legal departments of both The Camping and Caravanning Club and the Caravan & Motorhome Club are able to provide members with more information about rights and restrictions.

▼ *Some caravans can be camouflaged using full covers making them less of an eyesore.*

▼ *On a compact housing estate, a large parked caravan can spoil the views of neighbours.*

When restrictions are absent, there are both advantages and disadvantages to storage at your place of residence. These are:

Advantages

» You can keep an eye on your caravan.

» It's easy to keep it clean on a regular basis and you can also heat the interior periodically when winter temperatures plummet or damp weather arrives.

» Within reason a caravan can provide useful storage space for summer chairs, a picnic table and your patio sunshade.

» If fitted with an electric moving device, a caravan can be positioned alongside your home with impressive precision.

Disadvantages

» When screening is difficult or if there's no access to the side or rear of your house, a caravan stuck in the front garden is not an asset to your home's appearance.

» If you take a holiday in your caravan, everyone in the area knows you're not at home. Indeed, a caravan can become a conspicuous landmark and you don't have to be a professional housebreaker to spot that a 'van is missing from its normal resting place.

So, there might be better storage strategies.

▼ *With a motorised mover, a caravan can be placed alongside your home with considerable precision.*

Commercial storage compounds

If you search for 'Caravan Storage' using your internet search engine, you're likely to see addresses of commercial storage compounds. Furthermore, if you're a member of the Caravan & Motorhome Club a list of storage specialists is available free from the club headquarters.

Outdoor storage centres vary a great deal in respect of security, service and price. It's no secret that caravan theft has been a growing problem and some commercial storage centres have security fences, alarms, closed-circuit cameras and a resident warden living on site. That's one extreme. At the other end of the spectrum, you'll find a few compounds merely protected by a five-bar gate and a tractor.

▲ *Security at many high-quality commercial storage venues includes CCTV camera systems.*

Caravan Storage Site Owners' Association

Recognising the security problem, a professional trade body was instituted in 1999 to represent caravan storage owners. Known as CaSSOA (Caravan Storage Site Owners' Association), this specialist organisation demands a high level of security at member storage facilities, and the growing national chain of approved centres is now in excess of 460 members.

An inspector checks all storage sites that apply for membership and if the venue meets the Association's criteria, a gold, silver or bronze badge is allocated depending on the level of security. This takes note of the site's location, protection from the elements, security, safety and control of access. An item like a sound, secure perimeter fence, for example, is deemed essential.

The scheme is currently supported by some specialist caravan insurers and in some instances policy-holders are given a discount if their caravan is stored at one of the Association's accredited sites.

On the CaSSOA website there's a search facility to find your nearest approved storage centre(s), either by carrying out a countywide search or by using your post code. For information visit *www.cassoa.co.uk* or telephone 0843 216 5802.

Not surprisingly, insurance companies ask for detailed information about the place where clients park their caravan, and some storage specialists fall far short of the minimum level of security that the insurers specify. So, check this point most carefully before towing your 'van to a compound and parting with money.

And one more point, not all owners using a storage facility choose one that's close to their home. Owners who particularly like to return to the same area year after year sometimes prefer to select a storage site near their holiday venue in order to reduce towing distances.

Once again, there are advantages and disadvantages to this storage option:

▲ At this storage centre, caravans can be delivered to and retrieved from the adjacent touring park whenever the client requires.

▼ Addresses of commercial storage compounds are often listed on the Yellow Pages website.

Advantages

>> Your caravan is not taking up precious garden space at home.

>> The level of security on a high-quality storage facility is likely to be much higher than it is at your home.

>> Some storage specialists offer additional services like caravan cleaning. A few can carry out servicing work as well.

Disadvantages

>> Out of sight, out of mind. Once the 'van is sited, some owners completely forget to remove their battery for winter charging. Equally, end-of-season jobs like the water drain-down are overlooked.

>> If you want to collect something from your caravan, or perhaps you need to do repairs, it isn't always easy to gain access to a storage compound at short notice.

▲ *Indoor storage ensures that a caravan is kept out of inclement weather.*

Commercial indoor storage

Specialists offering indoor storage for caravans and motorhomes are relatively uncommon. However, there are a few in Britain and one of the largest is Calvers Caravan Storage in Bedfordshire. Not only are the caravans here owned by UK residents from all over the country; there are also clients from as far away as South Africa and the United States of America. These are people who enjoy touring the United Kingdom and other European countries but who prefer the versatility and flexibility of a caravan rather than stopping at hotels.

Taking this particular storage centre as an example, caravans are closely packed inside darkened and thermally insulated storage buildings. Items like the upholstery or curtains are thus unlikely to fade and the caravan is not exposed to the extremes of weather.

The intricate task of manoeuvring a caravan into or out of its bay is undertaken by personnel at the storage centre and clients simply drive up to a parking area near the entrance to collect or return their caravan. During a six-month or twelve-month storage period there are no restrictions on the number of times you request the use of the 'van.

Whereas a layer of dust will inevitably accumulate on a caravan stored under cover, there is no likelihood of leaks, algae deposits or bird droppings leaving their unwelcome marks.

Advantages

>> There's greater security when a caravan is locked away and packed tightly amongst many others in a storage building.

>> A caravan remains cleaner when kept indoors and any model afflicted by occasional leaks in very bad weather will benefit from indoor storage pending repair work.

Disadvantages

>> The fees charged for under-cover storage are usually quite high.

>> There are not many covered storage centres in Britain.

Storage at caravan sites

Both The Camping and Caravanning Club and the Caravan & Motorhome Club offer storage facilities at some of the sites they own. Appropriately the compounds are not always conspicuous and it's a useful service for members that often passes unnoticed.

In practice, storage is only available on selected club sites, although you don't have to choose a venue close to home. Equally, many other caravan sites and holiday parks also get involved in storage as a sideline. Take Highfield Farm Touring Park near Cambridge, for example, this is a privately owned site that is part of the Premier Parks network. Manicured lawns and screened sections are part of the charm and it is not unusual for visitors to be wholly unaware

that there's a small storage compound at the site. This is because it is appropriately shielded by trees and has strong steel posts to provide security at the entrance. This is just one of the hundreds of caravan sites around the country which offer a discreet storage service. So, if you stop at a caravan park in an area you find particularly pleasing, you might like to enquire about storage. But be aware of the advantages and disadvantages of this arrangement.

Advantages

>> You can easily return to an area you enjoy with the knowledge that your caravan can quickly be transferred from the compound to a pitch.

>> Towing – which for some owners is a chore – is reduced, and for a quick weekend getaway that's especially beneficial when fighting Friday traffic.

▼ *This storage facility is one of several offered at sites owned by the Caravan & Motorhome Club.*

Disadvantages

>> Don't be surprised to find a dusty and streaky caravan on your arrival. And remember to make arrangements for its transferral from the locked compound.

>> Levels of security vary and some sites don't have the sophisticated surveillance equipment found on many purpose-built commercial storage centres.

▲ Entry to Club sites sometimes requires either a swipe card or a security code.

>> One is less inclined to have a caravan regularly serviced when it's stored some way from home. Furthermore, most site owners do not allow you to wash or repair a caravan once it's transferred to a pitch.

Short-term seasonal pitches

On both club and privately owned sites it is often permitted to leave your caravan on one of the pitches for an extended period. This is not strictly storage in the normal sense of the word, but it enables you to have a base away from home. The term 'seasonal pitch' is used for this facility.

From a site owner's point of view it is always a gamble knowing how many pitches to allocate for long-term use. On occasions, caravans with drawn, faded curtains and a fair share of long grass around their perimeter can detract from a site's appearance. Equally they effectively curb the chance of more lucrative pitch lettings if the season is blessed with long spells of summer sunshine. But, of course, it's a guaranteed income for a pre-agreed period of time.

As far as the co-ordinating staff of the club sites are concerned, they constantly review the position, knowing that touring members will not be pleased if they find pitch availability much reduced on account of 'sitting tenants'. Consequently, the position is reviewed regularly and venues offering seasonal pitches are intentionally changed from year to year.

As far as a caravan owner is concerned, this is a splendid way to establish a 'second home' and a place of escape. You can even keep an eye on the weather and defer an away-weekend until the last minute. However, the booking conditions relating to seasonal pitches are strict. For instance, the sub-letting of a touring caravan is normally not permitted and you would need to read the 'small print' carefully.

Also, be aware that a caravan kept on a pitch in the main part of a site is unlikely to be as secure as it would be in a locked and fenced compound.

On the other hand, at some Club sites, entry for all visitors is via a security barrier for which you need a card or key number. This is certainly a praiseworthy provision.

Seasonal pitches are organised both at Club sites and privately owned sites.

At some Club sites, the level of security is especially good.

▲ *If you leave a clamped caravan on a seasonal pitch, make certain you can be easily contacted by the warden, especially if it's near a watercourse.*

As a postscript, it is also crucial that you keep in close touch with the site proprietor, particularly at times of severe weather. The photograph above shows a situation during extreme wet weather in 2001 when the owner of a wheel-clamped caravan on a seasonal pitch couldn't be contacted by the warden. Anxious 'phone calls went unanswered and floodwater from the nearby River Trent kept rising. Unclamped 'vans, meanwhile, were pulled to safe ground by tractor.

Advantages

>> During the caravanning season, you can have a leisure base properly established and ready for occupation.

>> Home storage inconvenience is eliminated for extended periods during the year.

Disadvantages

>> Being 'locked-in' to one site discourages you from travelling more widely.

>> Security on a pitch in the main part of a site doesn't match the level of anti-theft provision achievable when a caravan is locked securely in a fenced compound.

>> Seasonal pitches can be costly, and if circumstances prevent you from using the caravan on a regular basis this strategy is hardly cost-effective.

>> Wardens cannot crop the grass close to a caravan parked for a long period, so you may need to take some shears to keep your caravan's perimeter tidy.

Storing on a farm

If you visit some of the certificated location sites that both The Camping and Caravanning Club and the Caravan & Motorhome Club list in their Members' Site Book, you'll find that many are farms. Bearing in mind that farmers have been experiencing tough times in recent years, it's hardly surprising that a number are willing to store your caravan in a barn or within the farmyard itself for an appropriate fee.

You might like to take up this opportunity, but don't overlook the realities of rural life. Farm animals sometimes break through a fence and it's always amazing what they decide to eat. You might also find that manure which is so beneficial on the land is less welcome on a caravan's drawbar.

So, whereas you might decide to leave an inexpensive elderly caravan on a farm, I'd seriously doubt the wisdom of adopting this arrangement for an expensive and almost new model.

▲ Farms' fees are often reasonable and may have room to store your caravan undercover, which offers protection from the weather.

Advantages

>> Points made earlier in respect of seasonal pitch arrangements and storage away from home all apply once again.

>> Farms which take no more than five caravans under special exemption arrangements described in the adjacent panel can be enchanting places to visit.

>> The fee to leave your 'van on a farm is often extremely reasonable and sometimes there's space in a barn which provides weather protection.

Certificated Locations and Certificated Sites

Both major clubs list 'five-van only' sites in their directories. These are known as Certificated Locations (CLs) with the Caravan & Motorhome Club (around 2,300) or 'Certificated Sites' (CSs) with The Camping and Caravanning Club (more than 1,300). These venues obtain a special exemption under the 1960 Caravan Sites and Control of Development Act and a large proportion are based on farms. A number are able to offer small-scale storage as well – sometimes under cover in outbuildings.

Disadvantages

>> Security is often open to question.

>> Movement around a farmyard – both of livestock and agricultural implements – can easily lead to a brush with your paintwork.

>> Be prepared to find a dirty caravan on every visit.

▼ *There are many caravan storage sites in countries like Spain, situated near to tourist hot spots.*

Storing abroad

Caravanners who embark on long trips to Southern France, Spain and other more distant European locations will often see advertisements for caravan storage. Signs announcing *Gardiennage Caravanes* are often seen in France and a number of farmers advertise storage opportunities on roadside notice boards. In addition, you'll often find a leaflet left on the door of your caravan when stopping at a large holiday site. Recognising that journeys to these warm venues are costly on fuel, costly on

ferry tickets and often rather tiring, it is no surprise that local entrepreneurs offer to store your caravan.

But the position is not straightforward. Current EU Law appears to allow these storage arrangements provided your caravan is strictly used for pleasure purposes. However, the legal responsibilities, insurance and security situation are complex. For instance, your roof light might get blown off in a gale-force wind, striking a neighbouring caravan in the process. This raises Third Party considerations, not to mention the damage to your own caravan, which will now get wet inside whenever it rains.

Similarly, it is normal for storage specialists to want to move caravans around to achieve access, so your request to fit a robust wheel clamp as a security measure will probably be refused.

On a practical note, it is also likely that the higher temperatures in more southerly countries will hasten the drying out of the sealant along your caravan's seams. Likewise, direct sunlight won't be kind to the sidewalls of your tyres. And, if you leave a caravan at a distant venue for several seasons, when will it be serviced and by whom? This is likely to be a problem when you finally decide to tow it back to the United Kingdom.

Add to this the fact that you'll need to take an awful lot of caravanning clobber in your car whenever heading for the distant venue, and you begin to see why this is a very questionable strategy.

In reality, the savings on a ferry and fuel are counterbalanced by a number of disadvantages. In fact, when a friend of the author was rather slow to renew

storage payment on his elderly caravan that he left at a site in Spain, he subsequently found that the impatient proprietor had destroyed it.

Advantages

>> You will save on ferry costs, fuel costs and avoid the aggravation of towing over large distances.

Disadvantages

>> Insurance problems, security doubts and damage to the fabric of the 'van from heat and hail stones are just a few of many imponderables that place a big question mark over this idea.

>> When and by whom will the caravan be serviced?

>> A touring caravan left hundreds of miles away cannot provide the pleasure of travelling around closer to home.

>> A lot of caravan equipment needs stowing in your car when travelling to and from the venue.

Insurance

These seven alternative approaches to storage provide a number of possibilities. However, it is most important to emphasise that all caravan insurance companies will want to know where your caravan is kept. This is clearly stated in their literature, and if you contravene the agreed arrangement it is likely that a claim will not be met.

Furthermore, if you check the insurance position with storage proprietors, they normally point out that insurance is your responsibility. Some storage centres are as secure as the Tower of London and have a blemish-free record. Others are less impressive.

With this in mind, it's a matter of considerable concern that caravan theft has grown significantly in recent years and determined thieves go to great lengths to secure certain models. Whereas some storage specialists happily take your caravan off your hands, they sometimes make it all too easy for thieves to take the 'van off your hands in a way you didn't anticipate. Even though there might be a high fence and an alarm system, you are urged to fit security devices as well.

So be especially careful, even if you park a caravan outside your home. Wheel clamps and other security products need to be considered too, and these are discussed in Chapter Four.

▼ *Provided a storage site owner doesn't insist that your caravan should be easy to move, fitting it with a security device is much to be commended.*

Chapter Three

Towing a caravan

▲ Guidance on tow cars and towing is provided at the practical manoeuvring courses run by the two national caravanning clubs.

Most people planning to purchase a caravan are constrained in their choice by the suitability of their car for towing. A few go about things the other way round. They become so eager to own a particular type of caravan that they're fully prepared to buy a more powerful car if it's needed.

Either way, a well-matched partnership is essential, so what attributes does a car need in order to tow efficiently, economically and safely? And how can you acquire the skills of towing a caravan on today's busy roads?

If the letters sent by readers to caravan magazines are anything to go by, there are a surprising number of potential owners who find it difficult to work out what size and weight of caravan their car is able to tow. To create a well-matched 'outfit', several factors are involved and this chapter looks at some of the key points. (Note: The term 'outfit' is used to describe a coupled car and caravan.)

Fundamental requirements

>> **Pulling power:** The engine of a towing vehicle has to be sufficiently powerful to pull the chosen caravan when it has been fully loaded up.

>> **Weight issues:** A packed caravan must not be heavier than the fully laden tow car. Moreover, the weight limits relating to a car, a caravan or the complete outfit must *not* be exceeded.

>> **Brakes and suspension:** A tow car's brakes need to be powerful enough to slow down the outfit. Similarly, a car's rear suspension needs to be robust enough to withstand the extra downforce of a caravan's tow hitch. In reality, most modern cars fulfil these braking and suspension expectations, although some vehicles derive benefit from an add-on suspension aid.

As a general rule the best cars for towing are:

1. Equipped with a powerful engine

2. Fairly heavy

Without doubt, a heavy tow car is better placed to help the stability of a combined outfit, as explained later, but its engine has to be up to the task of pulling a substantial weight too.

▼ *Though not an essential requirement for caravanning, it certainly helps if a tow car is fairly heavy and has a suitable engine.*

Car weights

As regards the weight of a car as specified by its manufacturer, this is correctly referred to nowadays as the 'Mass (of vehicle) in running order' (MRO). However, the older terms 'kerbside weight' and 'kerbweight' are also still in use. These, and other terms, are defined in the panels on pages 44 and 45.

The data section in your vehicle's owner's handbook should provide the all-important figures that you need to know. Alternatively, a Type-Approved vehicle will have elements like the maximum towing weight stamped on its VIN plate; this is usually mounted in the engine compartment. Incidentally, the term 'mass' is preferred by physicists; for our purposes, and in this context, we'll regard this as 'weight'.

Car and caravan weight relationship

As the panels overleaf indicate, there are several weight limits that influence the type of caravan that your car will be able to tow. There are other legal constraints too. For example, a vehicle whose Maximum Authorised Mass (see panel for definition) is no greater than 3,500kg is only permitted to tow a caravan whose:

>> Maximum technically permissible laden mass does not exceed 3,500kg.

>> Overall width does not exceed 2.3m.

>> Overall body length, excluding the drawbar and coupling head, does not exceed 7m.

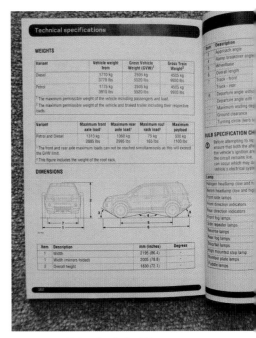

▲ The vehicle's handbook should have a section on technical specifications detailing weight limits.

If you want to tow a caravan that exceeds these limits, such as an imported American model, you need a heavier type of vehicle which is typically a commercial product.

In addition to complying with these legal issues, you will also want your coupled car and caravan to form a stable 'twosome'. Not surprisingly, stability is strongly influenced by the car's weight and the weight of its fully laden caravan. It was stated at the beginning of this chapter that the best cars for towing are usually fairly heavy, especially when compared with the weight of a coupled and fully laden caravan. However, this doesn't mean that lighter vehicles don't make good tow cars; some perform very well, as long as the towed caravan is appropriately light too.

WEIGHT (MASS) TERMINOLOGY – The towing vehicle

MASS OF VEHICLE IN RUNNING ORDER (MRO): Also referred to as 'kerbside weight' or 'kerbweight'. Defined by the vehicle manufacturer, normally this –
Includes:
>> A 90% full tank of fuel.
>> Other liquids forming part of the vehicle's operating systems.
>> The driver.
Excludes:
>> The weight of passengers.
>> Any load apart from essential tools such as a wheel brace and jack.
>> The weight of towing add-ons like a bracket, 12V sockets, mirrors, etc.
Note: Add 25kg as a typical figure for towbar, towball and other 'add-ons'.
Some manufacturers do not include a driver's weight in the quoted MRO figure.

MAXIMUM AUTHORISED MASS (MAM): Also referred to as Maximum Permissible Weight (MPW) or Gross Vehicle Weight (GVW). This is the total weight of a vehicle that must not be exceeded. It includes the driver, passengers, all carried luggage, and the noseweight of a caravan's coupling head when the outfit is stationary.

MAXIMUM PERMISSIBLE TOWING MASS (MPTM): The manufacturer's stated weight limit of any caravan or trailer that is towed. Also note:

TOWING LOAD LIMIT: Sometimes specified by a car manufacturer and often based on the maximum towing weight that a car's restart ability can handle on a 1:8 (12.5%) uphill gradient.

GROSS TRAIN WEIGHT (GTW): Also referred to as Maximum Train Weight. Defined by the vehicle manufacturer as the maximum permissible combined weight of both the laden tow car and the laden caravan. GTW is the total sum of the coupled outfit, which includes the weight of the occupants, the weight of all loaded items in the car and the weight of all contents in the caravan.

TOWBAR LOAD LIMIT: A trailer or caravan should be towed with a certain amount of 'noseweight', which has to be supported by the towball. The maximum permitted vertical load when a tow car is stationary will be given by the towbar manufacturer. On recent products this is known as the 'S' value and it is stated on a plate normally affixed to the towbar.

▲ *The 'S' value marked on this towbar plate as its 'noseload' must not exceed 50kg.*

WEIGHT (MASS) TERMINOLOGY – The caravan

The terms below are defined in the European standards for caravans (EN 1645 Pt 2). Terms used before these definitions were adopted are also given.

MAXIMUM TECHNICALLY PERMISSIBLE LADEN MASS (MTPLM): Formerly Maximum Authorised Mass, Maximum Allowable Mass or Maximum Technical Permissible Weight. Stated by the manufacturer and displayed on a plate. The factors on which a caravan's MTPLM are based include elements like tyre ratings, suspension weight limits, material rigidity etc. This represents the absolute weight limit of a caravan when it is fully laden, and includes: any accessories that have been fitted retrospectively; liquids, fuel (eg gas cylinders); and all personal belongings. To exceed this figure would not only be an offence, it could also represent a serious danger to road-users.

MASS IN RUNNING ORDER (MRO): Formerly Unladen Weight. Weight of the caravan with factory-supplied equipment as defined by the manufacturer and shown on its plate.

▼ *The MTPLM shown on the plate affixed to this Bailey Orion caravan is 1,345kg.*

USER PAYLOAD: Formerly Caravan Allowable Payload. This figure is calculated by subtracting the MRO from the MTPLM. The user payload is made up of three elements: **Personal effects payload:** items you take including clothing, food, drink, cutlery, crockery, cooking utensils, bedding etc. A formula sometimes used to confirm if the available payload is appropriate for a particular model is: (10 x number of berths) + (10 x length of body in metres excluding draw bar) + 30 = minimum recommended allowance in kg for personal effect payload. **Essential habitation equipment:** any items, including fluids, deemed by the manufacturer as essential for the safe and proper function of equipment for habitation – including toilet fluids, fuel, drinking water etc. **Optional equipment:** the weight of optional items like a cycle rack, an air-conditioning unit, and an extra bunk must now be itemised by caravan manufacturers, and figures usually appear in their brochures. The weight of items subsequently installed by the owner, eg a solar panel, also fall within the optional equipment total.

ACTUAL LADEN WEIGHT (ALW): This is what your caravan actually weighs when it is loaded up with the essential habitation equipment and personal possessions. The ALW can be established by taking your 'van to a weighbridge. When this weight is known, you can verify that you are not exceeding the caravan's MTPLM. The figure also enables you to compare its weight relationship with the car and to calculate the 'van's ideal noseweight.

Experienced caravanners are well aware that the weight relationship, or car/caravan weight 'ratio', is one of the key contributors to stability when towing. In this regard, the caravan clubs both strongly advise that **the weight of a loaded caravan should not be greater than 85% of the tow car's Mass in Running Order.** Both Club sites offer a tow car and caravan matching service that will help you identify the best combinations, but you do need to become a member in order to access this service.

This is a useful ratio to remember, but if a tow car is capable of pulling a heavier caravan whose weight is much closer to its own weight, experienced caravanners often exceed the 85% relationship. Of course, the outfit may be more likely to suffer from instability, and it's important to remember that **a caravan or trailer must *never* weigh more than the towing vehicle itself.** If you totally ignore this crucial element, there's a great likelihood that the 'tail' (ie the caravan) might start to wag the 'dog' (ie the tow car). It is at this point that the stability of a towed caravan is under severe threat.

Recognising the importance of having a stable outfit, striving to achieve an 85% or lower ratio is a good starting point, especially for drivers who are towing for the first time. Of course, the car/caravan weight ratio is not the only issue at stake where stability is concerned. Two further matters of importance are:

1. Achieving the ideal noseweight at the coupling head (ie 'hitch') of your particular caravan.

2. Making sure that you position heavy items being carried in your caravan as close to the axle (or axles) as possible.

Both 'noseweight' and 'load distribution' issues are explained in Chapter Six.

Using a weighbridge

Unfortunately, a surprising number of owners overload their caravans with no regard for safety. In consequence, the Police are carrying out an increasing number of roadside weight checks. Not only does towing an excessive weight present a greater likelihood of stability problems, but overloading a caravan or trailer can also lead to prosecution and may render an insurance policy null and void.

Without doubt, the best way to get accurate information regarding your caravan's Actual Laden Weight (see panel for definition) is to take it to a public weighbridge. These can be found using an online search, but you can also contact your Local Authority's Trading Standards Department (Weights & Measures Section) for addresses of weighbridges near your home. A visit to a weighbridge enables you to verify the weight of your loaded car and the Gross Train Weight of the car and caravan when coupled together.

Once you've obtained these figures, you can then calculate the ideal downforce or 'noseweight' imposed on the car's towball by your caravan's coupling head (ie 'hitch'). This matter is explained in Chapter Six.

Incidentally, it is not being suggested that every time you plan a trip away in your caravan you need to load up and head for

The stability of an outfit is potentially dangerous if a loaded trailer or caravan is heavier than the car that's doing the towing.

a weighbridge. However, you should check important weights at an early stage of ownership and it is most regrettable that many caravanners never bother to do this.

So, let's go through a preliminary trip to a weighbridge to confirm that your car, caravan and combined 'outfit' is fit for the road. This 'case-history' trip explains how to get three weights, each of which will be recorded on a dated printout issued by the weighbridge operator. Normally a report also includes the date, the tow car's registration number and the caravan's identification number. Fees vary, but at the time of writing each recorded weight at my local weighbridge cost £10.00 plus VAT.

Typical calculation exercise

OBTAINING THE WEIGHTS OF A LOADED CARAVAN, LOADED CAR AND COMPLETE OUTFIT

Pre-arrival preparations

>> Load your car for a 'dummy run' using all the gear you normally take on board for

a typical holiday. Let's imagine that you have also stowed in the car a lightweight universal awning that fits your caravan. Four lightweight camping chairs have also been tied to its roof rack.

>> Your reliable bathroom scales have revealed that your partner, yourself and your two young children weigh 190kg when you're clad in holiday clothes.

>> Take note of the caravan manufacturer's stated Mass in Running Order (empty weight) and then load the 'van with caution. If you normally include heavy items like a large crate of bottled drinks or a crate full of tinned food, you might be wise to check these on the bathroom scales. That's because you need a rough indication that the loaded weight isn't going to exceed the caravan's Maximum Technically Permissible Laden Mass (MTPLM) when towing it to a weighbridge for the first time.

>> Telephone the weighbridge to confirm its opening hours and to enquire if there are busy periods which are best avoided.

>> Check the tariff of charges.

>> Just before reaching the weighbridge, fill your vehicle to the brim with fuel at a service station – just as you might when genuinely travelling to a holiday destination.

Typical procedures

At some weighbridges there are certain procedures that have to be followed, such as the approach on to and off the weighing plate. Seek advice about the arrangements. Note, too, that a car's weight is not normally taken until its driver and passenger(s) have disembarked and left the weighing plate.

>> Provided it fulfils the weighbridge station's procedures, start by taking the total weight of the car and caravan while coupled. This produces the Gross Train Weight (GTW).

>> Uncouple the outfit and drive the car away to a suitable parking spot. The Actual Laden Weight (ALW) of the loaded caravan is now taken.

>> At a later date, the subtraction of a caravan's ALW from the GTW reveals what the tow car itself weighs. However, to obtain a more accurate reading, take a separate weight check of the car in its solo state. It then won't be saddled with a caravan's noseweight bearing down on its towball.

▲ *This holiday-laden caravan has been put on to a weighbridge to measure its Actual Laden Weight (ALW).*

>> Settle up and make sure that the issued certificates for each weight check show all the information you require, including the date, car reg number, caravan VIN or chassis number and recorded weight.

Post-visit conclusions

>> On your return home, compile a list of all the key items that were loaded into the car and caravan at the time of the weight check. For example, jot down if one or two gas cylinders were being carried in the caravan's gas locker. Also record the capacity of the cylinder(s); if they are already part-used, you could weigh them on some bathroom scales. Since this trip provides your benchmark for the future, the more detail regarding the contents the better.

◀ *Having driven the coupled car and caravan onto a weighbridge plate, you can now find out its laden Gross Train Weight, albeit without the occupants.*

» Add to the recorded gross train weight the combined weights of the driver and passengers. Also add this element to the tow car's reading if the weighbridge recording was completed without occupants in the car.

» Compare all the weighbridge readings with limits stated by the respective manufacturers. If your caravan's recorded weight exceeded its listed MTPLM, decide what items to leave at home in future.

» When you know the Actual Laden Weight of your caravan in a typical holiday state you can subtract this figure from the MTPLM to find how much scope remains to add more gear and extra accessories. That figure is most important to know, especially if you're planning to fit an electric motor mover or an air conditioning unit at a later date. Both are especially heavy accessories, and some people fit them without bothering to check if their caravan can accommodate them and still remain within its MTPLM.

» Once you know a caravan's Actual Laden Weight, you are then able to calculate the ideal noseweight needed for towing. This is described in Chapter Six, *Hitch-up and Go.*

Other towing considerations

Let's now consider the subject of engine power and that time-honoured phrase about 'horses for courses'.

Engine characteristics and torque

A fast, powerful horse likely to win a flat race at Newmarket might seem an impressive equine performer, but if required to pull a cart laden with beer crates it would be pretty ineffective. Conversely, a large shire horse which displays stunning strength when required to pull a heavy farm cart would hardly feel at home running in the Cheltenham Gold Cup.

Cars are much the same. In fact, many of the 'GT' types of 'sports' cars are swift performers but achieve their peak power characteristics (or 'torque', as it's usually called) when the engine is running at high revs. One of these cars being driven in top gear and at high revs would easily achieve an illegal speed of 130mph or more. That's fine on a private track but of no interest whatsoever to a caravanner, who in the UK is not permitted to exceed 50mph on single-carriage roads (where there is not a lower enforced restriction in place), or 60mph on dual carriageways and motorways.

What the caravanner wants is a car which achieves its best pulling power when it's in top gear and the engine is running at low revs. Hence you'll hear technically-minded caravan specialists saying that it's best to own a car which achieves its maximum torque at a low engine speed.

It's worth commenting that diesel engines are especially noted for achieving their best pulling power when the engine is turning over quite slowly, but there are plenty of petrol-driven cars which achieve good torque at low revs as well. Although diesel vehicles often make good tow cars, you certainly don't have to buy a diesel car to tow a caravan.

Most of the caravanning magazines publish tow car test reports, and in a thorough appraisal, issues relating to torque peaks and gearing will be discussed.

Automatic versus manual models

In recent years it has been claimed with increasing frequency that a vehicle with automatic transmission often makes a good tow car. That used not to be the view held by car enthusiasts, but it is now recognised more and more that an automatic affords relaxing driving, especially when progressing with stop-start irregularity in a traffic jam. It is also easier if you're required to drive a caravan up a steep slope from a standing start, because automatic transmissions provide maximum torque at very low revs.

Suspension

The suspension of a towing vehicle faces extra load when a caravan coupling head (or 'hitch') is bearing down on the towball. Caravan noseweight, as it's called, is an important contributor to stability as explained in Chapter Six.

Moreover, when a vehicle has a long overhang rearward of the back axle, a downward thrust on a towball (which is borne by the suspension) is then magnified. In some cases, the rear of the tow car will then start to sag excessively. This condition causes headlight beams to lift to an unacceptable level and also has the effect of reducing the load on the front tyres. On front-wheel-drive cars, this can also cause a loss of traction between the tyre tread and the road.

It's true that many vehicles have a stiff enough suspension to cope with noseweight but others need reinforcing products to assist the standard springs. Seek advice on this subject – especially from the customer service department of the car manufacturer. The technical departments of the caravan clubs also

▼ *Vehicles with an automatic gearbox usually make good tow cars, as long as the transmission fluid doesn't overheat in extreme temperatures.*

have useful free literature on this subject available for members.

The trouble with some remedial devices is that by stiffening-up the suspension for towing there's a hardened ride when the car is being driven solo. However, there are other devices on the market that offer progressive resistance; that means they only harden the suspension when a caravan or trailer is coupled-up.

Tyres

Good stability is also dependent on having car and caravan tyres of the appropriate type, in good condition and correctly inflated. Some car handbooks suggest that tyre pressures are increased when the vehicle is heavily laden and this usually relates to towing as well. It's not unusual, for example, to increase the rear tyre pressure by 4psi to 7psi (0.3−0.5 bar) prior to towing − but to avoid false readings, only alter pressures when the tyres are cold.

If your tow car is not supplied with a standard spare wheel, check with a main dealer what procedure should be followed if you sustain a puncture when you're towing a caravan.

Off-road 4x4 vehicles

Some owners presume that the 'ultimate' tow car for caravans is a 4x4 all-terrain vehicle. That's not entirely true. Certainly, on a campsite in muddy conditions this type of vehicle is ideal for hauling a large caravan from a slippery pitch; and on the road, the weight of this type of vehicle also helps in the vehicle/caravan weight relationship. But there are other elements that are less advantageous including the tendency of 4x4s to have a poor turning circle.

A further problem with some 4x4 off-road vehicles concerns towball height. Even though the height is required to fall within certain limits, there are some instances where manufacturer-supplied towbars for all-terrain vehicles leave the ball too high, even when a drop plate is fitted. Although its elevated position might be fine for towing agricultural trailers, it can cause a caravan to tow nose up and tail down.

Stability aids

It is important to emphasise that a well-balanced outfit with a good weight ratio should provide a pleasantly stable towing experience. However, there are often external forces like a strong gust of wind, a bad road surface, or the suction effect from a passing high-sided vehicle that can cause sudden sideways deflections. Normally a caravan soon comes back into line and it is most unlikely that the instability will get worse and develop into a condition referred to as 'snaking'.

As stated already, these moments of instability are caused by outside forces and their effect can be reduced to a large extent if a stabilising device is fitted. It's important to recognise that these devices should not be fitted in an attempt to cure an inherently unstable or badly matched outfit. Nor should they be used to provide a quick-fix cure for a major fault, like a twisted chassis. However, they can help to suppress the effects of external forces that briefly upset a caravan's stability.

Many stabilising products employ a friction component to suppress unwanted movements, and some of these are built into the coupling head.

▲ *Many of the caravans constructed on an AL-KO Kober chassis are sold with a stabilising coupling head as standard.*

Products have also been designed to perform similar functions in caravans. For instance, AL-KO Kober introduced the ATC Trailer Control in 2007 and this compact unit is mounted near the axle of a caravan. If its lateral acceleration sensors housed inside the unit detect instability, a caravan's brakes are promptly applied for a few seconds to re-establish a safe driving condition.

Of course, there are thousands of caravans being towed behind well-matched cars that are not being helped by control systems like these; what's more, their owners seldom complain about instability. On the other hand, it is pleasing that products are continually being developed in the quest to make caravanners' towing experiences both safer and more pleasant.

▼ *As long as a towball is kept clean and free of grease, this friction pad helps to dampen lateral movements.*

The ATC trailer control is either fitted from the outset by a caravan manufacturer or it can often be added retrospectively.

Towbars

When a vehicle is fitted with a towbar (sometimes referred to as a towing bracket), the assembly of steel members has been designed with a particular type of towball in mind. In fact, four main types of towball are manufactured:

1. A fixed 'swan neck' towball. *(There are a number of different stem patterns.)*

2. A detachable 'swan neck' towball. *(Sleek design with the advantage of being completely removed when not in use.)*

3. A fixed flange towball. *(The towball is bolted onto a faceplate and is permanently attached to your vehicle.)*

4. A detachable flange towball. *(Similar to the fixed flange with the advantage that it can be removed when not in use.)*

There are many patterns of swan neck towball, many of which provide unsuitable mounting points for accessories.

Towball height and drop plates

Nowadays, towbars are manufactured to comply with the towing heights given in Directive 94/20/EC. Problems arise, however, with some older caravans that have an unusually low coupling head. The same effect occurs, too, if a car is only partially laden and is riding high. In these instances, it would help if a towball was slightly lower.

Unfortunately, the height of a swan neck towball cannot be altered. However, drop plates are sold which allow you to lower the height of a bolt-on towball. In fact, if your towing vehicle was registered before 1 August 1998, fitting a drop plate is permitted and this measure can immediately remedy the problem of a caravan that assumes a nose-up inclination. But this practice is not permitted on the more recent Type-approved towbars unless a drop plate or spacer was fitted when the bracket went through its Type-approval tests. Check this with the towbar manufacturer.

▲ *This removable towball is neatly designed; some products are less easy to operate when the ball needs to be detached.*

Note:

1. Although a drop plate can be used in some instances to lower a towball, it should never be used to raise the height of a towball.

2. If there's a problem, take the matter up with your vehicle manufacturer. There are some modern vehicles whose approved towbars do not allow a caravan to assume its required stance.

▼ *It is most important that the tightness of the bolts securing this type of towball is checked using a calibrated torque wrench.*

Electrical connections for towing

It seems strange today, but at one time tow cars were fitted with just a five-pin socket to run the modest array of road lights required on the rear of trailers and caravans. Then, as more road lights were being fitted on vehicles, a seven-pin plug/socket arrangement was introduced in the early 1960s to take its place.

The use of a single seven-pin plug and socket continued until October 1979, at which point two seven-pin sockets were fitted to vehicles intended for towing caravans. The 12N black seven-pin socket was used for road lights; the 12S grey (sometimes white) seven-pin socket was intended to run several of the caravan's 12V accessories using power drawn from the tow car. Meanwhile, boat and goods trailers continued using just a single 12N connection.

The idea of having a pair of sockets was generally approved by UK caravanners, although the pin allocations did have minor changes in the mid-1990s. For the technically-minded person, these developments are described in considerable detail in *The Caravan Manual (Fourth Edition, 2009)* by John Wickersham. Wiring diagrams are provided too, which show the changes to pin allocations as ideas evolved.

However, in mainland Europe some caravanning countries didn't adopt twin plug/socket connections. In Germany, for example, a single 13-pin socket was developed instead. As a result, German cars imported by UK dealers in the 1990s and purchased for towing purposes were often fitted with an imported towbar complete with a 13-pin socket.

This was not always well-received and a costly adaptor lead was usually purchased to couple up to a UK caravan's twin-plug arrangement. But one thing was clear, the precise and positive coupling system employed on these 13-pin sockets produced a better electrical connection than was achievable with 12N and 12S products. A few caravanners have even found that 12S sockets can get warm because of sparks jumping across poor connections.

Recognising that standardisation offers many benefits between European neighbours, it was decided after lengthy debates that UK caravans built from 1 September 2008 would be fitted with a 13-pin plug that complies with ISO 11446. To make sure that UK caravanners are not faced with tiresome problems, a variety of adaptors are on sale. Let's have a look at the products now being used.

Towing adaptor connections

Most modern caravans are fitted with a 13-pin plug and your tow car should be fitted with a matching socket, all should work well. Just one small warning though, when a car is fitted with a 13-pin socket at a franchise garage, it's not unusual for only the pins serving the caravan's external road

▼ It is more important than ever before to appoint a towbar installer who understands both the mechanical and electrical complexities of modern cars.

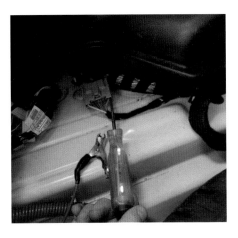

From October 1979 to August 2008, UK caravans and tow cars have been fitted with both 12N and 12S connections.

lights to be connected-up. Some garages are not familiar with the supplementary connections needed to run a caravan fridge during towing, or the principle of charging a caravan's battery from the tow car's alternator. In consequence, a knowledgeable towbar fitter is needed to add the appropriate wiring. This can be an exacting task and it isn't a cheap undertaking.

Some older cars and caravans may be equipped with a 12N and 12S connection. If the pins on both the plugs and sockets are correctly wired and everything works as it should, there is no need to make any changes.

Now let's look at the mismatch situations using photographs to show a suitable adaptor.

The 13-pin socket and its partner plug achieve an improved engagement compared to seven-pin connectors.

Situation 1

The tow car has a properly connected 13-pin socket, whereas the caravan is fitted with 12N and 12S plugs. This adaptor will make the right coupling.

Situation 2

The car has a pair of 12N/12S sockets connected up in compliance with the pin allocation that has been applicable since 1 September 1998. The caravan has a 13-pin plug.

Situation 3

Your car already has a pair of 12N/12S sockets that work well. However, you've ordered a caravan that will be supplied with a standard 13-pin plug. You want to collect your new caravan but haven't managed to get hold of the adaptor shown in Situation 2. The alternative small adaptor shown here is an inexpensive way of bringing the new caravan home with all its road lights working correctly.

Solution to Situation 1: The blue-collared plug on the right fits the 13-pin socket on the car; the twin sockets on the left accept the caravan's 12N and 12S plugs. Secure the adaptor to the caravan's draw bar.

Solution to Situation 2: The black and white plugs at the top are connected to the twin sockets on the tow car; the socket at the bottom needs to be secured to the caravan's draw bar to accept its 13-pin plug.

Solution to Situation 3: These inexpensive adaptors sold in car accessory shops fit into a 13-pin plug on one side and the 12N black socket on the other. They enable the caravan's road lights to operate but none of the internal caravan functions – those depend on a supply from the car's 12S socket.

In summarising the electrical connections that have to be fitted to tow cars, the complexity of wiring in modern cars has ended the efforts of DIY installers. The use of electronic aids in cars has brought safety benefits, improved fuel economy, provided better performance and so on. However, the downside of these changes is the fact that you can no longer couple cables to the rear lamp clusters on your car and take power feeds into the 12N socket for running the caravan lights. The advent of multiplex wiring in cars and the use of computer systems to send data signals to activate accessories has created a minefield of complexity. For this reason, a car must be wired up for towing duties by an experienced and fully trained automotive fitter. Even the electricians in 'main dealer' garages have wired up sockets incorrectly in a few reported cases.

To keep pace with all the radical changes in car electrics, the National Trailer and Towing Association (NTTA) has created a national programme of training courses for towbar installers. Equally, there's an ever-increasing chain of accredited towbar specialists. For example, the NTTA's establishment of its nationwide Quality Secured Accreditation scheme ensures that the installation of a towing bracket and its electrical connections is carried out correctly and to the highest standards.

The NTTA Quality Secured Scheme

This scheme means that accredited centres:

» Have qualified fitters with the right knowledge, skill and training.

» Have adequate resources and the right equipment.

» Are subject to regular assessment and approval by independent assessors.

» Adhere to the National Trailer and Towing Association code of practice.

» Use the best-quality components and work to established standards.

» Charge a fair rate for each job.

» Offer good customer care.

» Give a guarantee of good workmanship and component quality.

The growing list of Quality Secured Accredited fitters can be checked on the NTTA website at www.ntta.co.uk.

Other vehicle accessories

There are many new automotive accessories that have been introduced in recent years. For instance, many drivers now use satellite navigation systems; equally, a surprising number of vehicles are being fitted with reversing cameras.

This is not the place to review a large range of 'must-buy' products and there are always issues that retailers fail to mention. For example, some routes recommended by navigation systems are fine for cars but too tortuous for caravans. However, satellite navigation systems like the Avtex Tourer Two takes into consideration the size of your outfit (tow car and caravan) and checks out routes suitable for caravans.

▼ *This tiny camera, retrospectively fitted by Alpine Electronics UK, enables reversing up to a caravan to be done on your own.*

There's also a tiny reversing camera fitted to one well-known 4x4 vehicle just to the side of its rear number plate. When the author endeavoured to reverse this vehicle unaided towards an imaginary coupling hitch, the camera's location made final alignments quite hard.

This was not the case when an Alpine reversing system was fitted retrospectively, with its camera mounted centrally. This central location, together with a controllable close-up viewing mode, mean that reversing up to a caravan can sometimes be done on your own.

All in all, driving aids take time to refine; but once they work well, they are often regarded as essential accessories.

Towing skills

Many drivers start towing a caravan without receiving any formal instruction. Whether this is a wise thing to do rather depends on your previous driving experiences. For example, if you have previously towed a small trailer, you will already appreciate that it is necessary to take a wider sweep than usual when negotiating tight corners. Ignore this in a town and your caravan might ride up on the kerb with potentially dreadful results.

Parking against a kerb is difficult too, because of the width of most caravans. And then there's that elusive skill of reversing.

There's no doubt that to acquire the relatively simple skills of towing, it is wise to join one of the caravan manoeuvring courses organised by the two major caravanning clubs.

Manoeuvring courses

Both The Camping and Caravanning Club and the Caravan & Motorhome Club run manoeuvring courses at private locations around the country. Typical venues are former airfields and agricultural show grounds – so there's plenty of space that's empty of traffic.

Illustrated technical talks, supporting literature and instructional videos usefully support the practical sessions. There's only one warning – these courses are popular and you usually need to book a place a long time in advance.

The topics usually cover items like selecting and adjusting extension mirrors, coupling-up a caravan with and without a helper, checking noseweight, and general safety tips about items like tyres.

▲ Manoeuvring courses normally start with a technical talk before starting the practical session.

▼ Club manoeuvring courses include advice on choosing and using extension mirrors.

The use of cones and guide poles mark out the course to be negotiated.

Learning to reverse on the offside is easier than learning to reverse into a nearside opening. Practice makes perfect!

▲ Participants at manoeuvring courses are taught useful signals to adopt when helping a driver reverse up to a coupling hitch.

Practical tasks include straight-line reversing, reversing into an offside location and the harder task of reversing into a nearside opening. Plastic cones usually define the target zones and are flattened on a regular basis by wayward caravans. But practising manoeuvres with an experienced instructor is the way to learn these skills, even though many drivers regard reversing as a black art beyond their compass.

Other issues

Driving test

Remember that if you passed a driving test or obtained a full driving licence before 1 January 1997, this automatically permits you to tow a caravan. If you passed the test after this date and wish to tow a caravan over 750kg, then you will have to take a further test (B+E category). Whilst some lightweight caravans are under 750kg your choice will be more limited.

Also, as of 1st January 1998, if you are aged over 70 years and your driving licence expires, then you must pass a medical test and an eyesight test.

For further information write to the DVLA Drivers Customer Services, Long View Road, Morriston, Swansea SA6 7JL or call 0300 790 6801.

Motorway lane use

When towing a caravan you are not permitted to use the right-hand lane of a motorway which has three or more lanes – unless special notices indicate otherwise. Permission may be given in special circumstances, such as when roadworks have caused lanes to be closed.

Parking

When parking a car and caravan, you are not permitted to use parking meter zones.

Passengers

It is illegal – and highly dangerous – to carry passengers in a caravan when you are towing on public roads.

Deflection and snaking

When towing on fast roads, large overtaking vehicles will cause your caravan to deflect from side to side. This buffeting is quite normal but if you're not paying attention to your rear-view mirrors these unexpected movements can be rather frightening. Once the vehicle passes, a well-balanced outfit will realign itself quickly, and if you take your foot from the accelerator the dissipation of movement is usually hastened. But don't try to cure deflections by braking heavily. Stabilisers that help to reduce lateral deflection have already been discussed earlier in this chapter.

Note: These deflections are NOT what is meant by a 'snake'. A snake occurs when an ill-matched or damaged outfit gets out of control with the help of strong side-winds and thoughtless driving. In a snake, the caravan swings so far to one side and then the other that the articulation of car and caravan approaches an angle of 90°. In the unlikely event that you experience a snake, the advice is to immediately lift your foot from the accelerator, resist the temptation to apply your brakes, and hold the steering wheel steady rather than trying to steer with the movement.

Hopefully, anyone heeding the advice in this book will enjoy their caravanning without ever experiencing reptilian attacks.

Chapter Four

Accessories

▲ *Portable dishes, satellite receivers and flat screen TV sets are popular purchases at present.*

To describe all the accessories available for caravanners would take a whole book – and a very thick book at that. Many products have arrived with a flourish and then disappeared without ceremony. Others are 'must have' items that are not supplied when you buy a caravan from a dealer.

Accessories like water containers, gas cylinders and a spare wheel are virtually essential. In addition, a good quality security device is a worthwhile purchase whatever the age of your caravan.

In recent times, caravan manufacturers have been required to supply a mains hook-up lead with their new products. In contrast, a corner steady winder has been a standard accessory for much longer. Current regulations even require that a step of stipulated size is now supplied with all new tourers.

This is pleasing if you're intending to take delivery of a brand-new model. However, most purchasers start caravanning with a pre-owned 'van – a strategy which always makes sense. Differences aside, this chapter draws attention to a wide range of accessories for both new and second-hand models.

Incidentally, towing items like extension mirrors are discussed in Chapter Six so they're not mentioned here. Nor, for that matter, are awnings, which are described in Chapter Five.

Matters of weight

The previous chapter emphasised the point that all types of caravan have a maximum weight limit (MTPLM). Features like its empty weight were discussed too, and then related to the maximum weight it's allowed to attain. Subtracting the empty weight from its MTPLM produces a figure that covers its permitted 'payload'.

In consequence, you can only load up a limited amount of personal gear together with items like gas, water and toilet chemicals. However, if you subsequently decide to add an accessory item, the weight it imposes takes up part of your 'payload'. For example, if your caravan was already running at its maximum weight,

installing an accessory will necessitate a corresponding reduction in the personal items being carried.

In practical terms, if your caravan's already running near its weight limit and you want to have an air conditioner fitted, that appliance equates with a veritable mountain of shoes, socks, shirts and dresses that would have to be left back at home.

Suffice it to say, reflect on your priorities and get a weight check of your caravan when it's packed for a typical holiday *before* spending money on heavy additional items (using a weighbridge was described in Chapter Three); and remember that products like motorised movers, portable generators, air conditioners and awnings are particularly heavy accessories.

Road items

Spare wheel

You can caravan for years without getting a puncture, but if it happens, the mishap can prove costly, especially if you don't carry a spare wheel with a sound tyre. Prior to the launch of 2002 models, most new single-axle caravans were built on 13-inch wheels, and when touring abroad, buying a tyre to fit a 13-inch rim is usually difficult.

So, in 2001 a few manufacturers introduced 14-inch wheels on their single-axle caravans. The idea gathered momentum and in the 2002 model year, most (although not all) new caravans had 14-inch wheels. Again, this is no help to owners of older caravans, and it's one of many reasons why you should always carry a spare.

▲ *It is most important to have a spare wheel and it's sometimes possible to stow this on an underfloor carrier.*

When you buy one, be absolutely sure it fits. It's surprising how often dealers supply a spare wheel where the fixings do not match those on the caravan, or where the tyre is incorrect. This often passes unnoticed until a puncture necessitates a roadside wheel change. That is neither the time nor the place to discover the error. As regards the tyre, it should be:

>> The correct size (both in diameter and width).

>> The correct type.

>> Of the appropriate speed rating.

>> Of the appropriate load rating.

Safety Tip

Throughout much of mainland Europe, motorists are required to wear high-visibility reflective jackets or waistcoats if they leave a vehicle to attend to a puncture or perform similar tasks. In some countries you have to carry such items (including a warning triangle) whether you intend to change a wheel or not. Check the requirements for countries you visit.

▶ *In many countries you are obliged to wear a high-visibility jacket when attending to roadside repairs.*

Tyron Safety Bands

When a car or caravan tyre punctures badly, the collapsing casing often falls into the well of the wheel, whereupon its metal rim starts skidding along the road surface. This sudden loss of adhesion can cause all sorts of problems.

To cure this, Tyron Safety Bands comprise steel sections that are bolted into the well of a wheel, thereby preventing a deflated tyre from dropping into the recess. In consequence, the rubber of a punctured tyre continues to intervene between the rim and the road so that the vehicle doesn't slip all over the place. Even though the tyre is likely to get ruined, both car and caravan can be driven with reasonable control and steered to a safe point by the roadside.

Towing demonstrations held on redundant airfields in which a tyre is punctured by a detonation device are extraordinary to witness. The Tyron Safety Band certainly achieves what its promoters claim and some caravan manufacturers have fitted them as standard. Alternatively, they can be fitted retrospectively by Tyron's recommended specialists.

▲ In spite of a high-speed blow-out, rubber from this tyre – rather than the rim of the wheel – kept in contact with the road.

▼ Tyre pressure gauges are available from car accessory outlets like Halfords.

▼ Once a deflated tyre has been depressed with a clamp, the Tyron Safety Band is installed in the well of a wheel.

Jacks

When lightweight chassis were introduced in the early 1980s, the positioning point for a jack became critical in order to avoid damage to the main longitudinal members. Many caravans are lifted using a portable jack, although more recent models now incorporate a side jacking system. It's a good arrangement and these lifting assemblies can sometimes be fitted retrospectively. However, this depends on the age and the type of chassis; manufacturers like AL-KO Kober can give guidance.

Where lifting clamps can't be fitted to chassis side members, you need a jack that can be positioned at the outermost ends of the axle tube, even when your caravan has slumped close to the ground due to a puncture. A compact scissors jack usually meets this requirement, but these devices take considerable arm strength to lift a heavy caravan. It's certainly worth doing a 'practice run' at home or in a storage compound rather than carrying out your first wheel change by the roadside.

▲ *This AL-KO Side Lift Jack makes changing a wheel much easier with minimal effort.*

▼ *Although this scissors jack has been positioned correctly near the end of an axle tube, elevating a heavy caravan can be tough.*

▲ *A telescopic wrench makes it notably easier to loosen over-tightened wheel fixings.*

Telescopic wheel brace and torque wrench

These inexpensive tools are invaluable should you ever wish to remove a wheel yourself. The additional leverage offered by an extending telescopic bar means you don't need great strength to loosen an over-tightened wheel bolt. Telescopic wheel braces are obtainable from most car accessory shops and are sold with sockets to fit four different sizes of fixing.

That said, it's very important that the fixings (ie wheel bolts or wheel nuts) that secure a replaced wheel are tightened to the specified level. There are reports of caravan wheels becoming mysteriously detached, and it's normally the nearside one which is the first to loosen. That's why a caravanner who's prepared to change a wheel is advised to purchase a torque wrench. The 'torque setting' should be given in a caravan owner's manual and this figure has to be set on a scale adjacent to the torque wrench handgrip. When the fixing reaches the tightness required, a ratchet goes 'click', whereupon the wrench will tighten no further.

▼ *Once you know the required tightness of a wheel fixing, the specified amount is set on a scale near the handgrip of a torque wrench.*

If you don't own a torque wrench and tighten-up using guesswork, a fixing that's insufficiently tight may come loose; equally disturbing, an over-tightened nut can deform its seating in the wheel, whereupon it then comes loose on account of the damage.

Chocks

These are obligatory in Germany, and if you have to change a wheel after a puncture, chocks are most important accessories. Chocking the wheels when you're parked on a steeply sloping pitch is also strongly recommended. Frightening stories of caravans rolling down slopes are well documented.

Regrettably, however, some of the plastic chocks on sale have a habit of slipping when used on a smooth road surface. This can cause a serious problem if you've just removed a wheel. Sticking a layer of rubber matting on the underside of the chocks often helps, but you might prefer to get some larger wooden wedges constructed by a carpenter in which the curvature matches the shape of your caravan's wheels.

Site items

Spirit level

There are several levelling aids on the market but a small spirit level takes some beating. Laying this on the floor directly above the axle is a logical place for both lateral and longitudinal checks. However, a few owners position a level on the A-frame at the front; others use the horizontal line of a front or rear window to check lateral levelling.

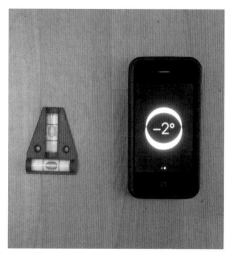

▲ *Small spirit levels are sold in many caravan accessory shops. Alternatively, download a spirit level app on your smartphone.*

◀ *Wheel chocks are inexpensive items that can often perform an important job.*

▲ *DIY caravanners often make their own ramps for lateral levelling.*

▲ *The Lock 'n' Level inflated cushion can help to achieve the perfect lateral level with ease.*

Levelling boards and ramps

Getting a caravan level from side to side is harder than levelling from front to back – which a jockey wheel achieves with ease. The classic and inexpensive answer is to pull your caravan forwards on to some wooden boards prior to unhitching. Some DIY enthusiasts make their own simple system. Alternatively, there are several types of wedge-like ramps on sale at accessory suppliers.

The Lock 'n' Level is an innovative bit of kit designed for caravans by caravanners. In order to achieve a lateral level, the caravan is positioned onto the Lock 'n' Level and the wheel lock is secured. Using a spirit level positioned on the floor near the central axle, a standard tyre pump is connected to the inlet valve and inflated until the lateral reading on the spirit level is central; this normally happens between 8-30 psi.

For ease and simplicity, consider automatic levelling devices. They use powerful hydraulic jacks that are operated via a fixed control panel or using a wireless remote control. At the push of a button, the jacks are deployed and within minutes your caravan is level. The jacks are so powerful they can lift a leisure vehicle's tyre completely off the floor making it easier for changing wheels. Companies like AL-KO, E&P Hydraulics and MA-VE are just a

◀ *Various types of ramp systems are sold in caravan accessory shops.*

few of the companies that can fit them retrospectively.

Corner steady pads

To prevent lowered corner steadies from sinking into soft ground, four small pads help to distribute the load. Small blocks of wood are perfectly adequate, although a number of owners like to use purpose-made moulded plastic pads.

These are often attached to corner steadies with a steel pin, however some versions have a habit of shaking around when you're towing. One type of pad used to be made with a channel that you had to fill up with water. This acted as an effective

moat, thereby preventing colonies of ants from climbing up corner steadies to share the caravanning experience.

▼ *On soft ground corner steadies need a base pad to prevent them from sinking.*

▼ *This E&P Levelling system takes away the hassle of levelling and winding down the corner steadies.*

Steps

There are plenty of step designs on the market, some of which offer uncertain stability. A number of caravanners take DIY steps that double-up as tool boxes. Heavy tools hold them in place, but there's the risk that their contents could be stolen. Milk crates with a ply top are also popular – and provide bottle storage when you're towing. Anyway, whatever strategy is preferred, it's essential that steps are stable and safe.

Service supply items

Hook-up mains lead, socket adaptors and socket tester are described in Chapter Ten and the quality of cable needed to connect with the hook-up pillar is clearly explained. There have been instances where sub-standard cable has been sold at an attractive price – but whose specification does not comply with European Standards.

Leisure battery

Choosing, using and understanding the purpose of a leisure battery is discussed in Chapter Eleven.

Fresh and waste water tanks

Trolley types, rolling barrels and simple jerrycans will all be seen on caravan sites. Some of these are described and illustrated in Chapter Eight.

Gas cylinders and regulator

Important tips on choosing the right type of gas and the subject of regulators are covered in Chapter Twelve.

▼ *There are many different styles of steps on the market, it is just down to personal choice.*

Security devices

There are two main concerns in respect of security: on the one hand there's the risk of a break-in while your caravan is unattended; on the other, there's the risk it might be towed away.

The latter has become increasingly worrying in the last few years and here are some points to bear in mind:

▲ *Many hitch locks include a plastic or metal insert which takes the place of a towball.*

>> It's claimed that 'buying time' is important. Most security devices can be beaten by an experienced thief, but more robust types take much too long to defeat. Anxious not to be 'caught in the act', most thieves move on to easier pickings.

>> It often pays to fit more than one device. Hitch locks are useful, but a well-designed wheel clamp is usually harder to overcome. Fitting both is an extra deterrent.

>> The locking mechanism is usually the easiest element to defeat. Devices employing an unsophisticated padlock are often easy to force open.

>> Note the difference between heavy duty wheel clamps designed to protect caravans when stored for long spells and lighter 'portable' wheel clamps intended to be taken on holiday for caravan site use.

▼ *This Milenco AKS hitch lock achieved Gold Standard in the Sold Secure Tests.*

>> Locking posts and barriers are often worth considering if your caravan sits outside your house on a drive. Some types are made to couple-up with a hitch lock as well.

>> Electronic devices are reliant on a battery and some have a nasty habit of leaping into life due to a false alarm. Whereas some are mainly to register a break-in, others include a switch that incorporates a blob of mercury that starts rolling when a caravan is moved, this immediately triggers the alarm.

>> Check the advice in the section overleaf regarding the Sold Secure testing scheme.

▲ Some wheel clamps are heavy duty models for storage use; this portable version, however, is more compact to take on holiday.

▼ This sturdy wheel clamp is more suitable for securing a caravan that's being stored.

Owner vigilance

Since there are skilful thieves looking for caravans, an owner should be constantly vigilant. If your insurance policy allows you to store your caravan at home with a wheel removed, and provided the wheel is hidden elsewhere, this is a surprisingly effective deterrent.

During a long winter lay-up it is also wise to remove all the upholstery items and store them somewhere that's both warm and dry. Soft furnishings, seat backs and bases are remarkably costly to replace and thieves are seldom interested in stealing a caravan if all its upholstery items are missing.

Taking these points into account, it is fair to state that some mechanically-based security products are tough to beat; others are less effective. In response to this, AL-KO Kober worked with the National Caravan Council to produce a wheel lock that operated in conjunction with an AL-KO Chassis. The AL-KO Secure Wheel Lock was then introduced in 2005 after a rigorous development programme. Today there's a wide range of installation kits that enable the product to be retrospectively fitted to caravans built on the Company's chassis from 2001 onwards.

The AL-KO Secure consists of two main elements. Firstly, there's a highly visual locking bolt component. Secondly, there's the bolt receiver unit, which is fitted behind the brake drum.

▼ *The AL-KO Secure Wheel lock has been tested to Diamond standard from Sold Secure and is fitted as a standard fitment on some new caravans.*

▲ *A wheel has to be in the right position to access the AL-KO Secure bolt receiver unit.*

These two components are secured with a nine-pin anti-pick radial lock, and this is the only caravan wheel-locking product to achieve Sold Secure Diamond Standard.

In practice, it is fairly straightforward to lock an AL-KO Secure to a single-axle caravan; fitting the version made for twin-axle models is not quite so easy.

Sold Secure Test House

It is extremely hard for caravanners to evaluate which security devices are most likely to deter someone who wants to break into a caravan, or defeat a thief who wants to drive off with the whole lot in tow.

So, the Sold Secure initiative is particularly noteworthy. Not only is this a way that manufacturers of security aids can gain recognition from an independent, non-profit-making agency, it's also a means whereby a caravanner can check which products have passed the very stringent attack tests conducted at the Sold Secure Test House.

Understandably, you won't be able to find out which products fail these tests, but at least the published Approved Products list gives you guidance on successful ones.

Note, too, that products passing the test are rechecked on a regular basis, just to ensure that no shortcuts or quality faults subsequently creep into the manufacturing process.

The testing involves a five-minute sustained onslaught by locksmiths with all manner of picks, together with heavyweight attacks with wrenches, bolt cutters, drills, hammers and so on. There's also a saltwater bath to check rust degradation and a parallel test facility for checking the integrity of electronic systems.

Caravan accessories are the main interest in this book and products tested by Sold Secure include parking posts as well as wheel clamps, hitch locks and other devices. However, for caravanners who take bicycles on holiday, there are also Approved Product lists for cycle locks. Other Approved Product lists cover house alarms, car alarms, motorcycle alarms and so on.

Information and Approved Product lists are available free by telephoning 01327 264687. Alternatively, information is available on the Sold Secure website at *www.soldsecure.com.*

Interior accessories

▲ *Duvalay's compact sleeping bag is a duvet and topper combination. Unlike a traditional sleeping bag you are not zipped in.*

Bedding

This is really a personal matter. Some caravanners take the sleeping bags they previously used for camping. They're notably easy to stow, whereas duvets can take up a lot of space in a bed box. Other caravanners hate being 'bagged up' and prefer a traditional bed in spite of the effort involved in using sheets and blankets. There has also been a recent arrival of specialist manufacturers like Duvalay and Jonic which have developed caravan-specific bedding products; both summer and winter grades are available.

Mattress Toppers

Some caravanners find the upholstery in caravans a little uncomfortable to sleep on, so invest in a mattress topper. They come in different thicknesses and offer support

and comfort to those that suffer from back, neck and joints pain. Duvalay offer a FreshTec option that is a cooling foam that offers pressure relief and comfort, but also actively fights heat retention.

▼ *Duvalay's sleeping bags come with an integrated mattress topper, which comes in a zipped, washable protective cover.*

Underlay

If a bed mattress rests on a sheet of plywood (as opposed to a slatted support), air cannot freely move around underneath. This leads to large damp patches appearing on the underside of mattresses and these soon encourage mildew if a mattress isn't turned and aired periodically. The phenomenon seems to be more prevalent in winter.

Putting large towels under mattresses makes a small improvement, but it's not a cure. However, there are several products now available that help air to circulate – some of which are sold by boat specialists too. These include:

>> The Natural Mat Marine Company's 15mm fibrous rubberised, non-slip underlay.

>> Vent Air-Mat from Hawke House Marine.

>> DRY Mat from Ship Shape Bedding.

Cutlery and crockery

This is another personal matter. To save weight, most owners buy plastic wine glasses, melamine dinner services or similar items from a caravan accessory shop. Only when you purchase a top tourer like a Carlight can you expect to find a bone china dinner service; this was standard equipment when a Carlight was originally sold new.

▲ *Carlight was a luxury tourer and was renowned for having a full glass drinking set with their name engraved on the side.*

▼ *Carlight's opulent interior also included a full bone-china crockery set.*

Fire precautions

Smoke alarms now have to be installed in all NCC-approved new caravans, but they're unlikely to be found in older caravans. Their inclusion makes good sense, although in the close confines of a caravan they have a habit of reacting extremely easily.

When visiting a caravan site, it's also wise to check the provision of fire fighting equipment and alarms. In addition, you should strongly consider the merit of fitting a fire blanket (made to EN 1869). The problem of fat fires in caravans, and the terrible mistake of trying to extinguish one with water, is often demonstrated with devastating effect at outdoor shows. This impressively reveals why a fire blanket is important, and once it has been put in place it should be left covering a pan for up to 30 minutes. This is because hot fat has an ability to reignite.

It's also wise to install a general-purpose fire extinguisher. A dry powder type is recommended as the best 'all-rounder' for typical caravan problems, although there are some products like the Firetool Portable Fire Extinguisher that claim to work on all types of fire, including liquid fires, gas fires and electrical fires.

▲ *Smoke alarms are fitted as standard in most new caravans. Remember to test them regularly.*

▶ *For some fires, a fire blanket is extremely useful to have readily to hand.*

◀ *It's always wise to check the distribution of Fire Points when you visit a site.*

▲ *The Firetool Portable Fire Extinguisher works on all types of fire and is maintenance free for 5 years.*

When fitting these items, remember to mount them within easy reach but not too close to a source of heat or enveloping flames.

Carbon monoxide alarm

These battery-operated devices are readily available and are often on sale in DIY superstores.

First Aid

It's obviously wise to take a First Aid kit on holiday stocked with all the medical supplies and medication you would have at home. Some modern cars include one as standard but if that's not the case, get one to keep in your caravan too.

Toilets

Caravans have been fitted with cassette toilets for a number of years. If you've bought an old caravan, a fixed cassette toilet can sometimes be installed retrospectively provided the washroom cubicle is large enough. Don't worry if that's not the case. The smaller portable cassette toilets from Elsan and Thetford are almost as convenient. Turn to Chapter Eight to find out about treatment chemicals and related matters.

Other accessories

TV systems

Many caravanners like to take their flat-screen TV sets with them on holiday. Some TVs come fitted with a built-in DVD player, which is ideal if you want to borrow one of the many DVDs on offer at some Club sites.

▼ *Some Club sites have a DVD library, which is ideal for its members to borrow on a cold, dark winter's evening.*

▲ *A directional aerial can be completely controlled from indoors.*

Also fitted inside recent TV sets are digital receivers, and that is important if you don't own a separate 'set-top' box (often called a 'Digibox'), because analogue transmission has been terminated throughout the United Kingdom.

However, digital television programmes are only available when a signal is strong. If the reception permits, a good-quality picture is a pleasure to watch. This all-or-nothing feature applies to both digital TV captured using an aerial and digital TV captured using a satellite dish.

In consequence, you need either a good directional aerial (for terrestrial TV) or a good dish (for satellite TV). Both need to be pointed in their required directions and both will be affected by obstructions. In addition, your aerial or dish has to be reset every time you move to a new site; similarly, your TV set often needs retuning as well. Being able

to watch TV in a caravan is undoubtedly more involved than watching programmes at home.

Given the options, some caravanners decide to use an aerial in order to watch terrestrial TV coming from land-based transmitters. With the Freeview service and a good reception, you can enjoy over 40 TV stations and over 20 radio stations from caravanning venues in the UK.

Other caravanners decide to change to satellite TV using non-subscription programmes from either Freesat or Free to Air systems. With a suitable set-up you can also pick up many UK stations when you're on holiday elsewhere in mainland Europe.

However, things are changing at such pace that it would be inappropriate to go into any more detail here. One of the best overviews of television in leisure vehicles is published each year in RoadPro's free

▲ *An increasing number of caravanners are purchasing portable satellite dishes complete with a tripod.*

annual catalogue. Furthermore, most of the terrestrial and satellite products offered for sale are tested in Europe by members of the RoadPro staff.

Terrestrial TV equipment

For several years, caravans have often been supplied with a roof-mounted TV aerial as a standard item. The circular types are known as omnidirectional aerials because they don't need to be pointed towards the nearest transmitter. That's a useful feature, but an omnidirectional aerial is not able to pick up signals as efficiently as a 'directional' type. This weakness has become particularly evident now that digital transmissions have arrived.

It is true, of course, that many caravan aerials are fitted with a 12V booster amplifier. This helps to improve a signal in a weak reception area; in addition, these devices can also reduce signal strength when a caravan site is too close to a transmitter.

Notwithstanding the merits of amplification devices, the advent of digital systems has found that caravanners are better served by using a pole-mounted directional aerial. The Status Digital Antenna Systems are made for permanent installation in caravans. Once fitted, the user is able to push the pole upwards and to rotate it from indoors while watching the results on a screen. In addition, there's a control handle to tilt the mast-head aerial through 180° to suit those transmitting stations which need an aerial's elements to be in the vertical plane. In summary, a Status aerial is a good product that can often be fitted in older caravans as long as its pole can be suitably hidden indoors.

A less expensive alternative is to purchase a sectional mast in order to mount a directional aerial on the top.

▲ *Get one of these coupling boxes fitted to an external wall if there's a cable to connect from an outside aerial.*

Caravanners often route the connecting cable for linking-up to their TV set through a part-open window, but a better arrangement is to have a coupling point fitted. Otherwise, a Freeview set-top box is needed, although modern flat-screen TVs have this product built in. **Note:** *Freeview is a terrestrial service that has nothing to do with satellite TV. Don't confuse it with Freesat.*

In summary, the success of a terrestrial system is strongly influenced by the location of a caravan site. That is equally true with satellite systems.

Satellite TV equipment

Some caravanners are choosing to purchase portable satellite systems in preference to improving their terrestrial TV reception. Several specialists are supplying the items required and guidance booklets are available from both Maxview and RoadPro.

Obviously, a dish needs to be set up every time you arrive at a new site, and many caravanners use an inexpensive satellite finder to establish when the signal has reached its optimum strength. Although satellites are moving through space, their speed is set to match that of the earth; doubtless this is an over-simplified explanation but it illustrates why a dish has to be set in a fixed position when you arrive at your pitch.

Although there are automatic satellite-seeking domes for installing on roofs, portable dishes are far less expensive and are usually easy to tilt at the right angle and to point in the right direction.

Another necessary purchase is the receiver, and at the time of writing dozens of free programmes are available using either a Freesat or a Free-to-Air receiver. **Note:** *Don't confuse these with Freeview receivers that capture terrestrial TV systems via an aerial.*

More information on these seemingly complex products in the fast-moving world of modern TV are obtainable from specialist suppliers.

◄ *A satellite finder enables a satellite to be found quickly using signal strength LEDs and an audible noise.*

WiFi

Some sites offer WiFi for free, whilst others may charge for the service. Bear in mind that the speed of the connection will depend on where you are located, for example, you may receive a poor connection if you are pitched in the woods or in the hills. Also, lots of other people on the site might be trying to use WiFi at the same time, which will slow things down.

WiFi booster kits, like the Kuma Wireless WiFi Hotspot kit, will help to boost an external wireless signal. It will allow you to connect items such as laptops, tablet, iPad, Kindle and smartphones all at the same time. The kit can be connected to a WiFi connection up to a mile away, then connect your devices to the Kuma kit.

Alternatively, you can hotspot off your own Smartphone WiFi, but I would not recommend streaming videos as you might end up with a very large bill.

Air conditioning appliances

Caravans can get extremely hot inside when parked in direct sunlight. When temperatures rise, caravanners use both 12V and 230V fans to improve their comfort, and suitable products cost around £12 to £30.

That's a sensible strategy, but if you regularly take holidays in really hot places you might decide to have an air conditioning unit fitted as well. These fall into two broad categories: refrigerative air conditioners, and water evaporative coolers.

Refrigerative air conditioners

A refrigerative appliance employs a compressor-driven cooling unit just like the types fitted in fridges used at home. Without doubt, one of these units will make a caravan very much cooler inside and some appliances are mounted in a bed locker; others are fitted on the roof and use

▼ In very hot conditions, a refrigerative air conditioner achieves impressive levels of cooling.

an aperture like the ones used for roof-lights. Some models are made to produce mild background heat in winter as well.

Although their performance is remarkably good, these appliances are not often installed by UK owners for a number of reasons. For example:

>> Roof-mounted models need a robust roof structure.

>> They are heavy; an average unit weighs 32kg (70lb).

>> They are costly; eg a Dometic FJ2200 costs over £2,000, plus fitting.

>> On most products, the cooling unit requires a 230V supply.

>> Some appliances are noisy and are irritating when left running at night.

>> Summers in several European countries have few days of high temperatures.

Water evaporative cooling units

To understand the water evaporative principle, cover your mouth with a wet cloth on a hot day and inhale. The intake of air will be cool until the rag eventually becomes dry. The reason for this is simple: when water evaporates it absorbs heat, although the phenomenon is far less evident in humid conditions.

The Totalcool is a portable evaporative air cooler. It is unlikely to create the level of cooling achieved by a refrigerative product but has several points of note. For example, the Totalcool 3000 model:

>> Weighs only 2kg (4.4lb) in a dry state.

>> Runs on a 12V, 24V and mains supply.

▼ *The compact and light Transcool cooling unit is ideal for cooling down the interior of your caravan.*

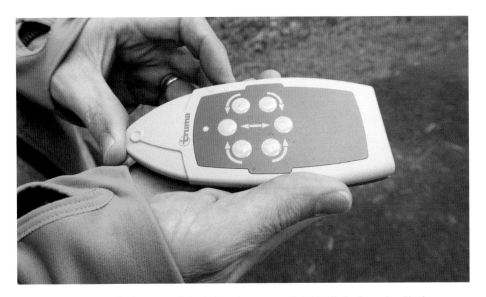

▲ This hand held controller has an aerial view indent of a caravan to help identify the forward and back directions.

>> Has little to go wrong in its mechanism.

>> Costs around £339.

Caravan motorised movers

When a caravan has to be manoeuvred into a difficult storage place, it can be an exacting job, especially if conducting the operation on sloping ground.

A solution is to have an electric motorised mover fitted which drives your caravan's wheels. When the Carver Caravan Mover was first launched it certainly allowed thousands of owners to continue caravanning, secure in the knowledge that they wouldn't have to push a caravan on to a pitch or into a confined parking place.

Carver ceased manufacturing caravan products around 1999 and several other manufacturers then started to produce 12V motorised movers as well, with a choice

of either auto engage or manual engage (depending on how strong you are and if you want to pay the extra for auto engage). Whereas the first models had a coupling cable for the hand-held controller, wireless control pads appeared very soon after. Once you've practised with the simple controls, moving a caravan is much like operating a child's radio-controlled car. Not that having a motorised mover is the sole preserve of elderly owners. On the contrary, there are caravanners of all ages who are not good at reversing a caravan with their tow car.

Many struggle when siting a 'van on a pitch with spectating neighbours witnessing their every mistake. Other owners want to keep their caravan parked in a tight spot at the side of their house. In situations like these, a motorised mover provides a practical answer.

▲ Parking a caravan tight up to a wall is simple with a motor mover.

Unfortunately, though, these devices are heavy in weight and greedy on power; they're not cheap either. Recognising that a caravan's leisure battery is soon left in a badly discharged condition after a few manoeuvres, some owners buy a second leisure battery, which adds even more weight.

Fine though caravan movers might be, it's a dreadful mistake to have one fitted if you haven't first checked your available payload. Even without its own battery, the addition of an accessory that tops the scales at around 35kg (77lb) represents a very large chunk of a caravan's payload. That's sufficient to put some holiday-packed caravans well over their MTPLM, as explained in the previous chapter.

To be certain that your caravan is legal for use on the road, a weighbridge visit must precede the purchase of heavy products like a motorised mover.

▼ The non-slip surface of the drive rollers ensures the required grip on the tyre.

Chapter Five

Choosing and using awnings

▲ *This large Isabella awning doubles the amount of living space.*

If you park a caravan on a pitch for an extended period, an awning can be a great asset. Not only does it add to your personal space, it provides undercover storage for wet clothing and bikes. Some caravanners use an awning in summer for food preparation or as a venue for campsite banquets.

Others fit a purpose-made sleeping compartment to provide an overflow bedroom. Even a small porch awning serves as a useful shelter when you're removing muddy wellies. It all depends on your needs...

▲ *This awning canopy is housed in a sturdy bag making it not just effective, but quick and easy to set up.*

A good way to gain extra living space without buying a bigger caravan is to purchase an awning. These useful accessories come in a wide range of sizes, styles and materials. Types currently on sale include:

» **Simple sun canopies** consisting of just a roof and supporting poles.

» **Sun canopies** that permit the addition of a zip-in front panel and side walls to increase protection against mild winds and moderate rain showers.

» **Small porch awnings** that are especially useful in winter to keep draughts from your caravan door and to provide a place for wet wellies.

» **'Combi', 'universal' or 'half-awnings'** which fall midway between a porch and a full awning. These are intended to fit a wide range of models – which is important if you're changing your caravan and don't want to spend money on a replacement awning.

» **Traditional full-sized awnings** whose size has to match your particular 'van. These usually have a rectangular floor plan and their side walls are stitched permanently to the roof panel. However, more expensive versions have 'zip-out' removable sides so that you can opt for either a roof-only sunshade or a full enclosure – depending on how long you're staying.

>> **Purpose-made awnings** that are made for particular types of caravans, such as folding models.

>> **Awnings that offer a facility for adding** an extra sleeping compartment to one of the sides.

>> **Massive multi-sided units** whose overall internal dimensions are far greater than those of the caravan to which they're attached.

▼ *A lightweight porch awning can be erected in minutes.*

▼ *Though larger than a porch awning, a 'combi' or 'half-awning' normally fits several types of caravan.*

▼ *This awning is intentionally made as an accessory to fit on a Carousel folding caravan.*

▲ The zip-on bedroom extension shown here simply takes the place of a side-wall panel.

▼ Though not the largest type of awning, this example would still weigh a lot when both its fabric and poles are packed.

Note:

1. Large awnings are especially heavy and it is often better if they can be carried in a tow car rather than a caravan. If you follow the advice in Chapter Three and take a holiday-loaded caravan to a weighbridge, it then becomes clear whether a heavy awning can be included without exceeding the 'van's Maximum Technically Permissible Laden Mass (MTPLM).

2. Universal and porch awnings are usually easy to transfer from one caravan to another. However, you need to check that there are no obstructions at the points where their sides rest against the caravan's wall. For instance, if they cross the face of an acrylic window, this is likely to get scratched when the fabric gets blown in the wind. Similarly, the canvas should neither cross a refrigerator vent nor obstruct the fridge's flue outlet.

3. A resourceful owner is usually able to erect an awning unaided, although it isn't always an easy task. When it's dark, and especially if it's breezy, it is sensible to wait until later. Either way it is much easier if you have someone who can help. Bear this in mind before buying one of the mansion-like structures that look impressive in catalogue illustrations.

4. Air awnings require a pump to erect them, so don't forget to pack it. They can also be surprisingly heavy considering there are no poles.

5. Instead of purchasing caravan-specific awnings, some owners prefer to use free-standing structures that can also be erected on the lawn back at home. Gazebos are particularly popular but they *must* be pegged down securely, especially when it's windy. However, these structures are less likely to suffer from wind-lift when zip-in side panels are added. Other types of free-standing enclosures are used for housing a portable toilet. In addition, Maypole Tidy Storage Tent is useful for hiding away campsite furniture, bikes, toys and barbecue equipment.

Materials

Many awnings are now manufactured using a synthetic fabric, and various forms of proofing are used. For example, ultra-light materials (often used for hike tents) are treated with a non-permeable coating on the inner face. These occupy little space when

▼ *A gazebo is more secure in winds if it has zip-in side panels; it can also be used on the lawn back at home.*

packed in a carrying valise, but the fabric isn't breathable so condensation quickly forms on the inside. That's one reason why natural cotton canvas is sometimes preferred, but it soon rots if packed away in a damp condition. Consequently, more expensive awnings are often made using breathable, treated synthetic products that feel similar to cotton.

Different types of poles employing various materials are also available, as the section below describes. Some pole structures use clip-together couplings which significantly speed-up the time it takes to set up an awning.

Rigid and flexible poles

>> **Coated steel rigid poles** – Strength is a point in their favour: weight is their disadvantage. An anodised finish is used on more expensive poles; cheaper products start to rust prematurely, especially when the coating gets damaged.

▼ *Steel poles are sturdy but heavy; when emptied from their bag they pose a daunting assembly problem at first sight.*

>> **Rigid aluminium poles** – At one time, manufacturers like Salou (now Bradcot) supplied alloy poles with their awnings. Alloy tubes are light and corrosion-resistant but usually lack the strength of a similar steel product. Today, awnings supported with rigid aluminium tubing are less common, although Fiamma uses this material to good effect on its Caravanstore awning canopy.

▲ *Aluminium folding poles are used very successfully in roller-blind sunshades like the Fiamma Caravanstore.*

▼ *Many Isabella awnings are sold with the option of either good quality glass-fibre poles or coated steel products.*

>> **Glass-fibre tubing** – This product will neither corrode nor discolour. It is also very light, though it tends to be costly. It also lacks the rigidity of steel tubing and if there are large areas of unsupported fabric, a pole structure can flex and might even break. In winter, for example, an overnight fall of snow will place considerable weight on a roof.

>> **Flexible hoops** – Influenced by the structures employed on many lightweight tents, more and more awning manufacturers supply flexible hoops instead of rigid poles. When fed through stitched sleeves in fabric panels, rods that are no thicker than your smallest finger assume a pronounced curve. Provided the sections only support light, nylon-proofed material, and guy ropes are used to resist deformation in strong gusts of wind, enclosures are often surprisingly rigid.

▼ *Flexible hoop assemblies, originally developed for backpacking tents, are now used on lightweight porch awnings too.*

Inflatable Air Awnings

The inflatable air awning has become increasingly popular with their integrated air poles and separate support poles. They can be quick and simple to erect, with options for pumping the whole lot in one go or inflating the poles individually. It all comes in one bag, rather than a bag for the poles and a bag for the awning. A word of warning – air awnings can be very heavy to lift (even the porch awnings) and a challenge to pack away!

Fabrics

>> **Cotton** – Depending on its grade, cotton is usually a light fabric and it has the advantage of breathability. This means that it doesn't suffer from condensation problems associated with several types of synthetic materials. At the same time, it's less tolerant to ill-treatment. Pack it away damp for several days and the rotting process starts. What's more, the inevitable marks left by mould are almost impossible to remove. On the other hand, if you look after a cotton awning it can last for at least 15 years of seasonal use.

▼ *Air awnings are quick to erect and surprisingly strong, even in gusty conditions.*

>> **Synthetic** – Several types of synthetic materials are used by awning manufacturers; some are as soft as cotton but more resistant to wear. Good quality synthetic fabrics can be surprisingly expensive and the proofing process means that many types are not able to 'breathe'. Having ventilation in an enclosure is therefore essential to disperse condensation. The condensation problem becomes particularly acute if you use your awning as a drying room. However, it's not as bad as it is inside non-breathable hike tents because there's a greater airflow in a large awning.

Features of synthetic products

Acrylic is light in weight, hard-wearing, virtually rot-proof, resistant to fading and it

doesn't shrink. **Polyester** fabrics can offer a small measure of breathability depending on the coating used. The product is lighter than acrylic but not as hard-wearing. To improve performance it is often coated with proofing treatments like polyurethane (PU) or polyvinyl chloride (PVC).

Note: In many awnings, more than one material is used. For instance, there are awnings where the roof is weather-resistant coated polyester whereas the sides are cotton. You may also note that there are often PVC-coated panels at the foot of the walls. This provision is particularly beneficial because it copes with splash-up damage in downpours and spray damage from canine leg-lifters.

▼ *The dark brown PVC-coated panels at the lower edges of this Isabella product offer useful practical benefits.*

Attachment to the caravan

Manufacturers use different ways to secure awnings and poles to the sides of caravans. Older models, for example, sometimes have large rubber suction pads fitted to the ends of the roof poles. However, these fail to achieve satisfactory suction on a surface that has a textured or smooth finish.

Other systems require eyelets to be mounted on a caravan's walls, and that necessitates drilling the external cladding. When mounting these eyelets you are seldom lucky enough to find a wood strut behind the aluminium or GRP skin to provide a firm fixing. In consequence, you have to rely on tight-fitting, self-tapping screws. Inevitably this addition produces potential leaking points, so it's important to use stainless steel screws and to bed the attachment plates on a flexible sealant. Since the act of drilling a new caravan might invalidate its water ingress warranty, some awning manufacturers have designed pads complete with a pole 'docking' arrangement which are slid into the awning rail as separate items. An alternative strategy is to slide roof support poles through sleeves that form part of the awning fabric itself. In some instances, you'll also find fabric pockets that are fitted with zips to retain the poles.

When comparing various attachment methods, it is undoubtedly better to have a roof pole support system that eliminates the need to drill a caravan's side wall.

Measuring-up

It is important that an awning fits well. If the fabric starts to flap in a wind, it not only keeps residents awake at night, it can also damage a caravan's side panels and the surface of acrylic windows.

▼ *At one time, awning poles were nearly always hooked into plastic eyelets that had to be mounted on a caravan's walls.*

▼ *Modern caravans no longer have the plastic eyelets on the caravan sidewall, so companies like Isabella use 'Fix On's' instead.*

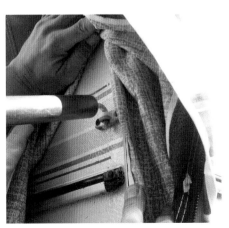

With a conventional full awning, as opposed to a porch or combi-design, it's most important that the measurement from the ground and all along the trackway is going to match the dimension of the awning you plan to purchase. In a good Owner's Handbook, the caravan manufacturer will advise what size awning is needed for your particular model of caravan. If this information has been overlooked you sometimes find that awning manufacturers and retailers hold records of measurements relating to the more popular recent caravans. Failing that, check the panel to the right.

Buying tips

>> When comparing products, check the quality of construction, especially the stitching. Look closely, too, at the zips; replacements can be costly to have fitted.

>> Check the 'optional extras'. Some manufacturers can supply a useful pocket panel for storing holiday items; others offer items like coat-hanger bars. Inner tents are also available if you want to use an awning as an overspill dormitory.

>> Look for storm guy fixing points. Some models are better suited to exposed, windy locations than others. There may also be storm straps listed in the catalogue. Failing that, several independent component specialists can supply these items.

Measuring-up tips

To establish the size of awning required you will need to carry out the following procedure:

>> Park your caravan on level ground and lower the corner steadies.

>> Hold a tape measure around the awning channel that normally runs round the perimeter of the side walls and the roof. Include in your measurement the bottom projection from each end of the trackway down to the ground.

>> Even better is to run a length of non-stretch cord around the trackway itself – just as you would the attachment cord of an awning. Carry both ends down to the ground, then remove it and measure it carefully.

>> Since the angle on the sides of an awning usually splays outwards, you need to take this into account when establishing the point where the bottom of the awning will touch the ground.

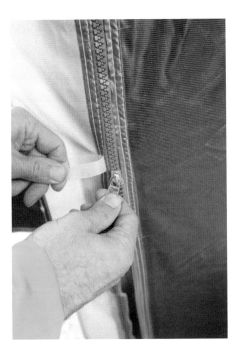

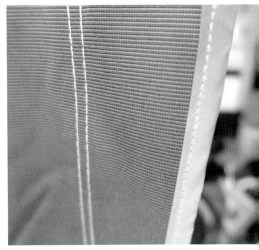

▲ *A good quality awning has taped edges and impeccable stitching on all the seams.*

◀ *When comparing awnings, look carefully at the quality of the zips.*

▼ *All sorts of 'extras' are available – including an inner roof designed to minimise the formation of condensation.*

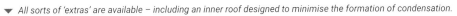

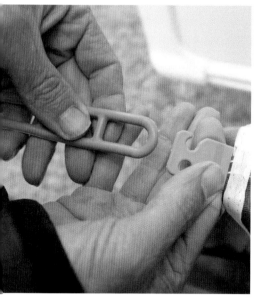

▲ *These ladder pegging points on a Doréma air awning are easy to fit.*

▼ *Fancy curtains offer a home-from-home feel and privacy.*

» Ask if there's an after-sales service in case of an accident. It's not unusual for a pole to fall over when an awning is being erected and sharp spikes on the top can easily puncture the fabric.

» Enquire if you can purchase spares like rubber expansion loops for the pegging points. Find out how easy it is to purchase a replacement pole. In a strong wind it's possible for a pole to become so badly bent that it cannot be straightened.

» Check the colours of awnings as well. Some manufacturers have moved to light pastel shades which look very pretty. However, colours that look good on their own might not match the colour of the caravan.

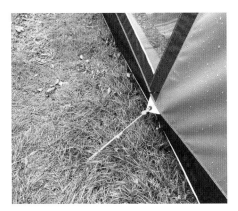

▲ *Note the storm guy fixing points, but use guys rather than 'bungee' rubbers.*

▲ *Storm straps are an important accessory to buy and it is recommended to always attach them as you never know when the wind will whip up.*

Ground-cover material

Think carefully about the type of ground-cover that you want to use. Traditional groundsheets kill the grass, so there are special carpeting materials with breathable characteristics. Some examples can be bought from the roll and priced according to size. Take note that some campsites will only allow you to use a breathable groundsheet on their pitches, so check before booking.

Interlocking foam tiles are ideal for hard standing pitches. They are also lightweight and relatively cheap.

▲ *Ground sheets left down for a long time can ruin a pitch; breathable floor coverings are much preferred.*

▼ *A stiff brush and a bucket of water will effectively clean a dirty groundsheet.*

▼ *Interlocking foam tiles are perfect on hard standing pitches.*

Spares and extras

>> If you need spares for an awning, it's likely that you'll be able to purchase these at an indoor exhibition or at an outdoor show. Smaller companies who specialise in awning components are more likely to attend the outdoor shows and rallies that are held in the warmer months of the year.

>> With the increasing use of hard standings on campsites, there's often a need to have a selection of heavy-duty items called 'rock pegs'. As their name suggests, these are also useful on rough ground, and several campsite operators sell rock pegs in the reception office.

>> If you have the misfortune of colliding with a tree or wall and compress the awning channel, W4 accessories has the answer – a tiny dumbbell with bullet-shaped ends designed to be tapped through the channelling with a hammer, thus re-establishing the shape of the aperture as it passes through. Don't prize open an awning channel with a screwdriver or pliers because you'll damage it.

▼ *Independent specialists sell awning spares – and you'll see them at outdoor rallies.*

▼ *Spray with silicone then tap the appropriate end of this re-forming tool through a damaged awning rail.*

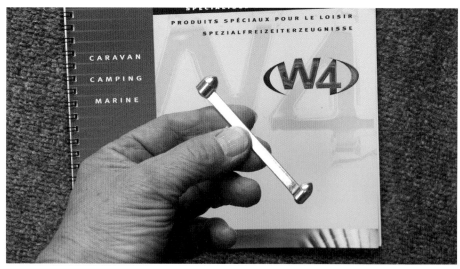

▲ *On rough ground like this, the plastic pegs supplied with many awnings are of little use.*

▼ *Rock pegs are useful additions and many caravanners also carry a hammer in their peg bag.*

▲ *There are many awning cleaning products on the market available from caravan accessory shops.*

Cleaners and reproofing products

Marks and stains are a fact of life, hence there are several specialist fabric cleaners available from caravan accessory and camping suppliers. For instance, Fenwick's Awning cleaner and reproofer has been especially popular in the last few years. Some awning manufacturers have developed their own cleaning products like Isabella's Isaclean and Aquatex Reproofer.

Bear in mind that stains like bird lime should be removed at the earliest opportunity, whereas mud is best left until it's completely dry. Other stains include tree sap. Apart from proprietary awning cleaners you can often shift marks using warm, soapy water – but never use detergent! Of course, there's sometimes a tendency for a tidemark to appear around the treated area, so you then have to extend your effort and clean the entire panel. However, this isn't always a problem because some marks are confined to a small panel with stitching boundaries.

▼ *Awning manufacturers like Isabella have produced their own awning cleaner and reproofer.*

The trouble with determined and regular cleaning is that this can hasten the need for reproofing. However, specialists like Fenwick's and Nikwax market a number of reproofing products and their application is straightforward provided the weather is on your side.

As a rule, it's best to erect an awning before tackling the reproofing work. It also needs to be clean. Ideally you want warm, dry weather – but not hot, direct sun. On the other hand, Nikwax Tent & Gear SolarProof is better when used on a damp fabric and not only is a waterproofer, but also a UV blocker. So before getting to work, check carefully the instruction leaflet supplied with the product that you intend to use.

Many treatments like Granger's Fabsil would normally be applied with a brush, although some owners use a pressurised garden atomiser spray, which is rather more convenient. Using a long lance attachment, for example, allows you to reach the roof panels much more easily.

Needless to say, a full reproofing operation will take an hour or more. However, if you merely want to reproof a small area – perhaps where you've carried out a spot-cleaning operation – you can purchase reproofers in aerosol cans for localised application.

Avoid bad locations

If you ever make the mistake of erecting an awning under a lime or similar tree that exudes a sticky sap, you'll never do it a second time. These substances soon coat the entire roof fabric and need washing-off at the earliest opportunity. Even then, you might find you remove the water-resistance of the fabric and need to reproof it.

▼ *A long, stiff brush will help to get to those hard to reach places.*

Packing an awning away

If circumstances force you to pack away a wet awning when leaving a caravan site, you need to open it up and dry the fabric as soon as possible. In a very short time, mould marks appear whatever the type of fabric. Hence on long trips back to the UK from abroad, many caravanners realise the importance of taking an overnight break to re-erect their damp awning to start the drying process.

At the end of a season, the need to ensure that its fabric is completely dry is again important. With some awnings costing a four-figure sum, these are expensive products needing care and attention. Although it's usually fine to store an awning in a caravan when the weather's warm, it can get too damp in a 'van during winter. So, if you've got room, transfer it into your home.

Repair work

Damage can occur in a number of ways, although a falling awning pole, complete with a spike, is one of the mishaps that tears a lot of awnings. Whilst a few owners subsequently use their domestic skills to carry out repairs, most seek the help of a professional equipped with industrial sewing machines.

Some awning manufacturers, such as Isabella (UK), carry out repairs for customers. In fact, this company can even make small alterations to an existing Isabella product so that it can be fitted to a larger or smaller caravan; that's a useful service for owners who want to purchase a different-sized caravan without getting rid of their current awning.

There are also independent awning repairers whose services are often listed in the classified advertisements of both caravan and camping magazines. In addition, both major caravanning clubs offer advice. For example, the Caravan & Motorhome Club list awning repair specialists in their Club Magazine. Repairers will also replace damaged zips, and some caravan breakers cut out zips from scrapped awnings and sell them in their accessory shop. It's not unusual to see a bundle of second-hand zips on display in various lengths and colours.

▼ *Specialists at the Isabella UK headquarters will repair or alter awnings the company has supplied.*

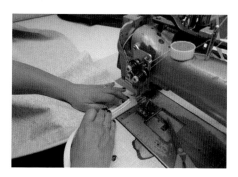

Erecting an awning

Some awnings are sold with very poor erection instructions. In fact, if you don't set up your awning on a regular basis, it's a good idea to colour-code the ends of each pole using PVC tape.

If the awning is being erected for the first time, you might also find that the feed

New awnings that leak

On some brand-new awnings, the sewing needles used to stitch the seams leave large puncture holes – especially in coated synthetic fabrics. When it rains, you then find that your new awning starts to leak. However, don't get too dismayed, provided the dampened thread and fabric swells, the tiny puncture holes diminish in size and the problem solves itself. Some manufacturers even advise purchasers to erect a brand-new awning before leaving for a holiday in order to spray it with a hose. It's a one-off job that seldom needs repeating, but if the leaks persist you might then have to apply a proofing compound along the stitched seams.

Incidentally, different people put up awnings in their own favourite ways. This is my preference, in which the sides are zipped out and reinstated later. It means the roof section, which goes up first, is lighter to handle.

▼ *Spray Isabella's Aquatex into the awning rail to help the beading slide through more easily.*

points on your caravan's trackway need widening slightly. Do this very carefully and try to use a blunt tool – the sharp corners on a slotted screwdriver can all too easily damage the surface of an aluminium extrusion. Alternatively, you can spray Isabella's Aquatex into the awning rail to help the beading slide through more easily.

Once this preliminary preparation is complete, the awning should go up fairly easily. The accompanying photographs show an Isabella Ambassador being erected, and my caravan's free-standing step proves especially useful when reaching up to the awning rail. Drawing the roof panel through the channelling can be quite a stretch!

Step-by-step guide to erecting an awning:

Step 1

Feed on the draught skirt first.

Step 2

Lay out the groundsheet to protect the awning from becoming dirty.

Step 3

Lay out the poles in groups. If you need a step to reach the roof, have it to hand.

Step 4

Find the openings in the awning track where the beading on the roof panel can be inserted.

Step 5

Once the roof panel is centralised, attach the fix-on's for the poles.

Step 6

Connect the poles starting with the middle pole and working your way to the side poles. Lean the legs towards the caravan to keep the awning at a workable level for doing the canopy.

Step 7

Connect the canopy poles and tension.

Step 8

Place the spike into the hole on the regulator tab at each corner and middle section.

Step 9

Insert the side panels, but leave partially unzipped at the top when tensioning the roof poles and cross members.

Step 10

It is important to zip-up all the doors of an awning before pegging-out the wall panels.

Step 11

For 'fine tuning', there's usually a facility to adjust the position of poles and telescopic couplings which allows the tension of the fabric to be altered.

Step 12

For that final touch, attach the curtains and tie backs for added privacy.

Hitch-up and go

▲ An assistant using prearranged signals is a great help when you're reversing a car towards a caravan's coupling hitch.

When getting ready for a trip away, there are several jobs to carry out before leaving. Packing a caravan correctly; checking its noseweight; and fitting the extension mirrors on your car are some of the points discussed in this chapter. Then you have to couple the car and caravan together. Nothing's particularly difficult, but several key tasks should be noted.

Let's imagine the situation: your caravan has been serviced for the season; it bears the same number plate as your tow car; you've turned all the gas cylinders off; the tyre pressures are correct; and you're now loading your personal gear. When your possessions have been duly stowed, that's when the caravan's noseweight needs checking.

Noseweight

The weight that bears down on the rear of a tow car is determined by the distribution of possessions inside. Their placement determines the load on the towball; this is referred to as 'noseweight'.

If the entire weight of a caravan is distributed so that everything balances over its axle (or axles), no weight at all will be bearing down on the car's towing ball. That might sound a wise strategy, but it's a recipe for disaster. You'll find that the balanced load above the caravan axle will see-saw up and down as soon as you start towing. The towing vehicle then receives relentless lifting and lowering movements and the outfit becomes alarmingly unstable.

For safe towing, noseweight is a crucial commodity. What's more, it's an easy thing to adjust. Repositioning heavy items of equipment inside the 'van, such as an awning or a toolbox, immediately alters the load on the towball.

To achieve the most stable arrangement, it is generally advised to create a noseweight that is around 7% of the total weight of your fully laden caravan. To calculate this in a precise way necessitates having your loaded caravan checked on a weighbridge (as described in Chapter Three). The total weight of the 'van is then divided by 100 and multiplied by seven to establish the ideal noseweight. That said, there are limits on the load that a towball can manage.

Both towbar and vehicle manufacturers prescribe the weight limits for their respective products. For example, the maximum carrying capacity of recent towbars is marked on a plate as shown on page 44. So, whereas towing stability might be at its best when the noseweight's 7% of a caravan's laden weight, there are instances when the calculated figure can't be used because it exceeds the car and the towbar limits. Check the panel on page 112 for further advice.

▼ *To measure noseweight, the coupling head is lowered on to a noseweight gauge.*

Technical Tip
Noseweight limits

As a general rule, stated maximum noseweights typically fall between 50 and 75kg (around 110–165lb). Moreover, it was mentioned in Chapter Three that nearly all towbars (sometimes called 'towing brackets') fitted to post 1 August 1998 vehicles have to bear a Type Approval plate declaring maximum loading capacities. One of the listed figures gives a towbar's noseweight limit, which is sometimes called the 'S' value.

It's true that a few cars have remarkably high limits. Examples include 4x4 all-terrain models and vehicles with self-levelling suspension, like some Citroën saloons. But that doesn't help if the permitted carrying capacity of the towbar you later have fitted is designed to handle much lower noseweights.

So remember:

» Generally, it's helpful to have as heavy a noseweight as possible, but this depends on a number of constraints. For example, you need to find out: (1) the towbar's noseweight limit, and (2) weight limits applicable to the towing vehicle. You must then ensure that you don't exceed these figures.
» Once these constraints have been noted, you can then ascertain how close you can get to the 7% noseweight, which is believed to achieve the best level of stability when you're towing.
» Unfortunately, if you own a particularly heavy caravan you might not be able to achieve this ideal figure. That's because the calculated 7% figure turns out to be higher than the limits applicable to your car or its towbar. That doesn't necessarily mean that you mustn't tow the caravan. To comply with these limits you can usually reduce noseweight to a lower percentage of the caravan's weight, provided you recognise that the outfit is unlikely to be quite so stable.

An alternative way to measure noseweight

If you don't own a gauge, a popular way to measure noseweight is to use a cut-down length of broomstick handle or a similar length of timber. When no one's looking, you then 'borrow' the family bathroom scales. Thereafter the procedure is much the same as it would be when using a purpose-made gauge. For example, one end of the wooden stick is inserted into the coupling head, the other is positioned on the central part of the weighing platform – preferably on a small piece of wooden board to prevent damaging the plate. Once you've lowered the 'van using the jockey wheel, take the reading from the scales.

Procedure for checking noseweight

Some owners use a purpose-made device. These products are used as follows:

1. Park the caravan on flat ground. If there's the slightest chance of movement, chock the wheels.

2. Make sure the jockey wheel is in contact with the ground and that the caravan brake has been engaged.

3. Raise all the corner steadies; then lift the coupling head using the jockey wheel handle.

4. Insert the top of the noseweight gauge into the coupling head and hold the device vertically. If you can't do this because the coupling head's too low, turn the jockey wheel handle to gain extra height.

5. Once the device is in place, lower the front of the caravan until all the noseweight is being borne by the piston on the gauge.

6. Take the noseweight reading.

If you prefer using electronic devices, a noseweight gauge is available from Reich UK.

▲ *Some caravanners purchase a purpose-made gauge to check the noseweight.*

▼ *Others check noseweight using a short pole, a pad and some bathroom scales.*

▲ An electronic noseweight checking device is available from Reich UK.

these heavy items tends to perpetuate a pendulum action. Even with a stabiliser fitted, the unwanted lateral movements take longer than usual to correct.

In consequence, if you need to *reduce* noseweight it's better to move items hitherto stored near the front of the 'van to a location much closer to the axle. In fact, as many heavy items as possible should be loaded low down over the axle. You certainly don't want a large amount of weight at the extremities. This is why you mustn't be tempted to use up all that inviting space in some of the latest gas cylinder lockers at the front. In fact, on some caravans, a correct noseweight can only be achieved by carrying no more than two small gas cylinders in this locker – even though there's space to accommodate much larger products.

▼ The space might look inviting, but it's all-too-easy to exceed the noseweight limit if you pack too much into a front-end gas locker.

Altering noseweight

Increasing or reducing noseweight is achieved by moving your stowed items either towards the front or the rear end of the caravan. But there's a warning, if there's excessive noseweight you might decide to eliminate this in one easy move by putting a heavy item at the extreme back of the 'van to compensate. That, however, is bad practice.

Loading heavy items at opposite extremities creates what is called the 'dumb-bell effect'; this means that if your caravan starts to sway from side to side when it's being towed, the inertia in

Loading a caravan

Not only does wise loading of your personal possessions help to achieve the ideal noseweight, it has other implications for stability when towing. For example, when negotiating a sharp bend, a caravan travelling at brisk speed is likely to develop 'body roll'. This is why heavy items should never be stowed in roof lockers. Caravans are fitted with rather a lot of lockers these days, but that doesn't mean you have to fill them all up.

Inclination

When you're towing at normal speeds, both the car and caravan should assume a level stance. This inclination should be checked on level ground when the outfit is stationary. However, it's worth noting that a slight nose-down inclination is often regarded as acceptable when a caravan is parked. That's because there's usually a small lifting effect brought about through turbulence which helps the 'van assume a level stance once you're on the move.

>> If you've achieved the correct noseweight but find that the rear end of the towing vehicle sags when the caravan's coupled, your car might need replacement rear springs or an approved spring-reinforcing device.

>> If it's the caravan's tail which sags, then you might resolve the problem by fitting a drop plate.

Loading food

The practice of loading up a caravan's cupboards with as much food as possible is fortunately losing its appeal. Even if a caravan site doesn't have a shop of its own, supermarkets are seldom far away – whether you're at home or abroad. So why give the tow car a tough assignment by transferring half your kitchen to the caravan?

To repeat the point made above, don't carry heavy items in roof lockers. Even if a roof locker might seem a logical place to store the marmalade jar on-site, it's not the place to keep heavy items when you take to the road.

As regards refrigerator products, try to pre-cool the fridge before taking to the road. Also ensure that you load it following the recommendations given in Chapter Nine.

▼ *The failure of a fridge door can leave quite a mess when you're towing.*

▲ *The Milenco Grand Aero 3 offers superb views down the side of the caravan to include the top and bottom of the caravan.*

Mirrors

The so-called 'through vision' created via a car's internal mirror is not likely to be very helpful when you're towing. Even if your caravan has large windows front and back, a few drops of rain will turn a rearward image into a fuzzy blur.

It is essential that anyone towing a caravan must be able to see 4 metres on either side of the caravan, at a distance of 20 metres behind the driver. Also, Regulation 33(4) (c) states that mirrors should not project more than 20cm beyond the overall width of the caravan. If your caravan is wider than the rear of your tow car, bearing in mind that 8-foot wide caravans are becoming popular, then legally you must have towing mirrors.

Many types have been marketed in the last 30 years and frankly the clamp style mirrors are the most popular choice of towing mirror, as they offer exceptional stability and are simple to attach. The mirrors themselves come in different shapes - from teardrop to larger mirrors like the Milenco Grand Aero.

Many people opt for convex rather than flat glass in an extension mirror because it provides a wide-angle image. Unfortunately, its greater capture of rearward vision is spoilt by the fact that any following vehicles are actually much closer than the reflected image suggests. For that reason, it is often recommended that an offside extension mirror is better fitted with flat glass instead. Once both external mirrors are mounted on your towing vehicle, carry out some checks to confirm their adjustment. A bit later, after you've left home, it's often necessary to pull into a lay-by to make further 'fine adjustments'. This is also a

Towing mirrors EU directives

Towing mirrors must meet with current EU directives, meaning they must show the 'e-mark' indicating that they comply with directives 2003/97 or 2005/27. The key information that you need to interpret can be found on the casing of the mirror:

» The lower case 'e' indicates that the mirror meets European Standard. If it was a capital 'E' it would meet International Standards (UNECE 46.01 or 46.02).

» The number following the 'e' identifies the country that the mirror was tested in, for example 11 represents the UK.

» The approval number should be 03 representing the 2010 compliance.

▶ *The Milenco Aero 3 towing mirror is a teardrop shape and complies with the very latest International regulations.*

good opportunity to double-check that the electrical coupling cable between your car and caravan hasn't started to sag more than you anticipated.

▼ *Strap on towing mirrors are quick and easy to fit.*

External mirrors

>> People who tow with a wide, commercial vehicle might not need extension mirrors added to the towing vehicle. But that's only a minority of caravanners.

>> A driver is required to have a good view down both sides of a caravan together with a sideways vision extending to 4m (157.5in) at a distance of 20m (787.5in) rearwards of the caravan. For most vehicles, this requirement clearly necessitates the addition of extension mirrors.

>> When your caravan has been unhitched, extension mirrors must be detached before you drive on the road.

>> The extension mirrors fitted to old towing vehicles should not project more than 200mm (8in) beyond the widest part of your caravan.

>> Extension mirrors now being sold have to be 'E-marked'; if you are using an older, unmarked product make sure that it is fitted with safety glass.

Coupling-up

Preliminary manoeuvres before coupling-up

Your car now has mirrors, the 'van is loaded and its noseweight is satisfactory. It's time to couple them together.

Reversing a car up to a caravan coupling head is undoubtedly easier if you've got assistance. Although a garden cane in soft ground can act as a useful marker when you're on your own, you'll still need to hop in and out of the car to check finer details. So, what makes a good assistant? Organising clear signals and agreeing on key words is important. For instance, the word 'good' is too vague, to a reversing driver it might mean, 'good . . . keep coming slowly' or 'good . . . you've got there'. Imprecise verbal communication might lead to a dent in the back of your car or a pointless dispute with your partner.

I wouldn't dream of giving adult readers a prescriptive list of commands. Develop your own but make sure they're not ambiguous – especially if you use different assistants to help you. For instance, it's not unusual to find that well-meaning neighbours on a caravan site employ a completely different sign language.

However, there are some common practices, such as, many assistants start by raising a hand vertically above the caravan's coupling head; this conveys a visual clue to the driver concerning the alignment of the coupling components.

Then, as the car reverses, agreed hand-signals will reveal progress, including a measure of the closing distance and deviations from the intended course. Note that a caravan's coupling head should be

Running out of jockey wheel elevation

Sometimes the threaded spindle inside your jockey wheel tube reaches the end of its travel. That's annoying if you still need to raise the coupling head even further to clear an approaching towball. Here's the remedy:

1. Temporarily lower the front corner steadies to support the 'van.

2. Wind up the jockey wheel with its handle so that the wheel pulls well away from the ground.

3. Unclamp the jockey wheel and lower it further in its clamp assembly than it was before. Make sure the wheel now touches the ground.

4. Tighten the clamp firmly once more.

5. Prepare to elevate the caravan using the jockey wheel handle. It will now have a lot more threads available on its spindle.

6. Since the front corner steadies have now completed their brief supportive function, raise them up once again.

slightly higher than the top of the towball; if that's not the case, wind down the jockey wheel to lift the coupling head.

In the final stages of reversing a tow car, some instructors discourage an assistant from standing directly between a caravan and a reversing car. It's certainly true that when grass is damp, a wet shoe might slip off a clutch pedal.

Some caravanners like to reverse the car until the coupling head is directly over the towball. Others are content if the coupling head is slightly to one side, because the flexibility of tyres allows minor alignments using a judicious nudge of a leg against a caravan's draw bar. On a light caravan, that can work without releasing a caravan's brake or removing the chocks, however, it's not so easy with a twin-axle 'van.

▼ *In the final stages of coupling preparation, experts recommend you give the driver progressional guidance from a side position.*

Step-by-step coupling procedure

Now let's reinforce the recommendations above with a visual step-by-step coupling operation. The sequence presumes that your caravan is loaded up in your preferred way, the noseweight has been confirmed, and the gas has been turned off at the cylinders.

▼ Using the hand lever, fully apply your caravan's brake.

Step 1

Step 2

▲ Use chocks on its wheels, especially if
the ground is sloping.

▼ Lift all corner steadies.

Step 3

Step 4

▲ Working with your prearranged signals, slowly reverse the tow car.

▼ Raise the coupling head using the jockey wheel, so that it is above the tow ball.

Step 5

Step 6

▲ Be precise in the final stages so that the coupling head causes no damage.

▼ Apply the handbrake on your car; release the brake on the caravan, recognising that the wheels have been chocked; lift the stabiliser lever; and check alignment with the towball.

Step 7

Step 8

▲ Lower the jockey wheel with one hand and lift the coupling lever with the other hand.

▼ When the coupling head embraces the ball, this indicator shows green.

Step 9

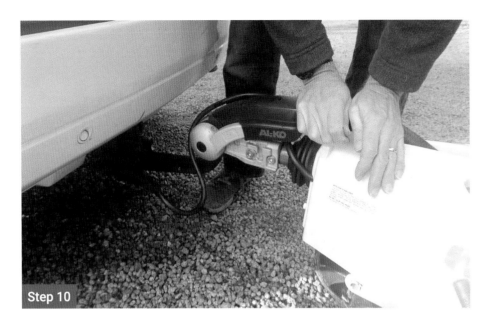

Step 10

▲ If there's a coupling head stabiliser, push this down to add ball friction.

▼ The safety indicator on the stabiliser coupling should show green to identify that it is correctly seated on the ball.

Step 11

Step 12

▲ With the car now supporting the
coupling, fully raise the jockey wheel.　　▼ Attach the breakaway cable.

Step 13

Step 14

▲ Check that the breakaway cable feeds straight through the guide eyelet.

▼ Connect the 13-pin socket (or 12N and 12S 7-pin sockets) to the car ensuring there is enough slack to turn corners, but not too long that it drags on the road.

Step 15

Step 16

▲ The green LED light on the AL-KO Trailer Control (ATC) indicates that the emergency system is fully functional.

▼ Retrieve chocks and carry out a rear road-light check before leaving.

Step 17

Breakaway cables

One of the most frequently misunderstood components is the 'breakaway cable'. Many owners connect these up incorrectly and there have been instances where this error has caused a caravan's brakes to fully engage and then burn out amidst billowing smoke. But why is this cable important?

Sacrificial operation

If, for some reason, a caravan becomes detached from a towball, a correctly fitted breakaway cable will tighten, apply the caravan's brakes, and then promptly snap on account of the load. This provision is intended to leave the 'van unattached, albeit with its brakes safely engaged. It is believed that parting company like this is better than having an unhitched caravan being dragged behind a tow car on the end of a sturdy safety chain. To achieve this preferred disconnection, a sacrificial clip, or crimped fitting, on a breakaway cable is intentionally designed to snap as soon as it has fully engaged the caravan's brakes.

Operational success

The effective operation of a breakaway cable is dependent on a number of factors. To begin with, it needs to follow a straight line from its fixed attachment point at the lowest point of a caravan's handbrake lever right through to its clipping point on the tow car. Within this path, it should be fed through a collar on the caravan itself, as shown in the earlier coupling-up sequence, and not tidily bunched-up with the electrical cables. Moreover, if coupled to a tow car's eyelet that's situated further than 100mm (4in) from the centre point of a towball, it's unlikely to engage a handbrake as needed.

Safety tips

» It's always very important to check that a caravan's coupling head (sometimes called the coupling hitch) has clasped itself fully around the ball and isn't merely resting on the top. If your caravan doesn't have the red/green safety button shown in the accompanying sequence, a simple way to confirm a successful union is to raise the locked-on coupling head a small amount using the jockey wheel. If the coupling-up has been correctly achieved you'll see the rear of the towing vehicle starting to rise on its springs.

» Once a caravan has been coupled correctly, completely raise the jockey wheel by turning its handle. Then release its clamp to pull the jockey wheel tube to its high-level towing position. Re-clamp the raised jockey wheel tube, ensuring that it's tight. Alternatively, some owners like to achieve better ground clearance by removing the entire jockey wheel assembly. This is then stowed in the back of the tow car. There are 'fors' and 'againsts' in both strategies and on some caravans a jockey wheel isn't readily detached.

» Always remember to turn off your gas supply at the cylinder(s) before driving an outfit away from its pitch. (To ensure the fridge keeps its contents cool when you're towing, switch its control to the 12V operating mode.)

▼ *This coupling eyelet is too far to one side of the towball.*

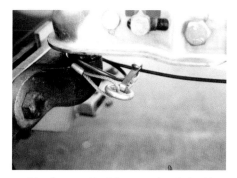

▲ *A breakaway cable of the correct length should never be wrapped twice round the stem of a towball.*

Being able to pull in a straight line is really important.

Burnt-out brakes

If a breakaway cable is inappropriately short, or if it has been wrongly wrapped twice around a towball stem, it will prematurely pull on a caravan's brakes. Similarly, if you are negotiating a very sharp corner this manoeuvre can also tighten an over-short cable and pull on the brakes. Unwanted brake activation also occurs on some off-road vehicles whose clipping point is too far forward of the towball itself. This equally leaves too little slack in the cable.

Each of these situations applies a caravan's brakes far too often, and that's when they start getting warm. However, the real problem occurs on caravan handbrakes that are fitted with a gas-strut spring. These well-intentioned products help owners to *fully* engage a brake without exerting a lot of muscular effort. In other words, the slightest tug on a brake lever that's supported by a gas-strut assister causes the brake to fly on to its limit. That reaction

is also triggered *if a breakaway cable goes taut prematurely.*

With most tow cars, you'd immediately notice that your fully braked 'van is very much harder to pull – so you'd stop to see what's wrong. However, some 4x4 vehicles are so powerful that their drivers haven't detected any problems and have kept on driving until they've seen smoke. A surprising number of brake systems have thus been totally ruined and that's one reason why breakaway cables must be coupled correctly. Careful coupling is particularly important on 'vans with gas-strut assisted handbrake levers.

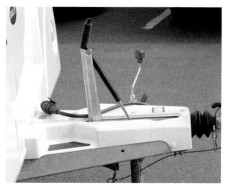

▲ *Just a small tug on this handbrake that has gas-strut assistance will fully engage a caravan's brakes.*

Clips and clipping

Although recent tow brackets have an eyelet to accommodate a breakaway clip, many offer nothing at all. Some owners buy a bolt-on 'pigtail' from an accessory shop which then affords a means of attachment. Others wind the cable once round the neck of the towball. This isn't the preferred method of attachment because in an emergency breakaway situation the

cable might flip over the top of the towball. It then couldn't pull on the brake. On the other hand, if there aren't any eyelets, this is sometimes the only way to fasten a cable.

As regards the clips themselves, the most common type which has been used for many years is not designed to attach directly to an eyelet. If you do this, a clip can chatter around during towing, settle in an upright position and then stand the risk of unacceptable distortion when it's needed to apply an unhitched caravan's brake. To ensure that the cable does function correctly, this type of clip should be passed right through the eyelet then clipped to its own cable to form a noose.

That's fine, but you also find that many of the eyelets are too small for the clip to pass through. Consequently, a new type of spring clip has recently been introduced that costs only a few pounds to have fitted instead. Based on the mechanism used in rock-climbing safety couplings, this revised product can be clipped directly to an eyelet. In fact, all caravans really ought to have one installed.

▲ *The new type of clip can be directly clipped to an eyelet, whereas the older version can't.*

▼ *This bolt-on plate offering an attachment point for a breakaway cable is too small for a clip to pass through.*

Breakaway cable replacements

It's extremely important that the brake assembly on a caravan is fitted with a breakaway cable of the correct length. Caravans built on an AL-KO Kober chassis use a cable with a *red* sleeve: BPW chassis should have cable with a *blue* sleeve.

Their respective lengths are not the same. Other chassis are often fitted with thin steel cable that lacks a coloured sleeve, and very old caravans were fitted with a small chain. Any replacement must be of the appropriate length.

▲ *This red-sleeved cable is designed to fit AL-KO Kober brakes; note that this one is fitted with an old-style clip.*

Plug connection

If your caravan is fitted with 12N and 12S plugs, these will need to be eased into their respective sockets, noting that a small notch in the plug in its 'six o'clock' position, engages with a lug in the socket. That ensures the plug is correctly orientated and inserted the right way up. There's a similar lug in the 13-pin plugs but the moulding also incorporates a twisting collar that helps to achieve a locking effect.

Make sure there's enough 'cable slack' for the caravan to articulate at sharp angles without trying to wrench the plugs from their sockets. At the same time, make sure there's not so much slack that the cable drags on the road. Some owners tidy up slack cable on the caravan drawbar using an elasticated strap. That's fine, but don't include the breakaway cable.

▲ *This new-style clip is fitted on a blue-sleeved cable whose length is made to suit a BPW braking system.*

With the plugs in place, now carry out a road-light test to confirm the connections are sound. This doesn't take long although it helps if you've got assistance from a partner. My preference is to follow a particular sequence and I always operate the lights as follows: right flasher, left flasher, brake lights, side and number plate lights, and fog lamp where fitted. The checker at the rear has to call out these words, to confirm the lights are working correctly or give a thumbs up. Incidentally, on recent caravans there's often a reversing light for checking as well.

Caravan road-lamp failure

1. If a lamp fails to light on your caravan, give the towbar plug a gentle shake in its socket. This sometimes improves a connection and signifies that some of its pins are probably dirty.

2. In rear light clusters, the holders securing the bulbs are sometimes starting to rust; an inoperative bulb may start to work when these sockets are given a clean.

3. There may be a faulty bulb – and you are always wise to keep spares in your caravan.

4. If there's a detached wire somewhere in the system, you may need to call a mobile towbar fitter.

5. Further advice is contained in *The Caravan Manual* by John Wickersham; this book is specifically concerned with caravan repairs.

Other issues

Finally, you may have a stabiliser to fit, or need to check the self-test results of an AL-KO ATC Trailer Control system. Stabilising products were discussed in Chapter Three.

Other routine tasks include checking that everything's secure inside the caravan, including items like roof vents, windows, cupboards, doors and so on. These procedures are also discussed in Chapter Seven, where Site Arrival and Site Departure checklists are provided. Have a look at these because they're equally applicable when you're about to leave home.

▼ *Make sure all skylights, windows, cupboards and doors are securely closed before departure.*

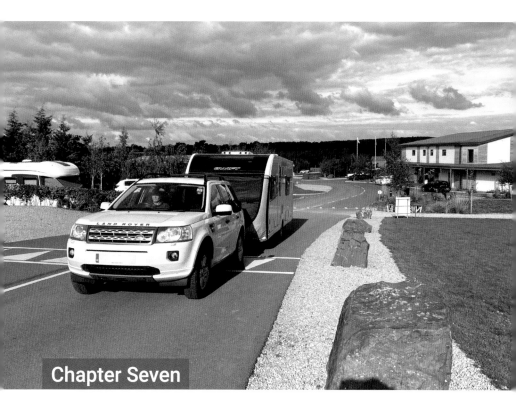

Chapter Seven

Choosing and using a site

▲ *Love2Stay is a Caravan & Motorhome Club Affiliated site set on the outskirts of Shrewsbury, Shropshire. It is a fine example of a modern, luxurious caravan site.*

Selecting a site, choosing a pitch and adopting a leisurely routine are some of the pleasures of caravanning. Here's advice on how to select the kind of site you like best and what to do when you get there. Sometimes the pitches are grass-covered, some are hard-surfaced, some are sloping and some have trees to avoid. Don't worry! The hints and tips here will help you find places that provide what you need.

Where can you go? And what must be done on arrival? These key questions are addressed in this chapter, so we'll take them in order and start with a warning. Newcomers to caravanning are initially confused by the diverse array of places to stay. Here are several examples:

Club sites

This category comprises venues that are owned and managed by (a) The Camping and Caravanning Club and (b) the Caravan & Motorhome Club. These are the two large clubs that look after the interests of Britain's caravanners. Many of their 300+ sites are purpose-built and are noted for their high standard of facilities providing first-class heated toilet/shower/washrooms, many of which have cubicle washbasins and provide appliances like hairdryers. The clubs' sites are kept notably clean and are run by experienced staff.

The Caravan & Motorhome Club also has some 'Management Agreement Sites', most of which are owned and maintained by Local Authorities or racecourse companies. The Club appoints site staff who undertake the day-to-day running of these facilities. Not all of the racecourse sites are used for caravanning during a race meeting, but for those that are, check what the arrival times are.

Similar co-operative ventures have been organised by The Camping and Caravanning Club. For instance, the establishment of 'Camping in the Forest' (formerly 'Forest Holidays') involves a partnership between The Camping and Caravanning Club and the Forestry Commission.

Some of the sites run by both clubs are exclusively for members, whereas others welcome non-members, albeit with a surcharge. You can often join the club on arrival as well.

▼ *The Caravan & Motorhome Club's Uttoxeter Racecourse Club site is set within the racecourse and is open to members on race day.*

▲ St Neots Camping and Caravanning Club site is on the banks of the Great Ouse, making it a popular location for fishermen or canoeists.

▼ A disused quarry near Buxton is a perfect setting for those that like to explore the Peak District National Park.

▲ *Many holiday parks are equipped with several swimming pools to suit the needs of their visitors.*

Holiday parks

Owners of caravanning facilities sometimes give their venues the title of 'park' rather than 'site'; places which adopt this practice often have a distinctly 'holiday' focus. For example, the provision of facilities at a 'holiday park' is usually aimed at families and you often find attractions like children's amusements, a swimming complex, climbing frames, club houses, restaurants, discos and on-site supermarkets.

One large holiday park in North-East England is especially diverse in the range of activities on offer; it even includes a fishing lake, an on-site theatre, a betting shop and donkey rides.

▶ *Sites in the UK are often equipped with climbing apparatus.*

Average-size commercial sites

Commercial sites vary in the facilities they offer in accordance with their owners' objectives. Fundamental provisions normally include a washroom, showers, toilet block, fresh water taps and toilet emptying points. Most sites also offer several pitches served by a 230V hook-up point, although in many parts of Europe, this extra feature incurs an additional charge. For a lot of caravanners that's all they need, whereas others look for commercial sites that offer facilities such as a children's playground, laundry facilities, a small shop, a dog exercise area, Internet coupling facilities and so on. Overnight charges will reflect what's on offer.

▲ Riverside Camp Site in Snowdonia is a typical mid-sized commercial venue with a restaurant for clients; in addition, it has stunning mountains nearby.

Restricted sites

Recently there has been a steady increase in the number of 'Adults Only' sites – a title that might imply they run sleazy nightclubs. In fact, they are usually quiet, football-free places, and one such restricted site accepts no one under 30 years of age. In fact, quite a number of elderly visitors enjoy taking their young grandchildren on occasional caravanning treats and have been deeply hurt when refused entry to this type of site.

▲ Banned! A growing number of sites are exclusively for adults, and children are not accepted.

This matter is very contentious and letters published in caravanning magazines reveal two extreme viewpoints. Some people are acutely opposed to any form of prejudice which affects caravanners' freedom, whereas others are strongly in favour of sites which impose some form of segregation or which exercise exclusion clauses in one form or another. 'No large, all-male groups' is one such restriction at a well-known Lake District site; bad experiences by the management have led to this ruling.

In addition to these discretionary measures, there are also sites where dogs are disallowed, especially on farm sites during lambing seasons. In contrast, other sites welcome dogs and have special 'dog walk' routes that provide for an animal's exercise requirements.

▲ *A growing number of sites now have special dog walks or fields where owners can exercise their pets.*

Some site owners also disallow travelling trades people; others refuse to accept caravans that are towed by commercial vans or lorries. In view of these restrictions, it's important to recognise that not all sites are open to everyone.

Camping in the Forest

The Camping and Caravanning Club formed a partnership with the Forestry Commission to create Camping in the Forest. These wooded locations can be found all around the UK; some have fairly extensive facilities,

▼ *Aldridge Hill is an idyllic site set in the heart of the New Forest, where ponies roam free.*

whereas others are more limited. If you like woodland and wildlife, these are delightful places. They're usually peaceful, too, and don't suit caravanners who want an on-site restaurant, a bar or bingo.

Information is obtainable from The Camping and Caravanning Club at *www.campingintheforest.co.uk* or by telephoning 024 7642 3008.

Small informal sites

Some caravanners seek out simple sites that offer no formally marked pitches, where grass in the field may rise above

the ankles and access roads are muddy tracks. Facilities are abundantly simple and overnight fees are a fraction of those charged at well-equipped sites. Be prepared to accept that other visitors may only be butterflies, birds and grasshoppers.

Certificated Sites and Certificated Locations

Some small venues are run by owners who are permitted to accept no more than five caravans or motorhomes at any one time. In addition, there's a maximum 'stay limit' of 28 successive days, and these five-unit sites are only available for members

▼ *Glenmore Campsite near Aviemore allows you to either immerse yourself in the forest or wake up to a mountainous view - the choice is yours.*

of the national club that has issued the appropriate certificate. The Camping and Caravanning Club calls the venues in their listing 'Certificated Sites' (CS), whereas the Caravan & Motorhome Club listing refers to their recognised venues as 'Certificated Locations' (CL).

Typically, a CS or CL is located in a rural area, and since a large number provide no more than a tap and a toilet-emptying point your caravan needs to be well-equipped. The modest fee is hugely different from the overnight charges at well-equipped sites and The Camping and Caravanning Club and the Caravan & Motorhome Club record several thousand examples in their Members' Site Guide Books. Although some caravanners don't want the peaceful solitude offered at these rural hideaways,

▲ *You'll often see these signs when driving around rural areas.*

some caravanners joining the Clubs have clearly stated that one of the main reasons for seeking membership was to gain access to the national chains of Certificated Sites and Locations.

▼ *This CL site near Ross-on-Wye is a great base for adventure sport like cycling, canoeing and walking.*

Year-round sites

This descriptive term usually implies there'll be some hard-standing areas – a provision that assumes special importance when winter weather renders grassy pitches unusable. Although not normally open for a full 365 days, a few site owners erect a large, heated marquee and organise Christmas Caravanning Packages complete with meals and seasonal cheer. However, these celebratory occasions are popular and have to be booked in advance.

▲ *Specially drained and gravel-topped pitches are a feature of sites that are open in winter.*

▼ *Well-placed for the National Exhibition Centre, Chapel Lane at Wythall is a Caravan & Motorhome Club site that's open all year; it accepts non-members.*

Choosing sites

Recognising that there are many different types of site, you need to make your choice carefully when consulting guidebooks. Using the benefits of modern technology, the publishers of some guidebooks work with a large computer data base of addresses. This means that an impressive list can be assembled, but experience shows that information sometimes gets out-of-date quickly.

There are also special marketing groups whose site owner-members pay for inclusion in a free promotional booklet. In this country, the Best of British chain is an example and the caravan sites of member-owners have to fulfil certain criteria before acceptance into the scheme. Typically, these are all high-quality 'five-star' holiday parks.

In France, Le French Time campsites were created from a merger between Les Castels (formerly called Camping & Castel Group) and Sites et Paysages. Les Castels offers high-quality sites that have a

▼ *Tanner Farm Park near Marden in Kent is one of the prestigious, five-star sites in The Best of British chain.*

chateau or historic building within the grounds. Meanwhile, the Sites et Paysages chain offers well-equipped sites in country settings. In most cases, site guide booklets published by these marketing groups are distributed free of charge at major indoor caravan exhibitions.

Then there are independent guides which only contain sites that have been inspected by specialist assessors. The *Alan Rogers' Site Guides*, for example, are published by a committed team of caravanning site assessors who travel all around Europe. The close scrutiny of each listed site takes a considerable time to complete and the owner is visited unannounced and at least every two years. In fact, if standards slip a venue is immediately taken out of these annually published guidebooks.

On a different note, there's also an increasing number of site-searching

As a member of Les Castels chain, Le Petit Trianon, five miles from Chatellerault, occupies the grounds of a French Chateau.

facilities on the Internet. Caravanning clubs, magazines and other organisations also hold databases with site information.

In addition, there are national competitions organised to find the best sites of the year in England, Scotland and Wales. There are various categories of site in these award schemes and the competitions are contested eagerly by owners. Not surprisingly, winning sites are always very impressive and well worth visiting. On a similar note, both of the caravan clubs conduct a contest to find the best Certificated Location/Certificated Site of the year.

Lastly, there are 'tick' and 'star' schemes run by tourist boards and the motoring organisations which add further measures of quality.

▲ *The Pencelli Castle site is a national award-winning location near Brecon.*

When it comes to booking a site, procedures vary from place to place. Normally the process starts with a telephone call and sometimes a deposit might later be required.

However, like other commercial ventures today, caravan sites can often be booked on the Internet and this booking procedure is becoming increasingly popular.

▼ *The awards displayed at the Reception of Pencelli Castle and Camping Site near Brecon speak for themselves.*

Arrival protocol

Prior to your arrival, it's important to establish when the site reception office is open, especially if you expect to arrive late in the evening. For security, more and more large sites are now protected by a barrier, and you need a code number or a swipe card to lift the bar.

If you can arrive on time, there may be an opportunity to make your own choice of a pitch. Whether a view over the sea is more important than a pitch close to a toilet block or the clubhouse is a matter for you to decide. However, try to avoid pitches under trees that shed sap; as Chapter Five on awnings points out, this can cause you a lot of work later. That said, on some sites a member of the reception staff will lead you to a recommended pitch – often with the help of a bike.

▲ Like a growing number of sites, Ferry Meadows near Peterborough has a robust security system.

▼ At this Camping and Caravanning Club Site, the manager often uses his bike to lead visitors to an allocated pitch.

If you decide to use a mains hook-up, ask how many amps the coupling supplies. The term amps is a measure of quantity and the amount you can draw at any one time varies from site to site. If you use too many appliances at once, the site's trip switch will automatically terminate your supply. So, the matter of amps is important, and guidance in Chapter Ten explains which electrical appliances you'll be able to use.

As regards late arrival procedures, some sites have a small compound near the entrance where you can stay overnight, pending the reopening of reception next morning. Most caravanners are unsympathetic with anyone who sets up on a pitch in the middle of the night. Even the most experienced owner is unable to position a caravan without making a noise.

▲ To prevent noise in the late evening, many sites have a 'Late Arrivals Area'.

For that reason, enquire before arrival when the gates are closed or when barriers come down for the night. Ask when reception closes too. If you arrive after the office is shut – and as long as there's no access barrier – a warden sometimes puts your name and allotted pitch number on a 'Late Arrivals' noticeboard. This system enables you to proceed to the allocated pitch, thereby leaving the completion of forms and payment of fees until the reception office is open next morning.

Finding the facilities

On arrival, nature often dictates that you'll seek out the toilet block first. Washrooms and showers will be checked, too, along with fresh water taps, waste disposal points, chemical toilet emptying points, ironing rooms, washing/drying rooms, and so on. Some sites even have dedicated washing-up sinks and vegetable preparation areas. It is also wise to establish where the fire points are situated.

▲ Many of the club sites are equipped with vegetable preparation and washing-up sinks with hot and cold water.

A few club caravanners place a fire bucket alongside their caravan, although it's a practice seldom pursued now. More and more caravans are equipped with a fire extinguisher and a safety fire blanket.

▲ *If you've ever seen the damage that can be done by a caravan fire, you'll appreciate the wisdom of checking the location of a site's fire points.*

If there's a swimming facility, check to see what safety precautions are in place. You won't always find a lifeguard on duty and some pools don't even advise which is the deep end. Several locations abroad are especially lax in these matters.

And the rest depends on you. Parents may want to find the children's playground, whereas owners of dogs might head for a dog walk.

Pitch spacing

With good sense and with safety in mind, the requirement on club pitches is that each resident's caravan should be sited no closer than a specified distance from a neighbour. Although this is mainly a precautionary fire measure, the stipulation also makes sense where noise is concerned. To give an example of a typical ruling, the Caravan & Motorhome Club makes the following statement:

'To avoid the spread of fire, there must be at least 6 metres (20 feet) spacing between facing walls of adjacent caravans, motorhomes or trailer tents and a minimum clear space of 3 metres (10 feet) between adjoining outfits in any direction.' The Caravan & Motorhome Club, Club Site Rules, 4 Using your pitch (c), Sites Directory & Handbook 2019/20.

No one likes too many rules and regulations, but the prescription above makes good sense. The wisdom of this becomes even more apparent when you see some commercial sites on a public holiday weekend where the tight packing of caravans is neither safe nor satisfactory.

◀ *There are many magnificent swimming pools on summer sites abroad, but safety measures vary in standard.*

▲ *These caravans and motorhomes are very tightly packed in at this festival.*

Setting-up procedure

When arriving at your pitch, the following tasks need to be carried out:

>> Unless there are site regulations prescribing outfit orientation, decide where you want to position the 'van, the car and perhaps an awning.

>> Either reverse your caravan or drive it forward on to the pitch.

>> In readiness for lateral checking, place a small spirit level or a part-filled translucent plastic water container on the floor.

>> Try not to step inside since this puts considerable strain on the unsupported chassis members and may upset the reading.

>> A side-to-side slope needs a remedy now. A few caravanners carry a special wheel-jacking accessory, but driving on to blocks is often easier. Angled plastic

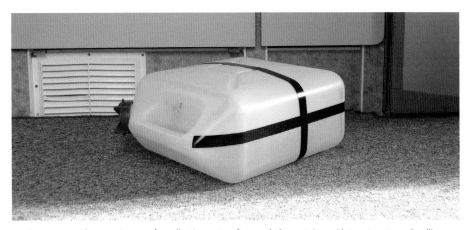

▲ *Caravanners who use a jerrycan for collecting water often mark the container with tape to act as a levelling device.*

▼ *Purpose-made spirit levels are sold at caravan accessory shops.*

▼ *Wood blocks or purpose-made ramps allow you to level up from side-to-side.*

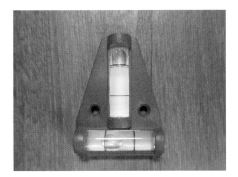

blocks are available from accessory shops. Leave the level-checker in place for later.

» Apply the handbrake on your caravan, and if the pitch is sloping chock the wheels. Chocks are important accessories to carry in a 'van.

» Unclip the breakaway cable; disconnect the 12V plug(s) from the tow car; lower

the jockey wheel to the ground; and tighten the clamp on the jockey wheel.

» Incidentally, if the ground's soft, put a small board under the jockey wheel.

» Lift the coupling head lever and hold it in the ball-release position while you operate the jockey-wheel handle. When the rising coupling head clears the towball, it's time to drive the car away.

» If it's greasy, fit the towball cover before you get marks all over your trousers. Also remember to remove the extension mirrors before driving your car solo on public roads.

» Again, refer to the spirit level or part-filled water container to check the caravan's front-to-back line of inclination. Lifting or lowering the jockey wheel by winding its handle soon gets this right.

» Once you've got your caravan level, lower the corner steadies. If they're not fitted with feet pads, use small blocks underneath each 'leg' to prevent it sinking into the ground. Some owners speed this process up by using a purpose-made socket that fits into a cordless drill.

» Position the step by the door and go inside.

▲ *Couplings are available for fitting into a rechargeable electric drill so that corner steadies can be operated quickly.*

» If you intend to use a mains hook-up, follow the strict coupling procedures given in Chapter Ten and leave spare cable loosely unravelled underneath the caravan.

» Turn on the supply gas cylinder and then get the refrigerator into operation as discussed in Chapter Nine. If coupled to the mains, you have a choice whether to run the fridge on gas or 230V.

» Set up the waste water container and couple the drain hoses as discussed in Chapter Eight.

» Top-up the fresh water container and couple to the caravan. Connecting-up advice is given on page 158 and guidance on pumps is also included in Chapter Eight.

» If the toilet hasn't been prepared for use, add one litre of water to the waste tank followed by a chemical additive. Top up

▼ *Blocks are needed under corner steadies, especially when the ground is soft.*

the flushing water and consider using a rinse-clean additive to keep the bowl shiny and clean.

>> If you're a TV enthusiast who uses a directional aerial, you'll need to get this pointing in the right direction to achieve the best possible signal.

>> Most caravanners fit a portable security device while staying at a site; thefts have become increasingly prevalent in recent years.

▲ Most caravanners fit a lightweight coupling lock or wheel clamp when stopping at a site.

Note

1. When setting up on a steep slope, the jockey wheel sometimes reaches the end of its travel before a level position is attained. The procedure for overcoming this situation is given on page 119

2. Where do you place a spirit level to check the 'van is level? This leads to opinionated debate among caravanners and here are some options to consider:

>> On the A-frame section of the chassis not far behind the coupling head.

>> On the lower edge of the forward-facing central window.

>> On the bottom of a sink to ensure waste water runs down the outlet and doesn't collect at one edge.

>> As far as a fridge is concerned, the shelf in its freezer section used to be seen as the point of reference, but now there are models without a freezer shelf.

>> Probably the best place of reference for the caravan as a whole is on the floor directly above its axle. This presumes the floor hasn't sustained damage and that a fitted carpet or floor covering material hasn't puckered. On a twin-axle caravan you can take readings over both axles and then make a decision.

Site etiquette

No one likes sites with an abundance of 'Don't Do This...' signs. At the same time, you'll come across instances where thoughtless behaviour spoils the pleasures of other caravanners. A common complaint is the fact that young children have a persistent habit of cycling around toilet blocks, which could obviously lead to an accident. But are youngsters to blame, or should parents be more aware of their unattended children elsewhere on the site?

On that note, the accompanying photographs show some problems to ponder:

Note: Thanks to the parents who gave permission for their children to appear in these 'staged' photographs cycling, kicking stones and playing with water.

▲ *Children often like playing with a hose and squirting water, but waste water disposal points are not appropriate places to play.*

▼ *Most caravan sites have safe places for children to cycle; repeated cycling around toilet blocks can be a nuisance to users.*

▲ *Many caravanning sites permit visitors to bring a dog, but as shown here, it should always be kept on a lead or a tether.*

▼ *It's easy to trip on badly laid cables when it's dark. Neither these TV nor mains cables had been thoughtfully uncoiled, and a rabbit agrees.*

▼ *Stones on areas of grass can damage a mower, so playing with stones on a hard standing is something to be discouraged.*

Departure procedures

Once you've prepared the car with its towing mirrors, prepare the caravan for departure. The list that follows looks at both indoor and outdoor jobs to attend to, but they are not presented in a particular order. For example, dealing with a mains supply appears in both lists.

Inside

Get into a routine here and consider creating a checklist. This might vary from model to model but is likely to include these reminders:

» Close roof light(s).

» Close windows.

» Secure cupboards.

» Clear the open shelves.

» Secure the fridge door.

▼ *If your refrigerator does not have an automatic switch over device, then remember to set it to 12V on the control panel.*

» Select the 12V operation on the fridge's fascia controls.

» Turn off the mains isolating switch on your caravan's 230V consumer unit as described on page 209.

» If it can't be loaded into your towcar, stow a packed awning over the caravan's axle.

» Secure a water container that has been part-filled with just enough water for picnic drinks.

» Stow the emptied waste container, the step, levelling ramps and other items.

» Make sure the toilet waste tank is emptied.

Note: Thetford's instructions have sometimes recommended that a flushing water tank is emptied, although most caravanners leave a little water in the system.

Outside

TURN OFF THE GAS SUPPLY AT THE CYLINDER

» Disconnect the mains supply cable, as described in Chapter Ten.

» Retrieve, coil and stow the mains hook-up cable.

» Remove water containers and coupling hoses.

» Retrieve any blocks of wood left under the corner steadies and wheel ramps.

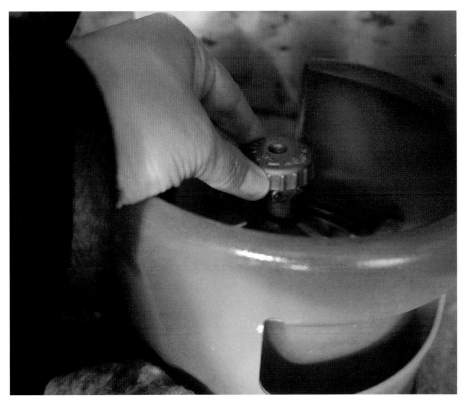

Hitching-up

It is imperative to turn off the gas supply at the cylinder.

Refer back to the illustrated step-by-step sequence in Chapter Six that goes through tasks involved in a hitching-up operation. Note, too, that when leaving an uneven pitch, a caravan sometimes lurches when releasing its brake, so chock the wheels where necessary. If it rolls forward a little, the coupling head can sometimes make unexpected contact with the back of the tow car; dents in the rear body panel of a caravanner's car are not unusual. Some owners reduce this risk by having an over-run bump plate fitted behind the towball.

Leaving the site

Road safety advisers sometimes assert that road accidents often occur in the first few moments of a journey. Without doubt, if the exit gate of a site takes you into a country lane that doesn't have road markings, extra vigilance is needed – especially in countries which don't drive on the left. A surprising number of sleepy British drivers leaving a foreign camping site have a momentary lapse of concentration and take up their position on the wrong side of the highway.

Chapter Eight

Water and sanitation systems

▲ *Some sites clearly mark the taps that are installed solely to provide your drinking water.*

In the 1950s, fresh water was often brought to a caravan in a white enamel jug that stood alongside the sink. Piped systems became popular in the 1960s with either foot-operated or hand-operated pumps delivering water to the sink from a container left outside. Water heaters appeared in the 1970s and electrically-operated pumps arrived around the same time. Shower rooms were then added and toilets were built-in as well.

Anyone who takes up caravanning after holidays spent in tents is often surprised by the sophistication of the sanitation systems. The provision of hot and cold water, a shower and a cleverly designed 'cassette toilet' means that you are pretty well self-contained. In fact, if you pull into a lay-by during a journey you can step from your car into a well-equipped home.This also means that you can stop at simple farm sites whose facilities are little more than a cold-water tap and a toilet emptying point. Self-contained independence undoubtedly has its advantages.

In spite of this, some caravanners still miss the simple arrangements of the past. Certainly, if you purchase an old 1970s 'van solely for summer touring and your intentions are to stop at well-equipped caravan sites, its lack of facilities is hardly a problem. Many modern sites have good showers, hairdryers, and designated washing-up sinks with hot and cold water.

Today, however, modern caravans are sold with every conceivable facility – whether you want them or not. It is probably true that most people purchasing new caravans expect to find on-board showers, even though many caravanners use sites' showers instead.

Notwithstanding anomalies like that, caravans have changed radically in the last few years. In view of the many improvements, this chapter adopts a broad overview of water and sanitation systems for these reasons:

» Many people start caravanning by purchasing an older caravan. Accordingly, the operation of earlier components is explained.

» Others purchase new caravans, so many of the latest systems are also discussed.

Within this review of products, the text and photographs show how things are put into operation. However, the information doesn't include repair guidance, nor does this chapter provide ideas for updating elderly installations. Practical projects of this nature are included in a companion book, *The Caravan Manual* by John Wickersham.

Setting off

You'll probably want to travel with a small amount of water on board for roadside picnics. In addition, a supply of water may prove useful if the tow car's windscreen washers need topping-up. However, don't completely fill a caravan's fresh water container because water adds considerable weight to the outfit. As a guide, a gallon of water weighs around 10lb; a litre of water weighs 1kg.

Also be aware of a further problem: surging water in a part-filled container can affect stability and braking. To avoid this, some caravanners carry their 'picnic' water in plastic bottles that they store in the fridge. Whichever strategy is preferred, always make sure that a water-filled container is well secured. If a large water container like an Aquaroll gets thrown around inside, it is likely to create serious instability when towing.

Connecting-up on arrival

Once your caravan has been levelled on its pitch, you'll need to set-up the fresh and waste water systems as follows:

>> The full fresh water container should be positioned near your caravan's fresh water inlet.

>> Remove the screw cap from the waste water container, store this somewhere safe, and put the container near the waste outlet.

>> Connect the fresh water coupling hose to the caravan's inlet – this might be fitted with a submersible pump on one end – as explained later.

>> Couple the waste pipe from the caravan's outlet (or outlets) to the waste water container.

>> Ensure that the water heater drain down valve is in the closed position.

>> Close all taps except one, which should be in the hot position.

>> Modern caravans have an electric pump so switch on the 12V system at the main control panel inside.

>> Check that water is delivered to the sink and let the tap run for several seconds on hot and cold to clear any stale water that may have been left in the pipes. Be careful - any air blocks will mean the water will shoot out like an exploding volcano.

▲ Position the fresh water container near the caravan's inlet; if it has a submersible pump lower this into the container.

▼ Couple the waste pipe to your waste water container; on some caravans there are two outlets.

>> Repeat this procedure with the other taps.

>> Put on the kettle for coffee or tea... at least, that's what most people do.

Direct coupling

There are a few sites in Britain and abroad where you can connect up directly to a mains water supply because every pitch is equipped with its own tap. These are often referred to as a Serviced Pitch. However, to enjoy this facility you need a special coupling hose that incorporates a pressure-reducing valve to protect the joints in your caravan's pipework. Direct coupling kits include:

▲ *If you forget to close the water heater drain valve, water will come in and go straight out again.*

1. The Truma Ultraflow Waterline, designed to couple with Truma Ultraflow inlets.

2. The Whale Watermaster Mains, which fits both Whale and Truma Sockets on UK vans.

Some pitches also have a pitch-specific waste water disposal point too. To take advantage of this you merely need to purchase a length of waste water hose, which will be fitted to your caravan's outlet nozzle.

Water containers

The connecting-up procedures described previously presume that you've already purchased fresh and waste water containers. These are seldom supplied with a new or second-hand caravan, and anyway, many people like a clean start.

It's a matter of choice whether you purchase an inexpensive plastic jerrycan, a rolling water barrel like the Aquaroll, or a trolley-type water container such as the Wastemaster. As a point of interest, many caravanners in mainland Europe don't like fresh water containers being left outdoors, so facilities are built to store them inside.

▼ *Some sites now provide fresh water coupling points to serve individual pitches.*

▲ *The Whale Watermaster Mains includes a pressure reducer so you can connect mains tap water directly into your caravan's supply system.*

▼ *This Whale Watermaster Mains is coupled up to a caravan and then connected to a tap reserved for the pitch.*

▲ *This caravanner used some rigid waste pipe and blocks to create a gradient – thereby creating their own draining facility.*

▼ *Some sites have serviced pitches with drainage for grey waste.*

Some UK manufacturers, *eg* Buccaneer and Compass, have noted this preference and a few models in their ranges have been built with an indoor tank compartment as well.

As regards waste water containers, buy one which is flat enough to stay close to the ground. That's because caravan waste water outlets are often fitted near the chassis and don't provide much scope for creating a downward gradient on the coupling pipe.

▼ *If you don't mind carrying a five-gallon jerrycan back from a tap, this is the least expensive fresh water container.*

▲ *The shallow height of a Wastemaster container just permits a gradient on this caravan's waste pipes.*

Technical tip

1. If you drape a waste water hose so that it rests on the bottom of its receiving container, as soon as the container starts to fill, the discharge of water from sinks and washbasins will slow down significantly. You'll find that water runs much more quickly out of a caravan's pipes if the end of the connecting hose is positioned near the entry point to the waste container rather than on the bottom.

2. Ensure that a fresh water container's inlet is covered to keep out slugs, snails and other inquisitive creatures. If your connection hose arrangement doesn't include a plastic cap or shield, dust covers or Aquacaps are available from Towsure or Leisureshopdirect.

▲ *Several purpose-made water barrels are available but models in the Aquaroll range are especially popular.*

▼ *Fiamma markets a wheeled container and some caravans have an indoor compartment where this can be coupled.*

Winter strategies

More owners are starting to use their caravans in cold weather, and when it's frosty it's wise to transfer the water containers indoors at night. Some intentionally carry back-up containers as well. There are also outdoor activity bag manufacturers that sell insulated fabric bags to prevent water containers freezing-up too easily.

Inboard tanks

A few caravans, including models from Bailey, Bessacarr and Compass, have been fitted with an inboard water tank. You shouldn't travel with this full, of course, because it would cause instability – and water takes up your valuable payload. So, take a couple of plastic bottles of water

▲ Winter caravanners often bring water containers indoors at night; some carry a back-up container too.

▼ For short-term protection, it's useful to put a water container inside an insulated bag when it's cold.

for a roadside brew by all means, but make sure the tank's left empty until you arrive at a site.

The trouble with an inboard tank is the fact that if you occupy a pitch for several days, you would have to tow your caravan to a site tap now and again to replenish the tank. That's a nuisance, so many people carry a long hose or even take an additional plastic container and a funnel to top-up the tank.

Fresh water and waste pipes

When checking the water systems inside caravans, plumbing components differ in several ways. At one time, *all* caravans used to be fitted with plastic hose that was coupled using fittings such as Jubilee clips. The trouble with flexible hose is the fact that unreinforced plastic tubing can develop kinks over a period of time. This seriously restricts the flow of water.

Modern caravans employ semi-rigid plastic pipe with push-fit couplings, which have been used domestically since the 1960s.

In the 1960s and '70s clear plastic hose continued being fitted in caravans, and since this allows the light to penetrate, algae and other deposits develop inside. This was one reason why opaque red and blue plastic pipes were later used for hot and cold supplies respectively.If you purchase an older caravan, clear plastic pipes are certain to look dirty inside. It's not a reassuring sight, especially when you consider that this is the supply route taken by your drinking water. The subject of

sterilising water systems is described in the following section and some caravanners also decide to purchase 'bottled water' for drinking purposes.

Then there's the waste water plumbing. Sadly, in many caravans this is the most primitive example of plumbing you're ever likely to find. Far too many manufacturers fit a convoluted plastic hose that features reinforcing ridges. These ridges might add strength, but on the inside they capture food remnants like rice, peas, meat and so on. Added to this is the fact that on some runs of waste pipe, a 'fall', or gradient, is scarcely discernible – which is one reason why caravan sinks empty so slowly. Sections of pipe might even travel uphill for short distances. Look under the floor and you may find that a lack of support clips causes the waste pipe to hang like a Christmas garland. In consequence, food remnants and greasy washing-up water accumulate in the dangling loops.

This criticism might sound harsh but in many caravans the waste water system hardly exemplifies state-of-the-art plumbing. Oddly enough, it's very easy to replace convoluted hose with rigid PVC-U

▼ *Some practically-minded owners upgrade poorly performing waste water systems.*

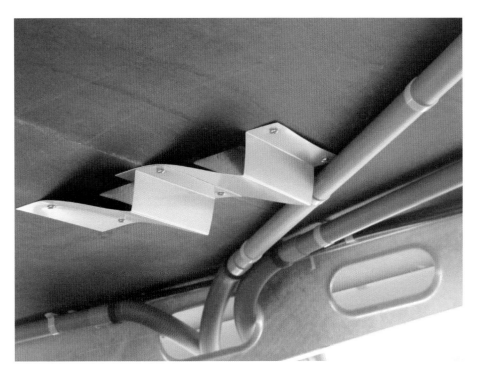

▲ *The 2013 Lunar Clubman Si is fitted with notably well-designed under-floor waste water pipework.*

pipe. This is fitted in our homes and is sold at builders' merchants. In fact, the upgrade work is described in more detail in *The Caravan Manual* by John Wickersham.

Keeping things clean

》 **Fresh water system** – At the start of every season (at the very least) flush this through thoroughly with plenty of water and then sterilise the pipes and your fresh water container using a product like Milton. This is the treatment used to sterilise babies' dummies, drinking bottles and so on.

》 **Waste water system** – A product called Wastemaster Superclean has recently been launched by F.L. Hitchman, manufacturer of the Aquaroll and Wastemaster. This is designed solely to clean waste water containers and tanks and *must not* be used on any of the fresh water components.

In addition, the waste system needs flushing out periodically and especially before a caravan is left in storage. One reason why a caravan interior smells unpleasant after a long winter break is the fact that odours from residual water trapped in the waste pipe creep up through the sink, basin and shower tray outlets. One way to prevent this is to put plugs in all the plug holes.

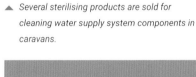

Sterilising and cleaning products, like TankKleen from C.A.K. Tanks, is simply added to the fresh water container/tank and drawn around the system by opening the taps.

Several sterilising products are sold for cleaning water supply system components in caravans.

Practical tip

If you purchase an older caravan and have doubts about the cleanliness of the supply and waste pipes, it may be wise to have them replaced. In some instances, the original system can be improved as well – some DIY projects can be found in Chapter Nine of *The Caravan Manual* by John Wickersham.

Filters

Some caravans have filters fitted, but note that there are essentially three different types, these are:

1. **Grit filters** – one of these is needed if a caravan has a diaphragm pump as described later. A grit filter needs checking and cleaning periodically.

2. **Taste filters** – these can be easily fitted and are a great asset if you visit venues where tap water tastes ghastly. However, remember that a taste filter improves palatability but does not purify water.

3. **Purifying filters** – in this system, a filter achieves levels of purification and taste improvement that allow you to drink water coming from all kinds of uncertain sources. For instance, products like the Nature Pure Ultrafine

from General Ecology are so effective that they even enable narrowboat owners to drink the water drawn from canals.

Needless to say, taste and purifying filters need changing periodically. Ignore this and the filter might even start to collect waterborne germs.

▼ *This Whale exterior water connection comes with a filter for caravans that have an onboard pump. The Silverised Carbon Filter removes unpleasant tastes and smells.*

▼ *Keeping the grit filter clean on a diaphragm pump is important.*

▲ This submersible pump has a debris protector cap.

▼ Some cartridge taste filters are mounted in the supply hose itself.

▲ The Truma Ultraflow replacement filter is for use with the Ultraflow Filter Housing and older Crystal II filter housing systems.

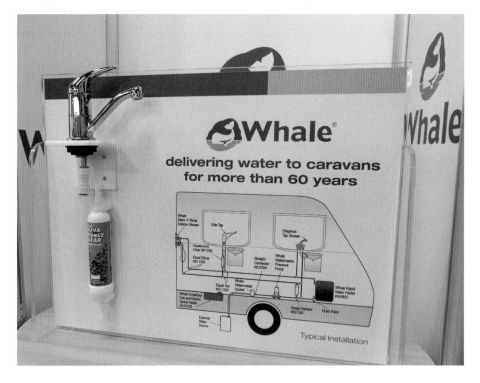

Electric submersible pump systems

Most caravans are now supplied with a submersible pump which is a relatively cheap, easily detachable and reasonably efficient component.

When arriving on site, you have to plug the assembled system into the caravan's wall inlet. This usually requires a firm and sustained push, because there's an 'O' ring in place so that a watertight seal is achieved, together with electrical contacts which have to connect tightly.

Once you've made the coupling, the pump is dropped into a full fresh water container to activate the supply. However, check the Technical Tip on page 170 if water doesn't start to flow.

▲ *For water purification, the Nature Pure Ultrafine is a remarkable product.*

▼ *The Whale Watermaster Exterior Water Pump with Easi-Press plug connection is compatible with both Whale and Truma Ultraflow sockets.*

Technical tip

For several years, submersible pumps didn't have an air release hole on their casings. If you own one of these earlier models, air bubbles sometimes get trapped inside – even when it is lowered into a water supply container. When this happens, its motor will still spring into life when a tap is turned on, but water doesn't arrive at the sink.

If you have this problem, the answer is to swing the unit around in the water container by holding its connecting hose and ensuring that it remains below the surface. Making the pump bump against the side of the water container while it's below the surface then helps dislodge the trapped air bubbles. Sometimes it helps to uncouple the feed hose at the caravan connection point before swinging the pump about; this provides a further escape route for trapped air. Having followed this routine, water should then flow from the taps.

▲ This coupling includes both a water inlet and brass 12V connections for pump operation.

▼ The 'O' ring on the water inlet nozzle ensures the coupling is water-tight but inserting the unit needs a sustained pressure.

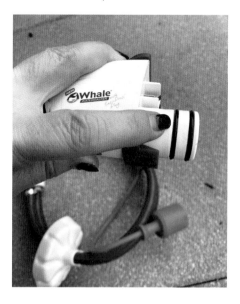

A submersible pump provision has both strengths and weaknesses. It's certainly wise to keep a replacement pump on board because these units can't usually be repaired. Equally, you're unlikely to find compatible units if you encounter a problem when touring abroad.

Advantages

>> **Cost:** submersible pumps are far less expensive than the diaphragm pumps described next.

>> **Self-priming:** whilst this type of pump has to be primed before it starts working, it achieves this automatically as soon as it's dropped into water.

>> **Damage:** the mechanism is merely a paddle wheel (or impeller) that's driven by a small motor. If grit or other waterborne debris gets into the mechanism, it is more likely to survive the intrusion than a diaphragm pump, which is far less tolerant of grit.

▼ *This Swift Conqueror has a Flojet water pump situated in the front locker.*

Disadvantages

>> **Repairs:** these are throwaway items and if the casing splits and water gets into the motor mechanism, it is irreparable.

>> **Battery dependence:** like all electric pumps, submersible models rely on having a 12V supply.

Electric diaphragm pump systems

Instead of having a submersible pump, some higher specified caravans have what is called a diaphragm pump. These are installed somewhere inside the living area, and on arrival at a site you merely need to connect a short length of hose from the external coupling inlet to your water supply vessel. Then it's 'all systems go'. Diaphragm pumps are well-engineered but are more costly than the submersible types.

▼ *Diaphragm pumps like this Whale Watermaster On Board Pump are noted for their high flow rates, reliability and robust construction.*

Advantages

» **Output:** these self-priming pumps usually achieve a notable flow rate.

» **Repairs:** most manufacturers and importers of these pumps offer a repair service.

Disadvantages

» **Noise:** diaphragm pumps can be noisy, although this is often through poor installation.

» **Damage:** grit soon damages the tiny pistons that create water flow and a special filter has to be checked and cleaned periodically.

» **Cost:** these items are considerably more expensive than submersible pumps, although a diaphragm pump is likely to last much longer.

» **Battery dependence:** like all electric pumps, a diaphragm pump relies on having a 12V supply.

Exploded drawings of the mechanisms, guidance on grit filter cleaning and installation checks are given in Chapter Nine of *The Caravan Manual* by John Wickersham.

Pump switching

Like all electric motors, the ones fitted in caravans' water pumps need something to switch them into action. In most cases, a pump motor is controlled by miniature switches that have been mounted in the

Handy tip

It's always wise to carry a spare microswitch. Even if you have no intention of carrying out your own repair jobs, the spare can be given to a service specialist to fit. This is particularly appropriate if you're travelling abroad because the water systems and associated products are often different.

taps and the shower controls. As you turn the hand-wheel on a tap or lift its lever, two things happen – firstly the water channel is opened up and secondly the microswitch is triggered.

This control arrangement is fine, apart from the fact that these diminutive switches cease working if damp gets into their housing. On some taps, you then have to throw the whole unit away and purchase a replacement. That might be costly and it is fortunate that most tap assemblies are designed so that a faulty microswitch can be replaced. Only the matter of access makes this a difficult operation, especially under a kitchen sink. It certainly helps if you're a contortionist, slight of build, and able to see in the dark.

Whereas microswitch systems are quite common, some caravans are fitted with a different switching system altogether. This involves a pressure-sensitive switch that detects when a tap is opened and then responds by setting the pump into action. In fact, a diaphragm pump usually has a pressure-sensitive switch housed inside its

▲ *The micro switch on this mixer tap is fairly easy to change.*

casing. Alternatively, it is possible to have a stand-alone pressure switch coupled-up within the supply pipe that serves the taps.

The only trouble with pressure-sensitive devices is the fact that they have a nasty habit of switching on a pump motor whenever a tiny failure in a pipe joint is sufficient to cause a slight air leak. That's why there's a pump isolating switch on many electrical control panels. In fact, it's always wise to switch off a pressure-controlled system last thing at night so that you don't get woken up by a pump making a brief pulsing action.

Pressure-sensitive switching systems can also be affected when a supply battery gets low. In anticipation of this possibility, both diaphragm pumps and stand-alone pressure switches usually have a screw control for making 'fine-tuning' adjustments. However, this is sometimes hidden so that

Handy tip

Many caravans have a double tap system for the hot and cold water supply. If a microswitch fails on one of the supplies – let's say it's the hot supply that cannot be switched into operation – you can sometimes solve this temporarily by 'cheating the system'. This is how you do it:

1. Open the hot tap a generous amount. Nothing will come out because we've established the microswitch has failed.

2. Now very, very gently turn the neighbouring cold tap (or any other tap in the caravan for that matter), listening for a tiny 'click' to indicate its switch is activated.

3. Don't open this tap any further – it just needs to be open enough to trigger the microswitch.

4. Hey presto! The pump will be set in motion but the water will come from the hot tap that was opened a generous amount.

owners don't tamper with the adjuster and upset its calibration.

To summarise, neither microswitch nor pressure-sensitive systems are perfect performers. Whereas some components work for years and years without a problem, others have less impressive reliability.

Which pumping system?

In light of the points made previously, anyone buying a new or pre-owned caravan would therefore be wise to ask:

>> What type of pump is fitted? And, in the case of a diaphragm type, where is it located?

>> Does pump switching rely on a microswitch or a pressure-sensitive device?

>> Are replacement microswitches readily available?

>> How is the sensitivity of a pressure-sensitive device (if fitted) adjusted?

>> Is it easy to purchase a replacement submersible pump of the appropriate type and with a connection to suit the caravan's water inlet?

▼ Bench-type cassette toilets from Thetford have been fitted in caravans for many years.

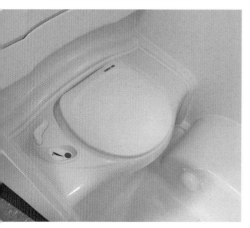

Toilets

It's a long time since the 'bucket and chuck it' toilet was used in caravans. Few modern caravanners would tolerate an open receptacle surmounted by a precarious seat. If using these toilets was primitive, caravanners' stories involving stumbling on the caravan's steps en route to the chemical emptying point with a full bucket were legendary, as you might imagine.

Most toilets are now built-in and this alternative style of 'cassette loo' has been installed in most British caravans for more than 30 years. There are two types of toilets - the 'bench-type' and the 'swivel-bowl'. Either way, the care, use and end-of-season servicing are much the same for permanently-installed models as for portable flushers.

▼ Swivel-bowl cassette toilets often fit better in small cubicles, which has made them increasingly popular.

▲ Many caravans have been equipped with a Thetford C260 toilet whose cassette is fitted with wheels and a retractable handle.

▲ On a bench-style Thetford toilet, there's a fold-out reservoir for flush water and additive in the cassette compartment.

When comparing all modern versions of these cassette toilets, several things remain much the same. They all need flush water, all use similar chemical treatments and all have a cassette that needs emptying – especially when its gauge reveals that it's full.

Not surprisingly, innovations appear now and again, and, to bring this overview right up to date, Thetford has now introduced a revolutionary smart sanitation system that is a macerator toilet, which has an automatic dosing module and an integrated discharging device allowing you to go off-grid for an average of 7 days.

▼ Swivel-bowl toilets fitted on caravans usually have a separate hatch and filler point for the flush water and additive.

Flush water

The procedure for adding a toilet's flushing water depends on the model. As the photos to the right show, a bench-type toilet has a fold-out reservoir, whereas a swivel-bowl model has a purpose-made hatch.

Chemical treatments

The cassette, sometimes called the 'holding tank', needs a chemical to break up solids, and there are plenty of products on the market. They appear in several forms, too, including liquids, granular crystals and dissolvable sachets. Pay careful attention to the mixing levels of the liquid products and always remember to put about a litre of water into the cassette first of all.

When purchasing chemicals, you'll find that some products are based on formaldehyde. This certainly breaks down solid matter, but there's growing concern that it is detrimental to the environment. Consequently, several 'environmentally friendly' chemicals have been appearing as alternatives.

Taking such concerns further, most treatments are formulated to bring a halt to biological activity in a toilet cassette tank. Unfortunately, constituents like formaldehyde and glutaraldehyde have also been claimed to pose problems at sewage treatment plants.

▼ *Chemical treatment fluid needs measuring out carefully and this cassette cap includes markings to make the task easier.*

In response to environmental concerns, new products are certain to appear, like Blue BIO which contains non-pathogenic enzymes. Their function is to break down the 'nasties', kill the odours and then continue to carry out these functions at the sewage treatment plant. This principle of operation is entirely different from more traditional approaches, and yet Blue BIO only has to be diluted at the parsimonious rate of one part product to 100 parts water. When used as a flush water additive, the prescribed dilution is then one part product to 500 parts water. Without doubt, this is a remarkably economic treatment.

▼ *There are many products available on the market to help keep your toilet hygienically clean.*

▲ Sachets and sanitation tabs are convenient, less messy and are a pre-measured dosage.

▼ Introduced in 2009, water-based Blue Bio is a cassette treatment which is also designed to be a flush additive.

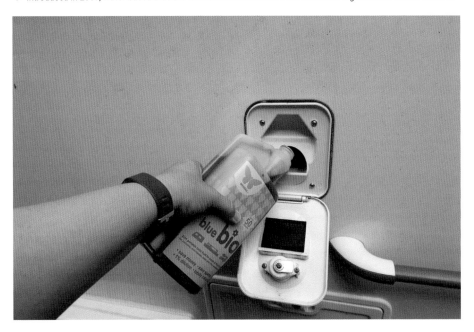

▲ *Dometic GreenCare Tabs are an environmentally friendly toilet additive made from eco-safe materials.*

Potty training

Many caravanners have 'house rules' that dictate that their toilet is only used for liquid waste. On most sites that's fine, but not when you stop at modestly-equipped farm sites where you have to be fully self-contained. The rule also ignores the reality of the 'human emergency'.

The time-honoured trick is to precede a

'performance' by flushing a small amount of water into the pan. Then a few pieces of toilet paper are carefully placed to float on the water like flower petals, making sure they make brief surface contact around the pan as well. This origami exercise may sound bizarre but it brings its rewards.

Once the 'performance' is complete, you find that as soon as the toilet emptying blade is swung open, the solids drop unhindered into the holding tank below and the paper encloses them completely with gift-wrapping panache. This means that

no stains are left on the pan, or – more importantly – on the blade and its sealing rubber ring. Don't forget that you see this rubber sealing ring every time the cassette is taken for emptying, so you don't want soil marks. If this all sounds unseemly, believe me – it works!

Emptying advice

There's definitely a knack to emptying a cassette, and using a brim-full container doesn't help you learn. Here is a step-by-step guide:

▼ **Lift the plastic catch to release the cassette holding tank.**

Step 1

Step 2

▲ Carefully remove the cassette using both hands as it might be heavy.

▼ Immediately put a removed cap in a safe place. This shows how not to proceed - the cap can easily get knocked into the caravan site's emptying chamber.

▼ Depressing the air release button while tipping a holding tank calls for dexterity, which comes with practice.

Step 3

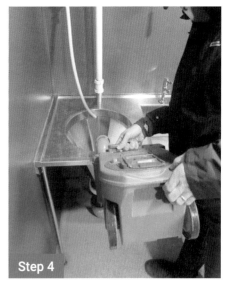

Step 4

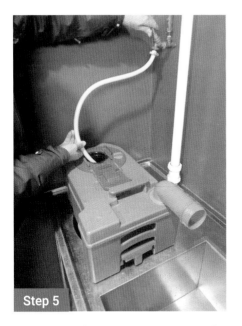

Step 5

▲ Add some fresh water and give a gentle shake from side-to-side to remove the last remnants of toilet paper. Vigorous shaking can damage the internal float mechanism that warns when a cassette is ready for emptying.

▼ Re-fill the fresh water tank, but don't over-fill it.

Step 7

Step 6

▲ Replenish the cassette with the correct amount of toilet chemical and water.

▼ *Love2Stay has a revolutionary fully automatic chemical cleaning station for those that don't like to get their hands dirty. It only takes 3 minutes to empty and prime your toilet cassette.*

Lay-up procedure

Obviously, it's catastrophic to leave a toilet un-emptied all winter, even though a cassette is built with a pressure-relief valve. But you won't make that mistake if you always remember to leave the blade in its open position prior to a lay-up period. Apart from acting as an emptying reminder, this prevents the blade sticking to the rubberised seal valve – which sometimes happens over a long storage period. You are also strongly advised to lubricate the seal prior to an extended lay-up period.

Do this as follows:

1. Clean the rubber seal using Thetford Bathroom Cleaner or a lukewarm diluted solution of washing-up liquid; never use a household cleaner, which can damage the seal.

2. Dry thoroughly then spray with Thetford's Toilet Seal lubricant. Alternatively, you can use olive oil, but never use Vaseline or any form of grease.

3. Leave the blade wide open throughout the period of storage.

▼ *An alternative to olive oil is Thetford's Seal Lubricant designed to protect toilet seals.*

Chapter Nine

Using a refrigerator

▲ *A modern refrigerator is one of the most useful appliances in a caravan.*

A refrigerator is one of the most useful appliances in a modern caravan. However, it is different from the fridges we've got at home, and to get the best from one it helps to have a rough idea of how it works. For example, unlike household refrigerators, the appliances fitted in modern caravans operate on one of three sources of power. First, they can work on gas; secondly, they can operate on 12V electricity while a caravan is being towed; and thirdly, they can work using a 230V mains supply.

The idea of equipping caravans with refrigerators gathered momentum in the 1970s. One of the popular types at the time was manufactured by Morphy Richards, and its gas burner was accessed by removing a hatch fitted to an outside wall. It then had to be lit with a match, which was always a challenge in breezy weather. This was one of the early appliances designed specifically for caravans. Other products appeared soon afterwards.

For example, the Electrolux range became popular too, which included portable refrigerators for use on picnics. In time, Electrolux leisure models occupied a special division within the parent company, which was well-known for a diverse range of domestic appliances. Then the leisure division became part of the Swedish Dometic Group, which is a prominent force in the caravan industry today.

Around the start of the new millennium, Norcold refrigerators, which had been eminent in the USA, were introduced to European markets. In the United Kingdom these appliances are now part of the Thetford Group, whose toilet systems have enjoyed a long-established presence in the leisure-vehicle market.

The refrigerants in products from Dometic and Thetford are circulated by the application of heat as described later. In contrast, there are cooling appliances made by Dometic whose refrigerants are circulated by a compressor pump rather than heat. These are often installed in

▶ *This Webasto Drawer refrigerator is a compressor fridge that runs on a 12V supply, but it's more commonly fitted in campervans, like this VW Grand California, rather than touring caravans.*

Technical Tip

In almost all caravan cooling appliances the refrigerants are circulated by heat. This is called the 'absorption' process. However, in your refrigerator at home the chemicals are circulated by a compressor pump, and you can often hear the hum of its motor when a thermostat brings it into operation.

The noise from a compressor fridge is seldom a problem in a large kitchen but the intermittent hum can be a nuisance in a caravan – especially at night. Nevertheless, compressor fridges are sometimes fitted in small 'camper vans' and this alternative approach to refrigeration might gain ground in the future. Time will tell.

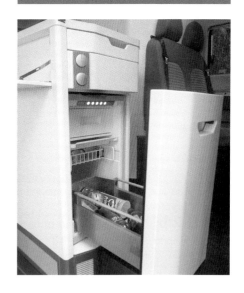

campervans but are not normally fitted in UK touring caravans.

Contact addresses for both Thetford and Dometic appear in the Appendix address list. However, Morphy Richards' contact details are not included; although the company's leisure refrigerators were sometimes fitted in early 1970s caravans, they were seldom seen after that period.

Three-way operation

Refrigerator manufacturers talk about three-way operation in recognition of the fact that three power sources can be used to run these appliances. Each has its merits and there's good reason for giving caravanners three alternatives.

Whichever option you choose, the supply is used to heat the refrigerant chemicals stored in the cooling unit at the back of the casing. Once heat has been applied, the refrigerant starts circulating around a complex assembly of pipes. During its circulation, the refrigerant chemicals change to a gas and then back to a liquid -– a process which is instrumental in drawing heat out of the food compartment. That's all you need to know about chemistry and cooling, although the Technical Tip panel on page 184 explains how caravan appliances differ from the ones in our homes.

Operation on gas

Applying heat from a small burner is particularly effective. Although this heat source is located low down at the back of the casing, a gas selector button on the front panel controls the level of cooling. As

shown in the accompanying photograph, this control raises or lowers the height of the flame. Incidentally, a caravan fridge is made to run on either butane or propane gas without any need for alteration.

When caravan fridges first became popular around 40 years ago, you had to light the burner with a match. Since the mid-1980s, an electronic system was introduced. Provided an appliance is switched on at the fascia, the electronic circuits will generate a spark automatically whenever the burner isn't alight.

▲ *Set the temperature using the button featuring an illustrated thermometer. One bar is the lowest cooling capacity and five bars is the highest cooling capacity.*

▼ *Older fridges were criticised for having complicated controls: this 2013 model is delightfully simple to operate.*

Technical Tip

Ignition systems only work if a spark gap is correctly set at the burner. Furthermore, soot is created when a fridge runs on gas and an excessive coating around a burner assembly similarly upsets an igniter's efficiency. That's partly why it's important to have a caravan fridge serviced periodically, as explained later. One of the tasks involves cleaning the system and realigning the electrode where the spark should appear.

Technical Tip

When you've set a refrigerator's selector switch to the 12V operating position, you will not be able to control the cooling level of the appliance as you can when it's running on either a gas or a 230V supply. On a 12V setting, the refrigerator runs at a steady level, and altering the fascia cooling controls makes no difference at all. However, don't be misled into thinking that 12V operation is any less efficient than it is when running on gas or mains electricity. That is not the case.

Operation on 12V

It is very unwise to run a fridge on gas when your caravan is being towed; in addition, it is illegal and potentially very dangerous to enter a filling station forecourt with an exposed gas flame. To avoid this, fridge manufacturers fit a heating element that runs on 12 volts as an alternative heat source. This means you can keep your fridge working while you're towing without using the gas system.

However, a refrigerator takes a lot of current to heat its refrigerants (around 8 amps) and the demand would discharge a 12V battery very quickly. So, it is entirely impracticable to run this appliance from a caravan leisure battery when you are stopping at the site. Accordingly, the caravan's wiring seldom includes a supply that links the fridge with its inboard battery.

Nevertheless, as long as your car's wiring has been correctly modified for caravanning use, a refrigerator is able to operate when you're towing and the engine is running. Current for the 12V heating element is drawn from the vehicle by taking advantage of its alternator charging system. In other words, the alternator keeps the car battery charged even though there's a power-hungry appliance taking some of its current.

Operation on 230V

If you select the mains option, a different heating element comes into use for circulating the chemicals.

This operating mode is not only useful on a caravan site. It can also be put into use when your caravan is parked at home and you're packing it for a holiday. For example, it enables you to pre-cool the fridge before setting off without having to use your gas supply.

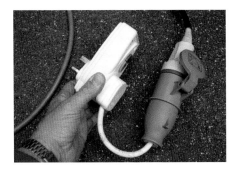

▲ *To run a fridge from a 13A mains socket at home, your hook-up lead will need an adaptor together with a portable RCD safety unit.*

To carry out this operation, run the fridge using your caravan's hook-up lead, thereby ensuring that the RCD safety unit in the 'van is providing protection inside. This safety component is described in Chapter Ten. Of course, you'll need a plug adaptor if you want to connect a hook-up lead to one of the domestic 13-amp sockets in your house. Moreover, it is strongly recommended to use a portable RCD unit in your selected 13-amp socket just in case anyone damages the external coupling cable running out to your caravan.

As regards fridge operation when stopping at caravan sites equipped with hook-ups, if you've paid to couple-up to a mains supply pillar, you'll obviously select the 230V mode rather than running your appliance on gas.

Possible problems and solutions

As a rule, a refrigerator that's serviced regularly and installed correctly will be notably trouble-free. However, the following tips may be useful, especially if you're

Technical Tip

On crowded sites in the summer, particularly in some European countries, the current draw on a mains system is considerable. This becomes especially acute in hot weather when fridges and air conditioning units are running flat-out. In some instances, heavy usage affects a caravan site's supply capabilities, and checks have revealed that some mains systems even drop below 195V. If this occurs, your fridge operation can be badly affected. Specialists at Dometic recommend that if you cannot get satisfactory cooling when running on mains, switch over to gas operation. This is likely to improve the performance, especially when you're using busy sites in hot locations.

experiencing problems when trying to get it started:

If you find the refrigerator doesn't work on gas, check these points:

a) Its supply cylinder still contains plenty of gas.

b) The gas valve serving the refrigerator is open.

c) If you can't ignite the burner after repeated attempts, arrange to have the appliance serviced.

▲ *If a refrigerator's gas burner doesn't ignite, check that the tap on the supply pipe is in the 'Open' position.*

If you find the refrigerator doesn't work on 12V, check:

a) The caravan's 12S or 13-pin plug is connected to the tow car's socket.

b) The fuse serving the refrigerator on the 12V supply panel is intact.

c) The 12V selector switch is in the correct position on the refrigerator fascia.

d) The tow car's engine is running – the 12V option is for use when towing only and is not available when the engine is switched off.

If you find the refrigerator doesn't work on 230V, check:

a) The 230V fascia switch is turned on.

b) If the fridge is coupled to a caravan's mains circuit using a 13A plug that normally stays in a socket, check that the fuse in the plug is intact.

c) Check that the miniature circuit breaker that controls the fridge supply hasn't tripped out on the 230V consumer unit.

Food storage advice

To get the best from a caravan refrigerator there are also a number of tips relating to food storage:

Pre-cooling

Refrigerator manufacturers recommend that the fridge will perform best if it has been in operation for three to four hours before setting off. During this period, some non-perishable items should be placed in the food compartment, eg bottles of water or some cans of drink.

Adding foodstuffs

When packing for a holiday, try to delay putting perishable foods in your refrigerator until its cabinet temperature has dropped considerably. If you are able to transfer items that are already cool from your kitchen fridge, so much the better.

Loading-up

Avoid packing food tightly in the fridge and try to position items so that air can circulate

▲ Cooling efficiency is greatly reduced if a pack of drinks is placed directly over the heat extractor fins.

▲ Wet lettuce must be wrapped in a sealed bag before storing it in a fridge.

around the cabinet. This is important because cooling is achieved by taking heat *out* of the food storage compartment.

Cooling fins

Heat withdrawal is carried out via a bank of silver fins at the rear of the food compartment and it's important not to cover these. Quite often poor cooling occurs when a caravanner stows an item such as a pack of drink cans hard against the cooling fins.

Covering food

Remember to pack strong-smelling commodities like pungent cheese or onions in a sealed plastic bag. Similarly pack any damp vegetables in a bag – especially freshly washed lettuce. Failure to do this leads to the formation of water droplets or frost on the silver cooling fins and this impairs performance.

▼ Heat from the food compartment is drawn out via silver heat extractor fins.

Door catches

Get into a fixed routine of checking that the door security catch is engaged before taking to the road. Many caravanners have the dreadful experience of finding the refrigerator's contents strewn across the floor on arrival at their destination. But you only make this mistake once!

Practical operating advice

Freezer compartment

If your refrigerator has a small freezer compartment, decide what types of food might be usefully stored inside. There is usually a tray for making ice cubes, too, but don't fill this with water just before hitching-up and leaving. As a point of interest, some Dometic fridges are fitted with a freezer compartment that can be dismantled if it isn't needed. This frees-up space in the main part of the food storage compartment.

Igniting the gas burner

If your caravan has not been used for some time, it may take several attempts to get the gas burner to light. This usually means there's air in the gas supply pipe and it may take repeated attempts before all the air is purged. However, if ignition difficulties persist, this often indicates that the spark is weak, the electrodes are dirty or the spark gap needs

▼ *This 2018 Swift Conqueror has been equipped with a refrigerator whose freezer compartment can be removed if it isn't needed.*

realignment. Problems like that typically show that it's time for an appliance to be serviced.

Checking the flame

On a refrigerator with electronic ignition, you will hear the unit clicking when it detects that the flame has been extinguished. These clicking sounds also indicate that the igniter is generating sparks automatically in an attempt to relight it. You will also note a flashing red switch on the fascia which again confirms the burner is *not* alight and that ignition attempts are not achieving results.

Flame-failure devices (FFDs)

Like most gas appliances, a refrigerator has a flame-failure device (FFD). This means that if the flame blows out in a wind, the gas supply to the burner will be shut off automatically. The FFD uses a probe (called a thermocouple) that is angled into the gas flame; when it gets hot it creates a small electric current, which, in turn, keeps a gas valve open in the supply line. However, when you start the fridge from cold you have to hold down the main control for several seconds to manually open the gas valve while the probe is getting warmed up. If you find the flame goes out as soon as you release the control knob, the FFD probably needs attention – and that's one of the jobs included in an annual service. Don't be tempted to jam the control knob open, since you will override the all-important flame-failure facility.

Note: *Further information about flame-failure devices is given in the Technical Tip panel on page 273.*

Efficiency

As long as a refrigerator has been correctly installed by the caravan manufacturer, and provided the user-recommendations are followed, Dometic refrigerators are able to operate efficiently in air temperatures as high as 38°C (100°F). Unfortunately, some caravan manufacturers have taken short cuts in the installation and these often prevent an appliance from achieving its full potential.

Ventilation

On an absorption refrigerator (as opposed to a compressor type), external vents are important contributors to the cooling process. For that reason, you should make sure that they don't get covered up. Occasionally sections of an awning can obscure a wall ventilator, and if this happens the fabric should be modified so that a clear airway is created. On some models a caravan's door opens directly across the vents, and this doesn't help either. Make sure a gap of at least 50mm (2in) is maintained when the door is held back, especially during warm weather.

▸ *On absorption fridges, efficient cooling is dependent on having external ventilators that allow air to flow across the cooling unit mounted on the rear of the casing.*

▲ *Fans are sometimes installed at the rear of the large fridge-freezers that are now being fitted in a few of the more expensive touring caravans.*

Note: If you buy a pre-owned caravan and find there's a small electric fan fitted on the inside face of the upper fridge ventilator, this is a modification to improve the flow of air across the cooling unit. This may improve cooling, although some manufacturers maintain that a fan is not normally necessary if an appliance has been installed correctly. However, small fans are sometimes fitted on the large fridge-freezers installed in a few 'top-of-the-range' caravans.

Door

In very hot weather, try to open the door of a fridge as little as possible. The wisdom of this is self-evident but young children may not appreciate that cooled air quickly drops out of the food compartments of upright fridges. Anyone who opens a door when wearing shorts is soon made aware of this feature; disciplined use of the door makes good sense.

Cold-weather caravanning

Most caravanners take their holidays in summer and poor cooling is often a matter of concern. On the other hand, if you use your 'van when outside temperatures are low, you can experience the opposite problem: over-cooling. It partly depends on the model fitted in your caravan.

Winter covers

Aware of the over-cooling problem, Dometic introduced an accessory referred to as 'winter covers'. If your caravan has recent Dometic ventilators, you can purchase compatible winter covers from your dealer. These covers are designed to restrict the flow of air across the rear of the appliance and you're recommended to clip them on to the ventilators whenever outside temperatures fall below 10°C (50°F).

Unfortunately, some of the cheaper ventilators fitted on caravans are of a different pattern and you can't buy covers that fit. As a rough and ready alternative some owners attach a piece of silver cooking foil over a small part of the upper ventilator. However, don't cover the lower ventilator, because on some refrigerator installations this also acts as a gas escape point in the event of a leak in the supply pipe.

Draughts

If a refrigerator has been installed in accordance with its manufacturer's instructions, the section at the rear of the appliance will be completely sealed-off from the caravan living quarters. In other words, if a strong wind blows towards the external ventilators, it is prevented from reaching the occupants inside.

It is a matter of considerable regret that a number of caravan manufacturers fail to seal off the rear section as required. Not only does this impair a refrigerator's cooling performance in summer, it also leads to draughtiness in cold, windy weather. Some owners wrongly presume that winter covers are intended to overcome this. In practice they might ease the problem, but winter covers were *not* designed to act as draught excluders.

Checking an installation

If you're buying a caravan – whether brand new or second-hand – it is often possible to establish if the cooling unit at the rear has been sealed off properly from the living area indoors. For instance, if you look through the external ventilators you should not be able to see into the kitchen. In fact, on the latest ventilators you can remove the grill by releasing the retention catches, which then reveals if there's a likelihood of a draught problem.

Alternatively, if you remove drawers in the kitchen near a fridge and peer towards

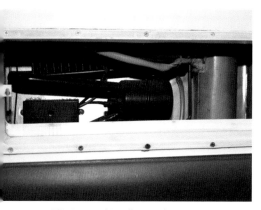

▲ *This is a good installation; when peering through a ventilator aperture it was impossible to see through to the kitchen.*

the wall vents, you shouldn't be able to see any light from outside. Indeed, you shouldn't even be able to see either the upper or lower ventilators from inside.

There's a further test that you can carry out to confirm if your refrigerator is suitably shielded-off at the rear. This check should be made when a fridge is running on gas. If there's a worktop or draining board directly

▼ *Removing a drawer sometimes reveals why draughts reach a kitchen; it's usually the result of a poorly fitted fridge.*

over the top of the appliance, put your hand on it. If it's warm, it's almost certain that the installation is not as good as it should be. Heat being produced around the cooling unit is not being confined at the rear as the refrigerator manufacturer prescribes.

If you carry out checks and find that an installation is disappointing, this is unlikely to constitute a risk to the occupants. Although the ventilation pathway at the rear should be sealed to create optimum cooling and a draught-free kitchen, don't get this confused with the flue system above the burner. Gases from combustion at the burner *do* have to be efficiently discharged outside via a flue, but that's a separate assembly.

A surprising number of refrigerators were fitted unsatisfactorily. Poor-performing appliances often get blamed for mediocre cooling, whereas it's usually a slipshod installation that provokes the problems. Furthermore, if you fail to get a refrigerator serviced regularly that can also affect performance. And without doubt, there are many caravan owners who stoically endure draughts in their kitchen whenever it's windy outside.

Cleaning and laying-up

On a 'housekeeping' matter, a refrigerator needs to be kept clean inside and free of mould.

» To keep the interior clean, Dometic recommends regular cleaning using a teaspoonful of bicarbonate of soda added to a litre of warm water. On Thetford refrigerators they recommend the use of Thetford Bathroom Cleaner.

To clean the inside of a Dometic fridge, the manufacturer recommends a solution of a teaspoonful of bicarbonate of soda mixed in a litre of warm water.

Thetford 'Bathroom Cleaner' is ideal for cleaning the inside of a refrigerator.

>> Do not use other cleaners; some brands slowly react with the plastic lining material of refrigerators and the resulting damage isn't always apparent until several months later.

>> Clean the condensate drain when necessary. If it gets blocked the condensate will collect at the bottom of the fridge.

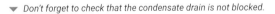

Don't forget to check that the condensate drain is not blocked.

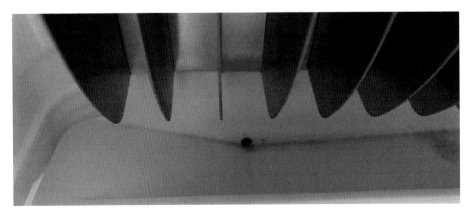

▲ *Most refrigerators have a catch that allows the door to be secured slightly ajar during periods of storage.*

>> Leave the door ajar when not in use using its security catch in the storage position. If the catch is broken or the 'van has a false wooden door to hide the fridge, rig up a system which will ensure the refrigerator door is held slightly open without being able to swing free if the caravan is moved during storage. The system must also prevent the normal magnetic closure device from pulling the door tightly shut.

>> Make sure that the ventilation grille on the outer wall of the caravan is free from dust and dirt, particularly spider's webs.

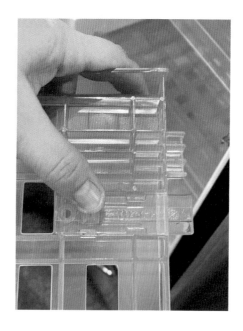

▶ *Some shelves, like on the Dometic 9 series fridge, have catches to stop the shelves shifting whilst in transit. Be careful not to pull too hard and break the plastic catch.*

Refrigerator servicing

Check your caravan's owner's manual for advice on refrigerator servicing intervals. For example, to ensure that their caravan refrigerators give good service, Dometic and Thetford recommend that their appliances are serviced every 12–18 months depending on the frequency of use. However, don't be misled into thinking that a fridge need not be serviced if a caravan remains stored for a couple of years. Rust will form in the flue and this can easily dislodge and fall on to the burner. Moths and spiders can also upset the fine operation of an electronic ignition system, or the gas supply itself.

One of the anomalies, however, is the fact that if you book-in your caravan for its 'standard' annual service, very little work is done on the refrigerator itself. Cooling is usually checked, and the appearance of the gas flame might be inspected by a gas engineer, but little else.

This is regrettable, and a full fridge service is usually regarded by caravan servicing specialists as a further task that is 'optional'. It is not an expensive operation, although one of the more time-consuming jobs is removing an appliance from a caravan to obtain better access. Several service jobs are virtually impossible to complete if appliances are left in situ.

Service jobs include:

>> Cleaning the burner, flue, FFD probe and ignition assembly.

>> Checking and realigning the ignition spark gap.

▲ *One of the most demanding parts of a refrigerator service can often be the business of withdrawing the appliance in the first place.*

>> Checking the operation of the flame-failure system.

Once a fridge has been moved to a bench, a servicing operation normally takes about an hour to complete. In a few cases the work can be done with an appliance left in situ, but that's unusual. Either way, the task should be entrusted to a qualified servicing specialist, and it is not a DIY job. Courses are run by refrigerator manufacturers so that caravan workshop staff know how to

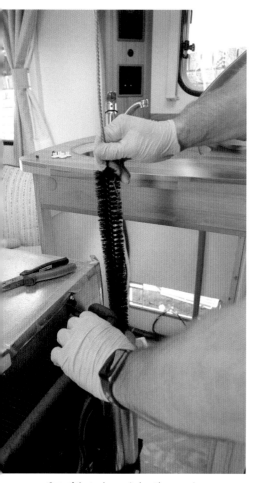

▲ One of the tasks carried out by a service engineer is cleaning the flue and burner assembly.

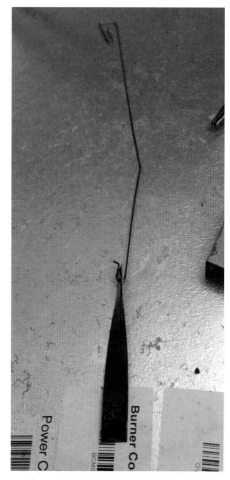

▲ The suspended twisted plate in the burner tube referred to as a 'baffle' also needs to be cleaned of any carbon deposits.

conduct service operations, diagnose faults and carry out repairs.

More detailed practical information on servicing, refrigerator operation and installation requirements are given in Chapter 11 of *The Caravan Manual* by John Wickersham.

Portable refrigerators

If you buy a very old caravan that hasn't been fitted with a fridge, it might be possible to have one installed. However, this can be a costly option, and alterations to your caravan's kitchen will probably be needed as well. A better alternative might be to purchase a portable refrigerator.

Don't get these mixed up with insulated 'cool boxes', which have a similar look but lack a cooling unit. Portable refrigerators are manufactured by several specialists, and many caravanners buy them to provide an additional cooling facility to use in an awning or to put into use back at home. These appliances normally offer three-way operation and it is important to read the instructions most carefully when putting one into commission. Operation from gas, for example, must follow all the usual safety procedures.

Nevertheless, the points mentioned already about food packing and pre-cooling are applicable to portable fridges as well. In addition, if you decide to change your caravan you can transfer a portable refrigerator to its replacement.

▶ Portable refrigerators can be especially useful appliances – both at home and on holiday.

▼ Occasionally a burner will need replacing following a refrigerator service.

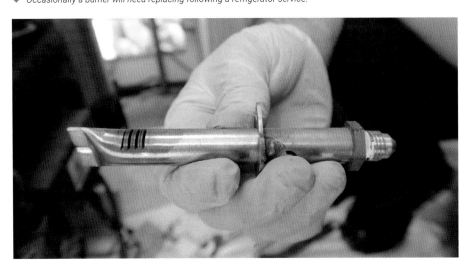

Chapter Ten

Using mains electricity

These hook-up pillars are often seen in Britain. This one also houses TV sockets linked to a large site aerial.

Being able to use mains lights and 230V appliances in your caravan is especially helpful. Indeed, in the last 25 years more and more sites have been offering mains connection points, called 'hook-ups'. However, two matters must be recognised. Firstly, it's essential to observe the important safety procedures; mains electricity can cause fatalities. Secondly, you won't be able to operate some of the power-hungry appliances often used at home.

If you purchase a second-hand caravan and find that its handbook is missing, you need to find out how to use the 230V mains 'hook-ups' which are provided on many caravanning sites. Even with a new caravan, some owner's manuals do not go into much detail about site supplies, hook-up pillars and issues encountered abroad. To help new caravanners, this chapter covers the following areas of interest:

>> An overview of components that are fitted in caravans to permit the safe use of 230V appliances.

>> A summary of the coupling items needed for connecting a site supply to your caravan.

>> Different types of hook-up pillars that you'll find in the UK and abroad – together with the use of adaptors.

>> Establishing what appliances you can and can't run in your caravan. This varies from site to site and you need to ensure that you don't overload a site's supply system.

>> The procedures, presented in step-by-step stages, for connecting up to a site supply.

>> The issue of 'reverse polarity'. This term refers to a situation where there are 'crossed wires' in a site's supply system.

>> The provision of a safe but independent 230V supply in an awning.

>> The use of portable generators and inverters.

On a technical note, it is worth adding that you don't have to understand terms like amps, volts and watts before switching on your lights at home. Nor, for that matter, is it necessary to have this knowledge before using electricity in a caravan. On the other hand, the matter of coupling-up to a caravan site supply is helped if you do have a rudimentary understanding of words like 'amps'. For this reason, the Technical Tip panel on page 202 is for readers who want to know why this is helpful.

The mains supply

New owners are often surprised to find that there are two separate electrical systems installed in modern caravans. These are: (1) a 230V mains system; (2) a 12V system that draws its supply from a battery. This chapter, and the one which follows, looks closely at the two installations.

Virtually all caravans currently manufactured in Britain are fitted with a mains electricity system as standard. In addition, many older models which were not originally equipped to run 230V appliances often have a mains facility installed retrospectively. This upgrading work can be carried out at a caravan workshop or by a qualified electrician who has a knowledge of the wiring products and special components needed in caravans.

In addition, DIY installation kits are sold, and these are ideal for owners who have the skill and knowledge to carry out conversion work themselves. An approved kit is strongly recommended, because the way that a caravan has to be wired-up is quite different from the way our homes are

Technical Tip
Amps, volts and watts

Expressed simply, the word 'voltage' refers to electrical 'pressure', and in Britain, a mains supply used to be rated at 240 volts (V). Other countries in mainland Europe often used lower voltages. However, as a result of European standardisation, supplies in EU states are now 230V AC – albeit with a permitted variation between plus 10% and minus 10%.

'Volts', therefore, relates to electrical *pressure* and isn't a measure of *quantity*. However, the matter of quantity is important, because some electrical appliances are certainly more greedy than others. Accordingly, the amount of power consumed is measured in amperes (amps or A), which is also referred to as the 'current'.

It is helpful for a caravanner to understand these definitions because the *amount* of electricity available from site hook-up pillars is also expressed in amps. What's more, the amount of current available varies from site to site, and that affects what types of appliances you'll be able to use. That's why you ask at a reception office how many amps are available from a site's hook-ups. With that information, you then need to know how many amps are used by your various mains appliances. You might think that will be easy to find out, but then discover that appliance labels refer to watts (W).

The watts information on a label refers to an appliance's *rate* of electrical consumption, and watts embrace a combination of both amps and volts. In fact, watts = amps x volts. Of course, it is widely understood that a traditional mains light bulb rated at 100W is brighter than a 60W bulb; it is also more costly to run. In fact, most electrical appliances are also rated in watts – which doesn't help the caravanner who really wants to know how many amps they consume.

But that's not a problem, you find this out by dividing the wattage of an appliance by the voltage of your electrical supply. So, a domestic 2,000W (2kW) fan heater being run from a 230V mains supply consumes nearly nine amps (2,000 divided by 230 = 8.70). Help! That exceeds the current supplied by many hook-up pillars – and that IS important to know. Trying to run an appliance like that on some sites will cause the hook-up supply to terminate automatically. Issues like this are explained later in this chapter.

wired. Moreover, you may find some kits – like the one from Powerpart – in which the mains consumer unit is already pre-wired. This means it is supplied with lengths of pre-connected cables which you see extending from its casing. The advantage of this is that most of the fitting operation involves basic carpentry and general practical skills rather than dealing with electrical issues.

▲ *This kit from Powerpart provides all the items needed to use a mains and 12V supply.*

With a supply system in place, all you then need to connect up your caravan to a supply pillar or 'hook-up' is a length of approved hook-up cable. Under no circumstances should you use any other type of flex, cable or coupling wire.

However, before describing the sequence of operations needed to make the connection, let's identify all the parts and find out their respective functions.

Electrical components

Irrespective of the age of your caravan, look for the following items:

Fixed components

These include:

>> An input socket.
>> The consumer unit.
>> A safety earth cable with bonding clamps.
>> Earth labels.
>> Internal cables and 13-amp sockets.

The input socket

In order to draw electricity from a site's supply point, a hook-up cable (described later) will have to be connected to a mains input socket mounted on your caravan. This socket has to be an industrial type that is suitably robust. At one time sockets were often fitted on the underside of caravans' floors, but in this location grit and rainwater can get into the connection when the 'van is being towed. It's possible, of course, to fit a protecting cap, but on balance it is better if the socket is mounted inside an external locker. Accordingly, it is sometimes fitted inside the box that also holds the leisure battery. On other caravans there are flush-fitting enclosures that are made just large enough to accommodate a socket on its own.

Consumer unit

Another essential component in a caravan's mains supply system is referred to as the 'consumer unit'. This not only enables a user to activate or isolate separate circuits, it is also an important safety device. Consumer units are situated in various places. Some, for example, are fitted in a caravan's wardrobe or a cupboard; others might be mounted in an external locker that provides storage for a hook-up cable and socket adaptors. There are also electrical component manufacturers who fit a mains consumer unit within an enclosure that's used to house 12V fuses and switches as well.

The all-important function of a consumer unit and a description of its controls are discussed in the later section entitled 'Switches on a consumer unit' (page 208).

▲ On this 2013 Bailey Orion, the mains coupling socket is mounted inside the battery locker.

◀ This consumer unit is neatly housed under the seating area with an easily accessible access door.

Bonded safety earth cable

For safety reasons, a consumer unit has to have a thick earthing cable that's bolted to the caravan's chassis. This is normally covered with a yellow and green insulation sheath. Near the chassis connection there should be a warning label and this will bear words such as: 'SAFETY ELECTRICAL CONNECTION – DO NOT REMOVE'. If your caravan has a metal sink or washbasin, this should also be bonded with an earthing cable and fitted with a label.

▼ *On removing this sink in order to carry out a refrigerator service, it is pleasing to see that this metal sink has an earth bonding cable which is connected to the chassis.*

Additional parts needed

You will also need the following items, available from a caravan accessory supplier:

» An approved hook-up cable.

» Adaptors if you want to couple-up to supply pillars abroad.

» An adaptor if you want to couple-up to a 13-amp socket at home.

» A system tester as shown at the end of 'Coupling-up procedures' (page 217).

Note

Any professionally built British caravan which displays a National Caravan Council badge of approval will have originally been wired to meet British and European Standards. However, if you purchase a pre-owned caravan it might include some owner alterations. For this reason, you are strongly recommended to get a dealer or qualified electrician with knowledge of caravan 230V wiring to:

1. Check the installation.
2. Confirm that it is safe.
3. Rectify anything which is faulty.
4. Issue a dated certificate affirming its integrity.

Note: Be aware that some DIY installations are wholly unsatisfactory

Technical Tip

The girth of the required three-core flexible cable is conspicuously substantial. For the technically-minded, each of the three individual cables within the cover sheath (usually orange) should have a cross-sectional area of 2.5mm² and comply with British Standard/European Norm (BS EN) 60309-2. On the ends of the cable, industrial connections compliant with this BS EN standard include one that has brass pins for coupling to the site pillar, while the other has deeply recessed brass tubes for coupling to your caravan.

Although these connectors are weather-resistant, they're not intended for submersion in puddles. Summer downpours occasionally take us by surprise, which is why extra lengths of cable should never be linked together.

Note: Thinner cable must NOT be used for hook-up purposes. If you see connecting lead being sold at an unusually low price, it might be sub-standard. It has been alleged that some orange-sheathed products sold in the past have enclosed non-compliant 2.0mm² cable inside.

▲ *Mains hook-up cable is sold in 25m lengths with a plug and socket pre-fitted on either end. It has to comply with British Standards/European Norms.*

always been the case, so connection leads are also sold at caravan accessory shops. Regulations are very precise about hook-up leads, which must have an approved heavy-duty flexible three-core cable as described in the Technical Tip box to the left.

Adaptors

If you travel abroad, mains adaptors are often needed. It's appropriate to point out, however, that the industrial-style couplings used in Britain are now being fitted on new installations in many European countries. Sometimes these are referred to as 'Euro sockets'. However, on several sites abroad you may come across both types of socket fitted on hook-up pillars.

For the most part, however, you are likely to need an adaptor to suit supply sockets used in countries outside the UK. It will be many years before a universal standard is eventually established throughout Europe.

In addition, you may want to couple a caravan's hook-up cable to the mains supply at your home. For example, in the

Hook-up cable

A hook-up cable of 25m (plus or minus 2m) is now supplied as standard equipment with every new caravan. However, that hasn't

previous chapter it was recommended that a refrigerator is pre-cooled before leaving for a holiday and most owners like to do this using mains electricity from their house. By purchasing an adaptor to suit a 13-amp domestic socket, this coupling can then be achieved.

This adaptor is for coupling to the traditional mains sockets in France.

This short adaptor lead allows a British caravanner to couple up to a French supply pillar.

This adaptor allows a caravan hook-up cable to be fitted into a domestic 13A socket.

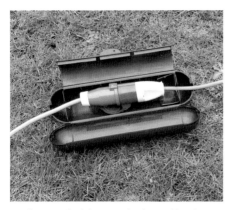

▲ *If you need to join up two hook-up cables, then a Plug & Coupler Safety Box will provide extra protection from the elements.*

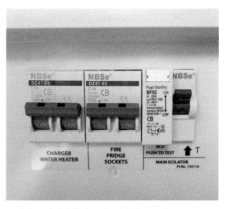

▲ *It is so helpful when the switches and test button on a consumer unit are clearly labelled like this.*

Plug & Coupler Safety Box

In the UK, a 25-metre cable should be ample for reaching the hook-up pillar. Some sites will not allow the use of extension cables. However, in my experience of travelling abroad, particularly to France, I have found that a 25-metre cable may not necessarily be sufficient. To prevent any embarrassment on your travels, take an additional 10-metre cable and a weatherproof Plug and Coupler Box as a back-up. The Plug & Coupler box will protect the connection from the weather. Ensure that your Plug and Coupler Safety Box comes with a padlock to prevent anyone from tampering with your connection.

Switches on a consumer unit

Irrespective of whether you purchase a new or pre-owned caravan, you should understand the function of the switches on a mains consumer unit. You will also be advised to operate these switches at several stages during the coupling-up procedure described later.

Consumer units may look different externally, and you'll come across both larger and smaller types according to the model of caravan and the extent of its mains supply facilities. Irrespective of the visual differences between units, the accompanying photographs show the key components you need to identify.

The purpose of each switch should be explained clearly in a caravan's owner's manual, but that sometimes gets lost. It is also extremely helpful if the switches are clearly labelled on the unit as well.

The Residual Current Device master isolating switch

Firstly, look for the master isolating switch which forms an integral part of the residual current device, or RCD. This is effectively the 'life saver'. If you want to know how it operates, check the Technical Tip box.

▶ *Pressing this test button simulates a fault and should immediately cause the master isolating switch to go into its OFF position.*

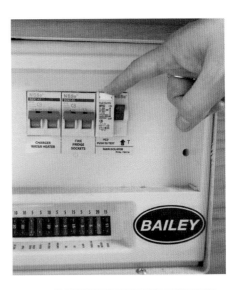

The master isolating switch that forms part of an RCD operates in one of three ways:

1. You can switch off the supply manually.

2. The supply switches off automatically in milliseconds if there's a fault in the system. It is also activated if a user accidentally touches a live contact.

3. There's a test button that will cause the switch to disengage instantly when depressed – just as if a real fault had occurred.

Provided the unit is in full working order, any of these actions immediately disconnects the mains supply to the wiring and sockets inside a caravan.

Miniature circuit-breakers

MCBs are a modern equivalent of rewirable fuses. In older houses, a rewirable fuse 'blows' (*ie* it melts and then breaks) when a fault develops in an appliance. However, in caravans – as in recently-built houses – there are MCB 'trip switches' instead; these are shown in the photograph overleaf.

Note that an MCB mustn't be confused with the similar-looking switch fitted on the RCD. Put simply, the principal function of the RCD that was described above is to prevent fatality through electrocution. In contrast, the purpose of an MCB is to prevent serious consequences, *eg* a fire, which might occur if there's a short circuit

Technical Tip: How the RCD identifies a fault

A residual current device senses any imbalance in the current passing along live and neutral cables. An imbalance occurs if a leak or a short circuit from either cable runs to earth. This would happen, for example, if you were to accidentally touch a live component or cable. In the event of this happening, the consequent imbalance in current flowing along live and neutral cables is detected in *milliseconds* by the RCD, whose master isolating switch instantly 'trips out' automatically. This immediate termination of the supply can prevent a fatality, although a very brief shock may still be experienced when the live component is initially touched.

Power Supply Unit

Test Regularly

RCD
40A 30mA   MCB1   MCB2   MCB3

▲ The three grey switches inside this consumer unit are miniature circuit breakers or MCBs.

If there are two MCBs, one is sometimes assigned to the fridge; the other serves the remaining 13-amp sockets. Be aware that you can operate the switches manually; in addition, they will cut off a supply automatically if a fault is detected.

Note: If your caravan's MCBs are not labelled, you can easily work out which appliances they respectively serve so that you can then mark them accordingly. When coupled to a mains supply, put all mains items into operation, then manually switch off one of the MCBs. Once you've checked which appliances then cease working, you'll know the MCB that controls their operation; repeat the test by switching off the other MCB(s).

The supply source

Hook-up pillars

A site supply is drawn from a hook-up pillar and the voltage in EU member countries has now been standardised. However, supply pillars don't follow a universal pattern and differ both in structure as well as the sockets they offer.

The accompanying photographs illustrate these dissimilarities, and the one shown on the opening page of the chapter includes TV supply sockets for aerial cables as well. At the base of this pillar there's also a locked door, and if the user overloads the supply a trip switch is activated and the site manager has to be notified. A member of staff will subsequently unlock the enclosure door and switch the system back on.

Other types of hook-up points are shown alongside.

in either the wiring or one of the appliances being used.

Most caravan consumer units have either two or three MCBs depending on the complexity of the mains supply installation.

▲ On this site in Wales, overload resetting switches are easily accessible, although it isn't intended that clients will operate them.

◀ This French site offers different levels of supply (in amps) and the user-fee varies accordingly. The site warden inserts one of the switch blocks shown here to activate a visitor's chosen supply.

▼ Some hook-up points abroad can be awash with wires and can pose a trip hazard.

▼ Temporary sites tend to only supply a maximum of 6 amps, therefore the total of all your appliances in use must not exceed 6 amps.

Putting a system into operation safely

Confirming which appliances can be used

Before coupling-up to a mains supply, you should ask at the reception office how many amps are available from the site's hook-up pillars. For example, some site hook-up sockets offer no more than 5 amps, whereas others offer 16 amps. To find the practical implications of this, refer back to the guidance and simple calculation given in the Technical Tip box 'Amps, volts and watts' at the beginning of this chapter.

Calculating which appliances will operate within your limit

To establish what appliances you can and can't run on your pitch, you first have to check the wattage of all your appliances. Here are some typical ratings taken from markings or labels affixed to appliances and from information given in their instructional manuals:

» Flat-screen colour TV: 25W.
» Laptop charger: 45W.
» Microwave: 1200W.
» Typical domestic pop-up toaster: 800W.
» Typical travel kettle: 750W.

Then you need to decide which appliances will typically be running at the same time in order to total-up their respective wattages. When carrying out your calculation, don't forget that a fixed battery charger is usually working in the background and may not have an on/off switch. So, include this item in your addition using a rough estimate

of its wattage. It can only be an estimate because its consumption rate will vary according to the condition of the 12V leisure battery it's charging. If your battery is generally well charged, an estimate of 200W won't be far from the mark. If it's in a poor condition, the charger will be working hard to revive it so your estimate might be 500W.

Once the combined wattage of your working appliances is calculated, dividing the total by 230 establishes how many amps they will all be drawing from the hook-up supply. On some small rural sites whose hook-up supplies only offer 5 amps (maximum), you'll probably have to reduce the number of items that you were hoping to operate. However, on Club sites offering a 16-amp supply provide you with much more scope.

Having to undertake these calculations might sound onerous, so for a quick check bear in mind that a site offering 5 amps allows you to run appliances whose combined rating doesn't exceed roughly 1,000W. If the site hook-ups offer a maximum of 10 amps, the combined rating of your appliances mustn't exceed 2,000W. If you find that your demands are too great for your hook-up supply capability, take account of the fact that a 'three-way' refrigerator will run well on gas. Similarly, you can avoid using an electric kettle by boiling water on the hob. Your supply of electricity could then be prioritised – let's say to keep the 12V leisure battery in a good state of charge, to charge a mobile device and to operate a colour TV. Naturally we all have different priorities when belt-tightening is needed.

If you do exceed your hook-up supply's

capability, the site system will 'trip out', whereupon you receive no power at all. On some pillars you are permitted to reinstate the supply by resetting the supply switch yourself. However, on many sites you have to summon a member of staff to do this for you. Naturally, if the problem occurs when the reception office is closed this may involve a long wait.

Note: On cold, dark, winter nights, a site's supply will be placed under heavy pressure, especially when all pitches equipped with hook-ups are occupied. Although an individual hook-up pillar might be able to provide a supply up to 16 amps maximum, a site's mains installation is not designed so that every pitch occupant can draw 16 amps at the same time. In consequence, you may see warning posters that advise visitors to be sparing in their use of electricity. Disregarding this request may result in a site being plunged into darkness.

▲ *Many caravanners take a special low-wattage electric kettle for use in their caravan.*

Coupling-up procedures

Once you understand the way a caravan mains supply system is controlled and you recognise the supply limit from hook-up pillars on your chosen site, it's time to couple-up your caravan to the mains. This step-by-step checklist describes each task and gives the correct order of action:

>> **Have a look at the site hook-up pillar nearest to your caravan.** Most pillars have several couplings and some might already be in use by caravanners on nearby pitches. If you find a multitude of doubtful-looking cables all around the hook-up, or have any concern about the safety of the supply itself, you might wisely decide not to couple-up your caravan.

>> **Check that all appliances in your caravan are switched off,** and as a precautionary measure move the RCD switch to its 'off' position. Presuming the hook-up point looks sound, now carry out the following operations.

>> **Insert the female connector of your hook-up lead into the caravan inlet.** That's the one on the lead that has the recessed *brass tubes.*

>> **Unravel the hook-up cable and work out a route for running it to the nearest hook-up pillar.** Make sure it lies flat on the ground and won't cause anyone to trip over when they're walking by in the dark. Also ensure that it doesn't go through low areas that might become puddles after unexpected downpours of rain.

>> **Before coupling to the hook-up point you'll see how much spare cable remains.** Do not be tempted to leave it tightly coiled on a drum, because it might overheat when high-consumption appliances are in use. In severe cases the insulation might even start to melt. The correct procedure is to place spare hook-up lead in loose coils underneath your caravan.

>> **The remaining plug is referred to as the male coupling and you'll note that it has three brass pins within its moulded casing.** The plug is pushed into the socket on the hook-up pillar, and on many hook-up installations the connection has now been completed. In other words, current will have reached your consumer unit.

▲ *If you feel uneasy about old hook-up pillars and a multitude of questionable cables, it may be safer not to use the supply.*

▼ *Always make the connection with the caravan before coupling-up at the hook-up pillar.*

This shows how not to lay out your cable. Loops can pose a trip hazard to other site users and the cable is immersed in a puddle after a heavy shower.

This might look tidy, but never leave spare cable on a drum; put it in loose, open coils under your caravan.

The male plug is inserted into this free socket on a typical hook-up pillar found on many caravan sites.

>> **On other hook-up installations, the power doesn't start to flow until you rotate the coupling clockwise and hear a click.** On the pillars where this is necessary, you'll see a red button near the socket and a label above. Unfortunately, however, the sun often bleaches out the label's instructions.

>> **Go to the consumer unit and check that the MCB switches are in the 'on' position.** Then move the RCD master isolating switch to its 'on' position.

▲ *Coupling and uncoupling is different on this type of hook-up and it is unfortunate that the instruction labels are sometimes missing.*

>> **At this point it's always advisable to confirm that the automatic 'trip-out' function of the RCD is working correctly.** So, press in the small test button to verify that the isolating switch 'trips-out' instantaneously. Once this has been confirmed, reset the RCD switch to its 'on' position, secure in the knowledge that this all-important safety device is operating correctly.

▼ *To confirm that the master isolating switch 'trips-out' correctly, press the test button on your consumer unit.*

Note: If the master isolating switch doesn't react when you press the check button, do NOT use the mains system. Seek advice from a caravan dealer.

>> **Now insert a test device into one of your caravan's 13-amp sockets.** Products like the one shown on page 217 are sold at electrical dealers. When the socket is switched on, the illuminated LEDs can highlight certain faults in your system including a case of reverse polarity. With good reason, 'reverse polarity' can be a source of concern.

Reverse polarity

In Britain, switches for wall sockets, lights and appliances are wired to the live cable. This means that when a switch is moved to its 'off' position, power can't reach an appliance at all. That's an important feature because it enables you to change a light bulb safely without having to switch off the entire 230V supply using the master switch that isolates your entire house.

Unfortunately, the safety of the British system is lost if the live and neutral cables are wired-up the other way round. For example, a switch that controls the flow of current on the way out of an appliance certainly prevents the appliance from working. However, in such an arrangement an appliance or light socket remains live, even though it isn't operating. This could be dangerous.

The problem doesn't arise in mainland Europe because the usual practice abroad is to fit switches which operate on both the live and neutral cables. These are referred to as 'double-pole' switches and ensure that an appliance still doesn't become live even if the live and neutral feeds are wired-up in reverse. In fact, on campsites abroad it's not unusual to find that the supply at hook-up pillars has been connected the other way round. This is referred to as 'reverse polarity'.

▼ *The display of light emitting diodes (LEDs) on this tester indicates that an earth connection is at fault. The supply should not be used until this has been rectified.*

▼ *This polarity tester device is indicating that it is OK to use the system.*

As a result, British tourists abroad need to check mains polarity as soon as they couple-up at a site. Sometimes reverse polarity is indicated by a red warning light fitted to a consumer unit. Alternatively, it can be revealed by means of one of the testers shown on page 217. So, what should you do in this situation?

>> Many caravanners acknowledge the potential danger and decide not to use the mains supply.

>> Some recognise the fact that polarity-sensitive appliances may receive damage and that their appliances will remain live, even when switched off. However, they decide to use the supply in spite of the inherent risks involved.

>> A few caravanners have a pole-reversal component fitted retrospectively in their vehicle.

▼ *If you often find that the polarity on site supplies is reversed, you can get one of these devices installed in your caravan.*

▲ *The live and neutral cables in the socket of this French hook-up adaptor have been intentionally connected in reverse. Red and white tape reminds the user that it has been modified.*

>> Many owners get an electrician to prepare a reversal adaptor using a short length of hook-up cable complete with a plug that's wired the other way round and *boldly marked*. You can't purchase these, but when one is fitted into a site pillar that has been wired in reverse, the supply is duly rectified at source; your hook-up cable can then be connected next.

Uncoupling from a mains supply

When leaving your pitch, disconnecting a mains hook-up is essentially a reversal of the sequence given earlier. In particular, it involves:

1. Switching off all your appliances and the RCD switch on the consumer unit.

2. Withdrawing the plug from the site pillar to terminate the supply. Normally this involves a sustained pull, but on pillars whose sockets have red locking buttons you have to depress the button first to release the plug.

▲ *On this type of hook-up pillar, the coupling plug can only be withdrawn when a red button is depressed.*

3. Withdrawing the plug from the caravan input socket.

On damp mornings you'll want to dry-off the hook-up lead before coiling it up and stowing it away.

Power from generators and inverters

Petrol generators

Modern portable generators are smartly designed, compact in size and much quieter than their industrial counterparts. However, they are surprisingly heavy, relatively costly to buy, and these leisure machines seldom provide as much current as you'd get from a site supply. To achieve that level of supply you would have to purchase an industrial generator and these models are costlier, heavier and noisier.

The output from portable leisure machines is typically from 650W (around 2.8 amps) to 2,000W (around 8.5 amps). Also be aware that generators often have two settings – 60Hz and 50Hz. To achieve a claimed 650W output you have to select the 60Hz setting; this provides a less stable supply that may not be suitable for operating sensitive appliances.

And a further warning. As the mains appliances in a caravan are switched on and off, you'll often hear the generator engine altering its note. On many models this is accompanied by a brief irregularity in the output. A similar change of note can occur when a generator is first started up and is running on its choke. Only a few models, such as the Honda EU10i and EU20i generators, offer clean and smooth power, making it safe for computers and other sensitive appliances that are suspectible to voltage spikes.

Technical Note

Circuitry in the most recent 230V portable generators from Honda includes a patented system referred to as 'inverter technology'. Models like the Honda EU10i and the EU20i employ this feature, which is claimed to eliminate power irregularities, unexpected surges and the attendant problems of damage to caravan appliances. The manufacturer also asserts that the delivered power is cleaner and smoother than electricity from a mains source.

▲ The Honda EU10i produces a smooth, surge-free output on account of its 'inverter technology'.

▼ This robust chain and lock is a wise purchase for securing this high-quality leisure generator. Thefts are not unusual.

▲ *The generator cover designed by Sew'n'So's provides good protection in rain and allows its exhaust fumes to escape easily.*

Good-quality generators are costly and there are often reports of them being stolen. Make sure you are able to secure a product you plan to purchase.

Also be aware that they must be covered when it is raining, but mustn't be used in an enclosed awning. Consider purchasing a purpose-made cover that's designed to allow the engine's exhaust fumes to discharge unhindered.

Finally, be aware that there has also been a recent influx of very cheap products imported from the Far East. If you intend to buy one of these, check that it's supported by a reliable after-sales, repair and spare parts service.

Inverters

When an inverter is connected to a 12V battery it will convert its 12V DC input into a 230V AC output. This can be useful, and even low-rated 100W inverters will enable you to run a laptop computer from a 12V battery.

However, the more you run through an inverter, the sooner your leisure battery will reach a state of total discharge. To give an example of this, if you were to buy a 250W inverter it typically draws more than 20 amps from a leisure battery (250W divided by 12 volts = 20.8 amps). In other words, a 60-amp-hour (Ah) caravan battery running only the inverter would be 'flat' in under three hours. In recognition of this, inverters often have low-voltage sensors that shut them down when a battery gets low enough to sustain damage.

Of course, a larger 90-amp-hour battery would work longer between recharges; the situation is also less acute when using an appliance that operates intermittently, such as an electric shaver. Similarly, if a compact 230V colour TV is used to show a half-hour episode of a favourite serial, a pure sine wave inverter might be the answer when using a site that's not equipped with hook-ups. On the other hand, long evenings of TV watching would soon leave you with a completely discharged battery. Hence why mains hook-ups are so popular.

Technical Tip
Inverter limitations

For sensitive equipment like TV sets and laptop power supplies, a 'pure sine wave' inverter is recommended, and these cost around three times the price of a 'modified sine wave' inverter. Inverters are complex products and one of the best explanatory guides is a leaflet supplied by Road Pro – telephone 01327 312233 or visit *www.roadpro.co.uk*.

▼ *The Sterling Power-Q range of inverters from RoadPro starts with compact models like this, which will run low consumption products.*

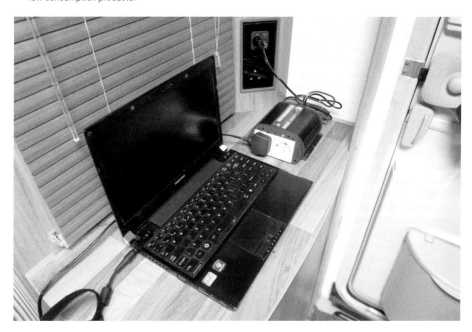

Chapter Eleven

Using 12-volt electricity

▲ A caravan's leisure battery carries out two jobs. Firstly, it supplies 12V DC electricity to run your caravan accessories. Secondly, it smooths out irregularities in the 12V power produced by a caravan charger when hooked up to mains supply.

Around 50 years ago, caravans were fitted with gas lamps. However, this changed when an Essex electronic specialist found a way to run a fluorescent light from a 12V battery. At first, the tow car's battery was used as the power supply. Then, a few years later, owners wanted to use this supply to run TV sets, stereo systems, heat distribution fans and extra reading lamps; and it immediately became clear that a caravan would need its own 12V battery. Overusing a car battery means you might not be able to get the engine started.

To get the best from a low voltage facility, it also helps to know something about the caravan's battery that's providing the power. There's also the wiring itself. So, let's look at these items more closely.

The 12V circuit

Everything starts at the battery. Two cables have to be connected to its live (+) and neutral (--) pillars.

▼ *The supply cables are clamped on to the live and neutral pillars of the leisure battery.*

▲ *The 12V system is soon ready for use after a few switches are checked on the main control panel.*

At the start of a circuit, the thick supply cables resemble the trunk of a tree. Having drawn power from its source, the trunk later divides into branches. In the same way, a 12V supply divides at a control box and then takes separate pathways to convey current to different components.

The cable used for these individual branches is normally thinner than the cable used for connecting-up to the battery. However, its actual size is determined by the amount of power that different components require. For example, a water pump is a more greedy consumer of current than a light fitting, so a pump's supply cable needs to be thicker than one that's serving a light.

As a rule, a 12V supply is divided up into three separate circuits. These serve:

>> The water pump.
>> The lighting.
>> Ancillary items like a TV socket, a heater fan and audio equipment.

Note: Each of the individual branches is usually controlled by a switch and a fuse of its own.

The only other point to add is that most caravans have a secondary facility whereby 12V electricity for running indoor components can be drawn from the tow car's battery instead. This presumes that:

1. The caravan is coupled to the car.

2. The towbar installer has wired-up a link from the car battery to the multi-pin socket near the vehicle's towball.

In reality, when you're stopping at sites you only take power from a car battery as a last resort. Today's caravans are fitted with so many 12V accessories, a vehicle battery wouldn't last very long. Therefore, with the exception of a caravan's road lights, the remaining items of 12V equipment normally draw power from what is referred to as a leisure battery.

Control panels

In design and appearance, control panels differ in various ways. There was a period, for example, when they bore a large number of switches, a galaxy of indicator lights, an array of analogue gauges and a clock. These elaborate displays were reminiscent of the flight decks on aircraft and seemed wholly inappropriate amidst the soft furnishings of ordinary touring caravans.

Today the control systems are more sensibly restrained. Some are simple panels that bear labelled switches whose functions are self-explanatory. Others are more elaborate and present read-outs on liquid crystal display (LCD) screens. Provided you peruse their instructions with care, the information available on the screen even includes inside or outside temperatures, and the amount of drinking water left in a tank.

▼ *This control panel uses a liquid crystal display to show a wide range of features including temperatures, current consumption and the time.*

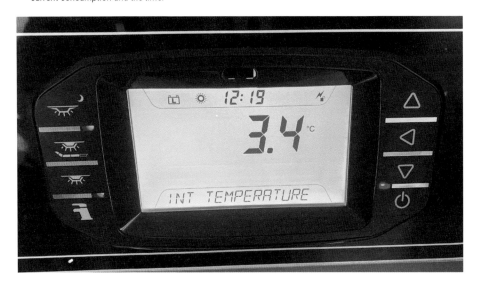

▲ The Swift Command Control Panel can be paired with a Swift Command App on your mobile phone, enabling you to control features like the heating or lighting remotely.

▲ This simple control has clearly labelled switches and a dial to indicate leisure battery level.

▼ In this Swift caravan, the lights not only have a master switch for all lighting, but also a dimmer switch to adjust the ambience of the lighting.

Other electronic gizmos are appearing as well. For instance, the Swift Command control panel can be paired to the Swift Command App on your mobile phone, enabling certain features like heating and lighting to be operated remotely or from the comfort of your bed.

Notwithstanding these differences in detail, here are the controls to locate:

>> **Master lighting control switch**. Although light fittings usually have their own switches, you can often turn them all out in 'one hit' by using a master switch. Typically, this is positioned somewhere near the entrance door.

>> **Water pump switch**. This is important to identify, especially if your caravan has a diaphragm pump rather than a submersible type. The reason for isolating a pump was given on page 173.

>> **Accessory master switch** which controls the supply of electricity to accessories such as a radio/CD player, a 12V socket for a TV set, and heating system fans.

In addition to these controls, it is normal to have a facility for identifying the charge level of your leisure battery. Some panels have a charge condition gauge, others have a warning light to indicate when a battery's charge level is low.

Now let's turn our attention to the source of the power. A basic understanding of leisure batteries is helpful because these are items that are not normally supplied when you buy a caravan.

Caravan batteries

A battery designed for use in a caravan, motorcaravan or boat is usually referred to as a 'leisure battery' and it is constructed differently from the batteries fitted in cars. Admittedly both products have a polypropylene case that houses lead plates and an electrolyte (either dilute sulphuric acid or an acidic paste). However, there are differences in the construction of the lead plates because car and caravan batteries have to perform dissimilar jobs. What's more, they don't do each other's jobs very well.

Different work patterns
A car battery has to provide a large amount of current to start an engine, but as soon as it fires-up the battery immediately

▼ *This digital readout clearly indicates the charge level of the battery.*

▼ *A leisure battery is constructed differently from a car battery, but on the outside they look very similar in design..*

receives a charge from the alternator. This is completely different from the work pattern of a leisure battery. In contrast, this has to keep low current appliances running for extended periods – often without the likelihood of receiving a recharge for a day or more.

If you use a car battery to perform the work carried out by a leisure battery, it soon needs replacing. That's because its lead plates are not suitable for the work regime described above. In contrast, leisure batteries are built with plates that *can* cope with repeated discharge/recharge cycles; accordingly, they're often described as 'deep cycling batteries'. Not surprisingly, though, a leisure battery is unlikely to perform well if you use it for starting a car.

There is also another function that a leisure battery has to fulfil. Although its principal purpose is to run a caravan's accessories, it also acts as a buffer (*ie* a protection device) that absorbs any power surges that might come from a caravan's built-in battery charger.

To explain this further, when you've connected your caravan to a mains supply its built-in charger duly provides 12V DC electricity. This is not just used to recharge a battery, it also provides some of the power that can be used to run your appliances. Unfortunately, a charger's output isn't always smooth and even a small surge is liable to damage sensitive accessories. This is less acute when a leisure battery is wired into the circuit because it has the effect of smoothing out irregularities. In consequence, a 12V supply that has been augmented by the output from an onboard charger is then more stable.

Lead acid

Most caravanners purchase what is commonly described as a 'wet' lead-acid battery. There are two types - open and sealed. The open lead acid battery has removable screw caps on the top, and inside each cell you can see a fluid. This is referred to as the electrolyte and it consists of a dilute solution of sulphuric acid. These batteries can be topped up using de-ionised water. Sealed lead acid batteries cannot be accessed for maintenance. They are not completely sealed, because a vent is provided for gas to escape and tipping will allow acid to escape.

Many battery engineers point out that from an electrical viewpoint, a lead-acid product is a better performer than its gel counterpart. It is usually much cheaper as well. With those points in mind, many UK caravanners opt for 'wet' lead-acid batteries, but it is important to make sure there are adequte ventilation facilities to deal with the release of gas when charging this type of battery.

Gel

The alternative is a gel battery in which the electrolyte is an acidic paste. Each cell is sealed and nothing leaks out if you turn the casing upside down. Since this type of battery has to be charged at a lower voltage than a 'wet' battery, it won't produce gas and therefore doesn't need a ventilation hole.

Gel batteries are obviously the preferred product for use on jet skis and quad bikes because they occasionally roll over. Presumably it's for safety reasons that they are now being fitted on some imported caravans too.

Absorbent Glass Mat (AGM)

This battery incorporates an absorbent glass mat which is its separator. The separators between each plate are fine white fibreglass material, which is similar to blotting paper in that it soaks up and retains the electrolyte (acid). This battery should never be opened.

They have a longer life and better starting performance (ideal for motor movers), and are spill-proof. However, they can be twice the price of a standard wet leisure battery.

▲ Gel batteries are occasionally used in caravans. They have no liquid to spill and don't create gas if charged correctly.

Lithium

These lightweight, compact leisure batteries are very powerful. They don't have many of the disadvantages of other batteries like slow charging, regular maintenance, sulphation and heavy weight. The claimed performance levels of lithium are excellent, however, it comes at a price. Visit RoadPro's website at *www.roadpro.co.uk* for detailed information about lithium batteries.

◀ AGM leisure batteries have a fine white fibreglass material between the plates which acts like blotting paper, soaking up the electrolyte.

▲ *Lithium batteries are ideal for those that like to go 'off-grid', but you will need to fit an inverter if you want to run 230V appliances when no mains hook-up is available.*

Battery capacity

The external dimensions of batteries differ and this is often related to their capacity, which is rated in amp hours (Ah). The greater an Ah rating – marked on its label – the longer a leisure battery provides power before it needs recharging.

Owners who normally stop at sites equipped with 230V hook-ups usually find that a 60Ah battery is adequate. At the other extreme, there are owners who seek as much self-sufficiency as possible and

prefer to stop at remote farm sites where mains power is seldom supplied. Similarly, there are caravanners who enjoy touring in winter when daylight hours are short and heating is essential. In those instances, it is necessary to fit a leisure battery with a higher Ah capacity.

In practice, many owners of modern caravans find that their leisure battery becomes discharged after only a couple of days. If that's the case, a 110Ah battery provides power for much longer, although the greater the Ah capacity the longer it takes to recharge it from flat. Also be aware that a caravan battery locker sometimes offers insufficient space to accommodate products with a high Ah capacity.

▲ *This 110Ah leisure battery just fits into the purpose-made battery box fitted in a Bailey caravan.*

Caravan battery locations

The Safety Tip panel on page 236 explains that a battery often gives off an explosive gas when it's being charged. This is why modern caravans have a purpose-built box with an outlet so that gas can escape. In practice, these outlets are often discreetly located to maintain protection from the weather.

To provide security there should also be clamps or straps to ensure that a battery doesn't topple over and spill its corrosive acid. Recent battery boxes also include a plastic tray that encloses the lower part of a battery's casing. As long as these purpose-built boxes are sufficiently capacious to house a higher capacity (Ah) battery (if needed), the arrangement is hard to fault. It's certainly a great improvement on previous practices.

▲ Straps are used to prevent a leisure battery from toppling over and spilling its corrosive acid.

There was a time in the 1980s, for example, when some caravan manufacturers provided a storage cage for a battery which was fitted in the gas locker compartment. This is potentially dangerous because gas control valves occasionally develop a leak. Equally, when you couple a connection to a battery terminal you sometimes create a small spark, so an accumulation of leaking gas could conceivably be ignited by a spark from the battery. That's why batteries and gas cylinders *must* be kept well apart. The problem of sparks at battery terminals

is another reason why clamping devices are better than crocodile clips for making a connection. They are less likely to create a spark if nudged accidentally and seldom spring off unexpectedly. To save the bother of using a spanner, some caravanners use coupling products that have a spring-loaded clamp. However, their contact surfaces must always be clean.

▲ Spring clamps are made to clip on to battery pillars, but the contact surfaces need periodic cleaning.

Before the advent of purpose-made battery boxes, many owners used to keep their leisure battery in a blanket locker; others used the bottom of a wardrobe. Either way, a battery stowed in these locations must be effectively secured so it cannot fall over in transit. Then there's the matter of ventilation. A caravan manufacturer is most unlikely to have fitted a high-level ventilator in a wardrobe or bed box, so a plastic ventilator tube is essential. If fitting a battery in an old caravan, it is often wise to purchase a purpose-made battery box with sealed lid to screw down in a locker indoors. However, it is also necessary to create an outlet hole through a caravan's floor for the flexible gas escape tube.

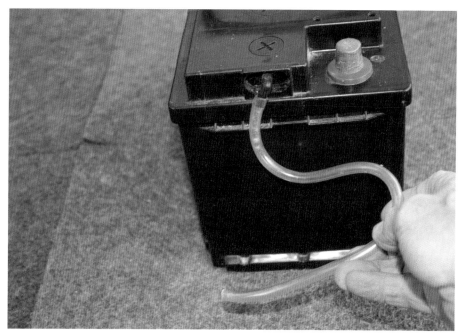

▲ Some lead-acid batteries have a ventilation tube; it discharges an explosive gas that's generated when a high charging voltage is used.

▼ To fit a battery in an older caravan, it's often wise to purchase a purpose-made battery box for mounting inside a locker, like this.

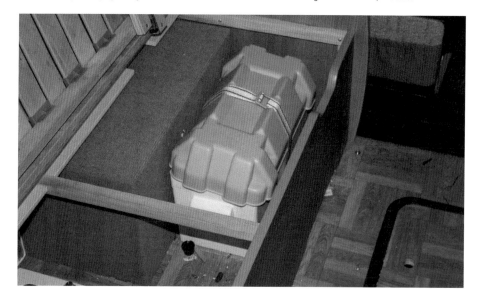

Life between charges

The length of time that you can run a battery before it needs recharging is partly determined by its amp-hour capacity. But that is only one of many considerations. For instance, there's a huge difference between caravanning in summer with long hours of daylight and caravanning in winter. During December's dark evenings, many hours are often spent around a TV and lights are frequently in full use.

Provided there's a restrained use of 12V accessories, a fully-charged 60Ah battery meets most caravanners' needs during a weekend in summer. Needless to say, a 75Ah battery contains more power and a 110Ah battery will last even longer.

If you seldom stop at sites that have mains hook-ups, you'll be entirely reliant on the battery for a supply of electricity. However, calculating a battery's likely performance period before needing a recharge can be an exacting task. As a further complication, temperature plays a part and so does the age of your battery.

Battery manufacturers also emphasise that you should never run a leisure battery to the point where it's absolutely flat. In fact, a battery is claimed to last many more years if you start recharging it as soon as its charge level drops to 50%. Whether the majority of owners heed this advice is anyone's guess.

Let's also return to that matter of a battery's amp-hour (Ah) rating. The figure quoted by manufacturers and marked on a label relates to its performance in an ambient temperature of 25°C (77°F). In reality there are many 24-hour periods in the UK when the temperature is much lower than that. The accompanying Technical Tip panel indicates the significance of temperatures and the effect that they have.

Technical Tip: Temperature effect on a battery's output

The stated Ah capacity of a battery presumes that there is an ambient temperature of 25°C (77°F). One well-respected battery manufacturer states that for every drop of 1°C below that figure, there's a 1% reduction in its performance capability. So, at 0°C (*ie* freezing point) the nominal Ah capacity is reduced by 25%. This means that a battery nominally rated at 60Ah effectively becomes a 45Ah battery at 0°C. Bearing this in mind, a battery mounted in an external locker performs less well in cold conditions than an identical one fitted indoors.

▼ *This label indicates the effect that a high rate of discharge over a short period of time will have on a battery's Ah capacity.*

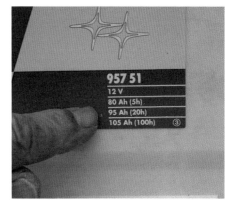

Lastly, if you use a battery to run a lot of appliances simultaneously, this obviously hastens the time when a recharge is needed. But it's worse than that, because a high demand in a short space of time also reduces an Ah rating even further. To highlight this, some battery manufacturers even quote different Ah figures on their battery labels to acknowledge this phenomenon.

Checking battery charge level

The control panel in modern caravans usually provides information about a battery's charge condition. To get a true picture, however, bear in mind that if the battery has just been receiving a charge – either when you've been towing or when a mains charger has been coupled – it should be left to settle for at least four hours before the reading is taken. Certainly, after a long charge on a workbench, a truer picture is obtained if you wait 12 or even 24 hours. This is because older batteries look misleadingly good when the charger is first disconnected, but subsequently lose their charge quite quickly even without being put into use.

Notwithstanding the warning light systems fitted on many caravan control panels, a more accurate assessment of condition is achieved by putting a voltmeter across a battery's terminals. Readings from a voltmeter are interpreted in the accompanying panel. Suffice it to say, a product that we refer to as a 12V battery carries a rather inaccurate title. If a voltmeter registers 12V, the battery is discharged. In a fully charged state, it should read 12.7V.

▼ *The reading of 12.67V displayed on this digital voltmeter reveals that the battery is almost fully charged.*

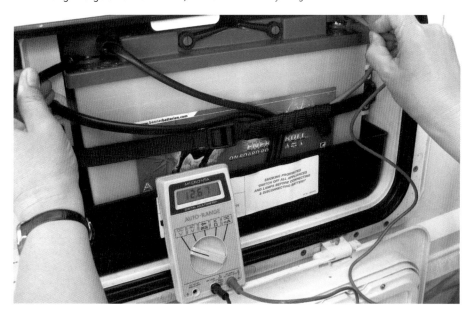

Technical Tip

Approximate indication of a battery's state of charge

Voltmeter reading	Approx charge state
12.7V or over	100%
12.5V	75%
12.4V	50%
12.2V	25%
12V or under	Discharged

Note:
1. *Some electrical specialists point out that this information should only be taken as an approximate guide.*
2. *Remember the advice about letting a battery rest for four hours or more after a charging period in order to get a more accurate reading.*
3. *Make sure every 12V appliance is 'Off' when taking a reading. This should include the clock, which sometimes gets overlooked.*

▼ *To ensure that its lead plates were immersed in electrolyte, de-ionised water was added to this battery.*

Looking after a leisure battery

In view of the cost of a leisure battery, always take heed of the manufacturer's advice. Here are some of the ways to get the best from a battery:

1. A battery's electrolyte should be checked periodically, but do not smoke when carrying this out. The inspection involves removing the caps over each cell and checking the level of acid inside. The electrolyte, as it's called, should just cover the lead plates that you can see in each cell. If the level has fallen in one or more cells, top-up where necessary with de-ionised water. This is sold at car accessory shops.

2. If a lead acid battery is left in a discharged state for a day or more, it will often be irreparably damaged. Attempts to recharge it may prove fruitless.

3. Avoid running a battery until it is completely flat. As stated earlier, always start recharging a battery when the control panel indicates that it's in a low state rather than after it's been used to the point of exhaustion.

4. When you want to remove a battery from its locker, always disconnect the negative terminal first. Equally, when you're installing a battery, connect the negative terminal last.

5. Sometimes you find that the terminals on a battery get covered with a white powdery substance. To prevent this forming, lightly smear the terminals with grease or petroleum jelly (Vaseline).

▲ *To prevent a deposit forming on the battery terminals, coat them with a thin film of Vaseline or grease.*

Charging a leisure battery
Using the tow car

When you are towing a caravan, some of the charge from the tow vehicle's alternator should yield a small input for the leisure battery. Since this isn't a particularly high input, it's referred to as a 'trickle charge'. In some older caravans the wiring is such that you have to put the battery selection switch on the control panel to the 'car' position in order to receive a trickle charge from the car. Guidance on this should be given in the caravan's Owner's Manual.

Using a hook-up on a site

If you use a mains hook-up, the caravan's built-in charger will keep the battery in a

Safety Tip: Emission of an explosive gas

When a battery is charged at a high rate, it creates an explosive gas (a mix of hydrogen and oxygen) that often lingers around the cells, even after charging ceases. Make certain that no one nearby is smoking when a charger is disconnected from the terminals. When batteries explode the casing often disintegrates and acid can easily get splashed in your face. Explosions also occur if there's a flame nearby – such as a pilot light on a gas appliance.

The gas normally only forms when a charging voltage exceeds 14.4V but it can be emitted at lower voltages if a battery cell is faulty. For this reason, always ensure there are *no* naked flames or a source of sparks near a battery when it's being charged or its cells are being checked.

Also note that this gas is lighter than air – so if a battery is fitted in a sealed compartment, there must be a high-level outlet to allow escaping gas to discharge and disperse outdoors. Alternatively, if a leak-proof tube and connecting elbow can be coupled to a battery, this may be routed down through the floor since gas will be forced downwards under pressure.

good state of charge. As mentioned already, some chargers can be left on all the time and electronic circuits prevent them from overcharging a battery. This kind of circuitry can also detect when a battery is fully charged, whereupon the charger goes into 'sleep mode' and ceases giving a charge current.

Fixed battery charger

Some chargers installed in caravans have an on/off switch but many start operating automatically as soon as a 230V supply is connected.

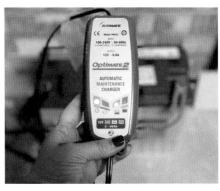

▲ *Portable chargers like this Milenco product constantly analyses the battery status and adjusts the pulse accordingly.*

Not only does the output from one of these devices charge the leisure battery, it provides a 12V supply to run the indoor accessories as well. These two functions operate simultaneously and that's why built-in chargers are designed not to yield more than 13.8V. The restriction means a battery won't start 'gassing' either and it's well within the 14.4V limit for charging a gel battery. Of course, it will make your 12V lights glow more brightly, but it's unlikely to cause them to fail.

Portable chargers

Unfortunately, lead-acid batteries respond better when recharged with an initial input around 15V or more, followed by a gradually reducing charge. This causes an emission of gas and a battery's cells need topping-up more often. However, periodic 'gassing' extends the life of a battery.

In order to meet this need, some electrical specialists are manufacturing portable chargers which offer 'stepped charging' regimes. Their electronic circuits are able to evaluate a battery's condition and also to monitor the battery's progress

while the charging process takes place. For example, a charging regime might commence with a boosting output of 15V that then tapers off as the battery responds. That is just what many batteries need. However, you wouldn't want your caravan's *built-in* charger to start at 15V, because it is usually running 12V appliances at the same time, many of which could get damaged. That is why many owners disconnect a leisure battery from the 12V circuits in their caravan and transfer it to a bench. Using a portable charger from manufacturers like Milenco, they can then provide a charge regime that suits a battery best.

Note: Further technical information on batteries and charging are dealt with in The Caravan Manual (4th Edition) by John Wickersham.

Trickle chargers

These products are designed to keep a battery (which is already in a good charge condition) fully maintained by providing an occasional input of power when it's needed. Trickle chargers are used by many owners of vehicles that have to be parked for extended spells, like classic cars, motorcycles in winter – and caravans too. Most products can be left permanently connected to both the mains supply and the battery because their electronic circuits monitor voltage and activate charging only when it's required.

The Milenco Solar Charge by Optimate will protect your battery and provide safe long-term maintenance without the need for access to a mains supply, making it ideal for caravans in storage.

Solar and wind generators

Neither of these products are cheap to buy and purchasers don't necessarily have them fitted with the hope of saving money. When conditions are right, both are able to provide a battery with a trickle charge, thereby helping to extend a battery's output before it needs a renovating recharge.

Solar panel power is measured in watts and you will find devices usually range from around 5W for a trickle charge to 300W for a large rigid system. Power ratings are determined under ideal conditions (bright, direct sunlight), though variables like cloud, low sun angle or dirt on the panel might affect the output. Hence, it is hard to predict exactly how much a given panel will put back into your leisure battery.

You also need to consider what power usage you need to allow for. As a rough rule of thumb, a 5-10W panel will provide trickle charging to keep a battery topped up whilst in storage; a 50W panel should cover usage of limited 12V devices (lights, mobile phone charging); and a 100W panel will cope with heavier 12V devices (water pump, TV).

Some caravanners use portable panels and have to take care that they don't get stolen. Other products are permanently installed on the roof and semi-flexible versions are remarkably light.

Wind generators are often fitted on boats and work best in exposed places where prevailing winds are strong. In large oceans they are a great asset. However, their use in caravanning venues is less convincing.

▲ A panel must be connected with a solar charge controller to regulate the voltage and current coming from the solar panels going to the battery.

▼ Rigid solar panels are often included in the price on high-end models, but can also be fitted retrospectively.

▲ Portable solar panels have the advantage that they can be moved to track the sun; but you have to make sure that they don't get stolen.

▼ Wind generators send a trickle charge to a 12V battery – provided there's enough wind, of course.

Using a portable generator

These products are compact and useful but they are also heavy and rather costly. Many models also provide an irregular output, and fluctuations can damage the circuits in 'switched-mode' electronic chargers that are fitted in the latest caravans. The subject of generators was discussed in more detail in the previous chapter, so check the advice given there.

National Caravan Council (NCC) Verified Battery Scheme

There are huge variations in quality, price and performance in leisure batteries, so the National Caravan Council (NCC) introduced a scheme in 2016 to grade leisure batteries. The aim was to assist consumers in making an informed choice on the type of battery that would best suit their caravanning needs.

The leisure battery is tested for its performance and categorised accordingly into either three categories:

Category A – these are aimed at people who frequently use their caravan without electrical hook-up.

Category B – aimed at those that regularly use sites with electrical hook-up facilities, but require a greater battery capacity to run items such as motor movers.

Category C – aimed at those who only require basic operation of their habitation equipment for short periods away from an electrical hook-up.

For further assistance in selecting the right battery for your caravanning needs go to the National Caravan Council website *www.thencc.org.uk*.

▼ *This leisure battery has been classed a Category B by the National Caravan Council, making it ideal for those that like to use sites with electric hook-up and operate a motor mover.*

Economy matters

Recognising that the demands placed on a leisure battery are greater now than in the past, efforts are being made to introduce less power-hungry appliances. Lights, for example, have been brought under scrutiny.

In the late 1960s caravans were fitted with gas lamps, and when tungsten 12V car bulbs were tried it was decided they drew too much current. However, the move away from gas gathered momentum when fluorescent lights were invented that could operate using a 12V supply. This was a turning point, and by the early 1970s gas lamps were phased out and fluorescent lights took their place.

▲ *The bulb on the right of the photo is a halogen bulb, which is fine but these products take quite a lot of current. They also get very hot and the bulbs don't tolerate current irregularities. The bulb to the left is a G4 side-pin LED.*

The light output from a fluorescent tube is good when related to the current it's using, but visually it appears rather 'cold'. By the 1990s halogen lights had started appearing in caravans too, and that's what many people wanted. However, halogen bulbs get remarkably hot and when several of these are in operation they draw quite a lot of current. Could anything else take their place?

For years we have had light-emitting diodes (LEDs) as the indicator lamps on

▼ *These LED lights consume little current, don't get hot and last for many years.*

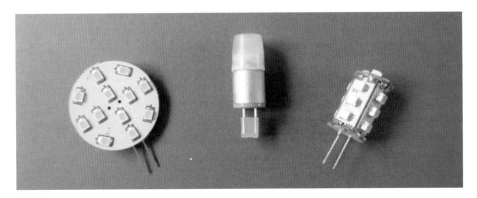

▲ *Modern caravan interiors have a multitude of LED lights from up-lighting on bedheads and lockers; spotlights with dimmer switches; and splashback lighting.*

electronic appliances. Stereo players, CD players and dozens of products have red or white LEDs on their fascias, but these tiny components were costly. Now the price has come down and they are produced in volume. LED light units draw considerably less current than a comparable output from a halogen bulb. Furthermore, an LED doesn't get hot either and usually lasts for many years. In consequence, LED light units are now used in caravans and as exterior lights on cars, caravans, buses and boats. On the 2018 Swift Conqueror caravan, for example, the interior is awash with LED lights. A drive for economy has undoubtedly helped these devices gain a foothold, especially when there's a limit to what a leisure battery can supply.

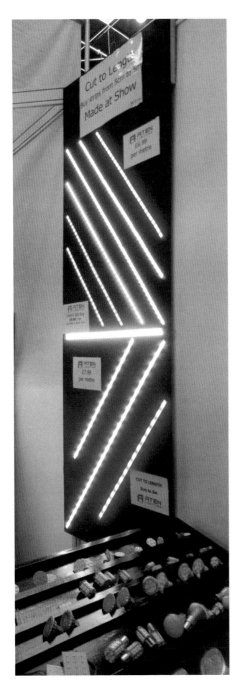

End of season

If there are long periods when your caravan remains unused, you should still arrange to keep the leisure battery charged. To do this, many owners take it out of the caravan and put it on a bench at home near a charger. However, this means that if your caravan has an electronic alarm powered by the battery it will then be disarmed.

When bench-charging at home, ensure that no one smokes near the battery and check there are no naked flames (*eg* a pilot light) nearby. Several portable chargers will keep a battery in good condition and examples were mentioned earlier.

Final thoughts

Older caravans were far simpler and a lot less sophisticated. For use in warm places in the summer when the evenings are light, it is hard to justify the expense of having an elaborate 12V supply system supported by a costly leisure battery.

On the other hand, today's modern caravans can be used all year round and offer all sorts of comfort features. Few owners could do without electric water pumps, twinkling spotlights, a TV supply socket and a warm-air distribution system. But this means you're hugely dependent on a good 12V supply, so the leisure battery needs to be kept in a good state of charge, even when the caravan is parked for long spells.

◀ *Aten Lighting has a wealth of experience in the lighting industry and is a specialist supplier of lighting for caravans.*

Chapter Twelve

Gas

▲ When the temperatures fall in winter, propane gas performs far better than butane.

The most popular fuel used in caravans for cooking and heating is liquefied petroleum gas, or LPG as it's usually called. It is available in Britain and abroad in cylinders that are sold in various sizes. Less pleasing is the fact that there's little standardisation in cylinder couplings. That aside, LPG is a good fuel – although it is highly flammable and needs to be treated with care, respect and understanding.

Safety First

Remember that LPG is highly flammable. It also has the potential to create explosions, which contributed to its development as an alternative fuel for road-going vehicles. In Europe, many cars currently use LPG as their main fuel.

Although caravanners have to learn how to use LPG safely and change cylinders when necessary, that is all that an owner is required to do. Do not attempt any work on your supply system, its components or its gas appliances. Tasks of this kind should always be entrusted to a competent gas engineer who has received formal training in the use of LPG in leisure vehicles. The Gas Safety (Installation and Use) Regulations 1998 provide further guidance on this subject.

It is also a statement of the obvious that this type of gas has to be used with the greatest of care. It also confirms why a caravanner is strongly advised to know something about LPG's characteristics, the way it can be safely used, and precautionary measures to take in the event of a leak.

If you detect a leak and the escaping gas hasn't ignited, the advice usually given is to:

>> Put cigarettes out at once and extinguish any naked flames.
>> Shut off individual gas control taps indoors.
>> Close the valve on the supply gas cylinder.
>> Open all windows, internal doors and the main entrance door.
>> Check if the leak seems to come from a gas cylinder valve.
>> Remove a suspected faulty cylinder from the gas locker.
>> Put a faulty cylinder in a well-ventilated space outdoors.
>> Consult a gas supplier regarding the safe collection of a leaking cylinder.

If there's any element of doubt relating to safety, do not remain in your caravan. Depending on the weather, however, you might choose to use the caravan as long as you cease using the gas system and any gas-operated appliances.

Safety when fitting and removing gas cylinders

When changing a cylinder, make sure there are no sources of gas ignition anywhere nearby. An electric heater, a gas water heater, pilot lights on an instantaneous water heater, an outside barbecue, a gas-operated portable awning lamp and so on should be extinguished if their proximity could lead to ignition. Equally, no one should be smoking nearby.

SWITCH OFF THE CYLINDER YOU WANT TO CHANGE. If you have an approved twin-cylinder coupling device with a manual or automatic changeover valve (described in the final section of this chapter), it *is* permissible to let the active supplying cylinder remain switched on. But you should still turn off the cylinder you want to change – there may be a small amount of gas still remaining, even if it's not sufficient to run the caravan's appliances properly.

▲ *Caravanners have to couple-up and turn on their gas cylinders themselves.*

▶ *Only approved coupling hose should be used. The markings here confirm that this is high-pressure hose that left the factory in September 2008.*

A gas cylinder is one of several important items that's not included when you purchase a new caravan. However, it's not difficult to obtain a cylinder of liquefied petroleum gas (LPG), or to purchase an appropriate regulator if the caravan doesn't have one fitted. Once these two items are in your possession, all that remains is to couple-up; turn on the cylinder; and enjoy the benefits of a clean, convenient fuel. But is it really as simple as that?

To begin with, anyone using LPG must be absolutely certain that they are handling the product safely. Linked to that is the importance of having an understanding of its characteristics.

Characteristics of LPG

An understanding of LPG's characteristics helps to reinforce why precautionary measures must never be treated lightly. Note the following points:

>> In its natural state, LPG is not poisonous.

Technical Tip
Terminology

Terms that are ambiguous or inaccurate should be avoided when dealing with LPG. For example:

1. Some people wrongly refer to LPG as 'liquid' petroleum gas, which is a contradiction because a gas is a gas and a liquid is a liquid; gas engineers correctly refer to it as 'liquefied petroleum gas'.

2. You will often hear caravanners state that they need another gas 'bottle', and that can certainly confuse a new owner. Beer might be sold in bottles but LPG is sold in purpose-made 'cylinders'.

3. A cylinder is usually connected to a system using a flexible 'coupling hose'. Sometimes this is rather confusingly referred to as a 'pigtail' – a term also used by towbar fitters for a linking connection near a towball. The term 'pigtail' is therefore avoided in this chapter.

4. With the exception of stainless-steel flexible pipes used for coupling-up, a coupling hose in a gas system is made of synthetic materials that include rubber. However, to call it a 'rubber hose' would be ill advised, because that might tempt someone to try coupling-up with an ordinary piece of rubber hose they found in their garage. Only approved coupling hose should be used which complies with current standards.

5. Coupling hose is available in Low Pressure (LP) and High Pressure (HP) varieties, as marked on the sides. The correct choice of hose is important, as described later.

For the sake of clarity, the terminologies preferred by gas specialists will be used in this chapter.

>> Caravanners use two types of LPG – butane and propane.

>> To warn of leaks, distributors add what is called a 'stenching agent'.

>> LPG does not have a smell, which means that leaks might not be noticed.

>> LPG is denser than air and if a leak occurs the gas sinks to the lowest point.

>> LPG reacts with some chemicals, which means that jointing compounds, pipes and coupling hose must be products that are specifically intended for use with butane and propane.

>> The gas escape outlets in a caravan are called 'drop-out holes' and should never be covered up.

>> When using an appropriate regulator, the gas appliances installed in British caravans run on butane or propane without requiring any adjustments.

>> Since LPG is highly flammable it must be stored in accordance with the LP Gas Association Codes of Practice.

Storage

At points of sale

Retailers and site operators supplying gas have to comply with strict rules when storing and handling LPG cylinders. For example, on rare occasions cylinder valves have become faulty and leakage occurs. Noting the earlier point that the gas is denser than air and sinks to the lowest point, storage facilities must allow leaking gas to disperse safely. That's why mesh cages are normally used and situated outdoors, well away from any potential source of ignition.

▼ *Never cover the drop-out holes in a caravan, which are there so that leaking gas can escape.*

In your caravan

Manufacturers have to comply with strict specifications and gas cylinder lockers must have low-level drop-out holes. The most common place for a cylinder locker is at the front of a caravan. However, caravans built by Bailey usually have lockers situated on one side and close to the axle.

A storage locker should also offer a minimum of 30 minutes fire resistance. However, in view of caravan structures some experts regard compliance with this expectation as unreasonably hard to achieve.

External access is required too, and the locker should be totally sealed from the living area. However, there have been models built in the past where a small hatch inside the caravan at the front enables a user to reach into the gas locker to close or open a cylinder valve. That was not considered good practice and the idea was dropped soon after its introduction.

▲ *Site operators often supply gas cylinders, but storage regulations have to be strictly observed.*

▼ *Unlike the majority of caravans, models from Bailey are usually fitted with a gas cylinder locker on one of the side walls.*

In addition, a gas cylinder locker must never be used to accommodate a battery, contain fuses, include a light or be used as a routeway for electrical cabling unless it is wholly sealed in a conduit. Anything

▼ *Don't make this bad mistake. The gas cylinder has been stored alongside a can of petrol and a 12V battery that could create a spark.*

that could create a spark is considered dangerous, although a few models now have recessed, sealed and covered niches that contain light-emitting diodes for illumination.

A robust and reliable way of securing cylinders in an upright position is also crucially important, recognising that bumpy roads pose a challenge to any fixing system.

At home

During a long lay-up period some owners remove their cylinders, but it is not safe to store them in a house. In fact, the worst place of all is in a cellar, since this is normally devoid of low-level ventilation outlets. In the event of a cylinder valve developing a leak, the heavier-than-air gas then has nowhere to escape, so it accumulates around the lowest parts of

Safety Tip
Always keep a cylinder in its upright position

It is not unknown for valves on cylinders to develop a small leak. For instance, if grit or grass gets caught in the spring-loaded steel ball that forms the seal on a Campingaz cylinder, the obstruction may lead to a seepage of gas. Sometimes you can even hear a faint hiss.

The problem is usually solved by taking a Campingaz cylinder outdoors, checking that there's no flame nearby and depressing the ball very briefly with a small screwdriver. A sharp blast of escaping gas occurs instantaneously and usually dislodges the obstruction, whereupon the steel ball reseats itself correctly. The valves on other types of cylinders can also develop leaks and it's therefore extremely dangerous to lay a cylinder on its side. A tiny drop of liquefied butane gas trickling from a cylinder resting on its side will multiply in volume around 233 times as it converts into a gas. The increase in volume of propane is approximately 274 times greater. The potential hazard of this is clearly apparent.

▲ *It can be extremely dangerous to lay a cylinder on its side. If a tiny amount of liquefied gas seeps through a leaking valve it will change into a large volume of gas.*

the floor. A garage is often unsafe too, especially if it's used for a car, to store a petrol can and to charge a battery. It's better to store a cylinder externally in a weather-protected and well-ventilated position.

Types of LPG

Two different types of LPG are used by caravanners in Britain. One is called butane, the other is propane, and their respective characteristics need to be recognised.

Butane

Key points about butane:

» It is widely sold throughout Europe. There are many suppliers, many different sizes of cylinder and, unfortunately, many dissimilar connecting systems.

» It has a higher calorific value than propane and since it burns at a slightly slower rate it's a more efficient heat producer.

» It presents problems in cold conditions because it doesn't change from its liquefied state into a gas. This occurs when temperatures fall to --2°C (around 29°F) at atmospheric pressure. Accordingly, butane is *not* the preferred gas for winter use or for visits to cold regions.

» It is heavier than propane. Taking the smallest cylinder sold by Calor Gas as an example, the propane version holds 3.9kg (8.6lb), whereas an identically sized cylinder filled with butane holds 4.5kg (10lb).

» A small volume of liquefied butane converts to a considerably larger volume of gas. The difference is about 1:233.

In Britain, butane supplied by Calor Gas Ltd and by Campingaz is sold in blue cylinders.

▼ *Butane cylinders from Calor Gas are always painted in blue.*

Technical tip

When temperatures fall, the rate at which liquefied butane changes to gas decreases progressively. So, even though the temperature in a gas cylinder locker might still be above freezing point, a significant reduction in the output of gas often becomes apparent, especially if you're cooking a meal and trying to run a space heater and water heater at the same time. On noting a lower-than-normal flame on the hob, many caravanners wrongly presume that the cylinder is nearly empty and fit a replacement prematurely.

Propane

Key points about propane:

>> This is the preferred winter fuel because it changes from a liquefied state into gas in temperatures as low as --45°C.

>> Outside the United Kingdom, it is harder to find propane in portable cylinders for leisure activities, although 11kg and 13kg propane cylinders are available in France, Italy and Spain.

>> Some processing companies add a small amount of propane to their butane cylinders in order to improve cold-weather performance.

>> It is lighter than butane in its liquefied state. If you check two cylinders of

identical size, you'll see from markings on the side that the propane one holds less in weight than butane.

>> A small volume of liquefied propane converts to a very much larger volume of gas. The difference is about 1:274.

>> It has a vapour pressure that is considerably greater than butane. Note how this affects the type of gas regulator required as described later in this chapter.

>> The 'off-take' rate of a propane cylinder permits it to run more gas appliances simultaneously than a butane cylinder. This is similarly beneficial when running appliances like a high-performance space heater that consumes a large quantity of gas.

In Britain, propane supplied by Calor Gas for caravanning is sold in red cylinders; the Calor Gas propane 'Patio Gas' cylinders are green. BP Gas Light propane cylinders are green and white.

▶ *Propane gas, which is sold by Calor Gas in red cylinders, is able to convert from its liquified form in temperatures as low as -45°C.*

Which gas should you use?

Having considered the differences between butane and propane, you will immediately appreciate why caravanners who only go away in the summer usually stick to butane. In contrast many year-round caravanners use propane all the time. Others run both types of gas, but the different cylinder couplings need to be recognised. For example, owners of caravans manufactured pre-1 September 2003 will need two cylinder-mounted regulators to suit the types of gas being used.

On later caravans there's a wall-mounted 'universal' regulator that's designed to operate with either gas. However, this necessitates the purchase of both a butane and a propane connecting hose because the respective cylinder couplings are different.

▲ Some owners use both butane and propane gas; on pre-1st September 2003 caravans this means that two cylinder-mounted regulators will have to be purchased.

Calor is the most commonly used gas in the UK. In addition to the company's wide variety of cylinders you also have a choice of butane or propane gas. You will also find that many dealers allow you to exchange an empty butane cylinder for a full propane one, and vice versa. Irrespective of these options, caravanners soon decide which products they like best and their preference is often determined by seasonal issues and destinations.

The range of supplier-filled cylinders

In the UK several specialists sell gas cylinders to leisure users, and the introduction of owner-refillable portable cylinders has also been well-received by many caravanners.

In this competitive field, Calor products are used in both the UK domestic and leisure markets. For instance, large cylinders are supplied to homeowners for their daily domestic needs, although Calor's 19kg propane products are too heavy and bulky to transport in touring caravans. Remember, too, that a cylinder should never be transported horizontally in case liquefied gas was to seep through its valve mechanism. Equally, a gas cylinder should always be mounted securely in a caravan gas locker. Standing a cylinder outside a caravan is potentially dangerous and the practice is strongly discouraged by caravanning clubs.

In spite of the popularity of Calor Gas in this country, the company's products are not available abroad. In contrast, Campingaz is available worldwide and cylinders are available in most European countries. But there are exceptions: Campingaz is not available in Finland or Sweden and is seldom stocked in Norway.

Also bear in mind that Campingaz cylinders only contain butane, which can present a problem for winter caravanners. It is believed that a small amount of propane is added to improve performance in cold environments but this strategy is not revealed on the cylinders' markings. Furthermore, only the 907 cylinder is suitable to meet the typical consumption requirements in modern caravans. This is the *largest* cylinder in the Campingaz range and it only holds 2.75kg of butane: even the *smallest* butane cylinder in the Calor Gas range holds 4.5kg of butane.

Notwithstanding the long-standing use of Calor Gas and Campingaz in Britain, the choices increased further when BP introduced 'Gas Light' cylinders in 2006. The corrosion-proof cylinders made of a composite plastic containing glass fibre

▼ Large cylinders used outside a caravan can cause damage if knocked over; the caravanning clubs strongly discourage this practice.

▼ The largest Campingaz cylinder, referred to as the 907, only holds 2.75kg of butane. The small one on the right is really only suitable for running a camping stove.

▲ *Two sizes of BP Gas Light are currently in production (5kg or 10kg) and their composite plastic containers are claimed to be half the weight of an equivalent sized steel cylinder.*

are claimed to be half the weight of steel cylinders of equivalent capacities. Part of its structure is semi-transparent too, so you can see the level of the LPG inside.

Two sizes of BP Gas Light cylinders have been introduced and these hold 5kg and 10kg of propane respectively. However, some caravan lockers are not able to accommodate the larger product, which is

571mm high; both have a diameter of 305mm. As regards coupling-up, Gas Light cylinders have a 27mm clip-on valve and many owners need to purchase an adaptor in order to use these products.

How full is the cylinder?

Finding out how much gas is left in a part-used cylinder isn't easy unless you use a BP Gas Light cylinder, which has translucent sides. To assist owners of other cylinders, several products are made which can reveal a cylinder's 'state-of-fill'. For example, Gaslow gauges are useful purchases.

In contrast, the Truma LevelCheck uses ultrasound to check a cylinder's state-of-fill, and the handy filling level indicator shows whether there is liquified gas within the measuring range. If the LED is green, there is gas in the cylinder. Alternatively, Truma's LevelControl makes reading the gas level easier and is more precise. It is fixed to the bottom of the gas cylinder and via Bluetooth the readings are sent to the Truma App, allowing you to check the levels, whilst sitting in your caravan.

▼ *The Gaslow Contents Guage allows you to assess how much LPG is available.*

▼ *The Truma LevelCheck uses ultrasound to establish how much gas there is in a Calor Gas cylinder.*

▲ *Truma LevelControl is attached to the base of a gas cylinder and via Bluetooth the gas levels can be checked using the LevelControl App on your mobile device.*

▲ *It is helpful to weigh a new cylinder on some scales and to note the findings. Further checks reveal how much gas remains after it has been used.*

Owner-refillable cylinders

The sale of refillable cylinders has become a contentious issue on safety grounds. For example, liquefied gas is delivered from many forecourt pumps at some force and any spillage on your hands leaves painful injuries. There are other safety issues too, just as there are when petrol is dispensed by a member of the public into a portable can.

Also be aware that a gas vessel should never be filled more than 85–87%, which is why it should be fitted with a European Pi approved filler valve. This device automatically shuts off the gas as soon as a tank or cylinder reaches its 80% limit. Some refillable portable cylinders *do* incorporate an approved, automatic cut-off device; however, others don't, and the user is expected instead to watch the rising level of the liquefied gas through a sighting zone in the side of the cylinder. This can be difficult. Controlling a fast-filling fuel dispenser with accuracy may prove challenging, and overfilling can have disastrous consequences. The situation is especially dangerous if you drive with an over-full cylinder in your caravan, because a change in air pressure can cause its contents to expand.

Not surprisingly, gas specialists became very concerned about the introduction of refillable gas cylinders that were not equipped with automatic safety cut-off valves. In acknowledgement of this and other concerns, a statement published by the LP Gas Association expressed the views of its members very clearly. The LPGA document asserts that permanently fixed gas 'vessels' intended for heating and cooking 'may be permitted to be re-filled at autogas refuelling sites *provided* they:

» remain in situ for refilling;

» and are fitted with a device to physically prevent filling beyond 80%;

» and are connected to a fixed filling connector which is not part of the vessel.'

In other words, appropriately installed tanks are deemed acceptable. So, too, are the specially-made cylinders sold by Gaslow, provided they are permanently installed and connected to an autogas filler point using Gaslow's stainless steel pipe. This filler should also be a permanent fixture mounted on the caravan. The components in this system carry a 10-year warranty, at which point the cylinder (which is marked with a date) must be exchanged.

Of course, not everyone wants to spend a three-figure sum to have a tank or a fixed cylinder system installed, but safe and easy-to-use systems are now available. Moreover, a Gaslow system can often be uninstalled, transferred, and refixed in another caravan without requiring major alterations. But is an owner-refillable system worthwhile?

Perhaps the main attraction is the fact that gas drawn from an LPG pump at a filling station is considerably less expensive than gas supplied with an exchange cylinder. In other words, an owner who goes caravanning regularly, especially in winter, might purchase a sufficient quantity of gas to recuperate the cost of a refillable cylinder and its installation quite quickly.

There are also advantages if you travel abroad; Autogas stations supplying gas-powered cars dispense propane, which is the chosen fuel of many caravanners. Sometimes a coupling adaptor might be needed but these are available from gas specialists.

◀ *The 6kg and 11kg refillable propane cylinders from Gaslow are fitted with a Gaslow multi-valve, which automatically switches off the gas when 80% is reached during filling; it also features an over-pressure relief valve.*

Technical Tip
The Gaslow refillable system

In response to the safety concerns described in the text, Gaslow, a long-established gas specialist, has designed a safe, caravan-specific owner-refillable installation. Products available from Gaslow include yellow portable cylinders, which are installed to act like the fixed tanks sometimes used on motor caravans. With capacities (in gas weight) of 6kg and 11kg respectively, these carry a 10-year warranty; after that period they can be replaced for a small fee. The cylinders are manufactured with a European Pi-approved filler valve that shuts off automatically when the gas vessel is 80% full. They also have an over-pressure release valve. Other components in a Gaslow installation kit include:

>> a 0.6m or 1.5m filler hose;
>> a filler coupling for mounting externally on the wall of a caravan;
>> and a stainless-steel regulator hose.

When the fitting work is carried out, a cylinder (or cylinders) must be installed in the caravan's locker and fixed permanently in place. A cylinder also has to be coupled-up to a wall-mounted filler, using the stainless-steel pipe provided. Three optional filling adaptors are also available as 'extras' from Gaslow, to match different European coupling systems.

To refill a cylinder in a Gaslow installation, the caravan has to be towed to a fuel station that's equipped with LPG pumps. Since this can sometimes be inconvenient, some owners pair a Gaslow product with a dealer-exchange cylinder. Various combinations of cylinder are permissible and Gaslow also supplies manual and automatic changeover regulators.

▼ An installation kit from Gaslow includes a 0.6m or 1.5m length of rubber-free, semi-flexible stainless steel tubing.

▼ One of these filler couplings has to be fitted externally on a caravan and comes in grey, white or black.

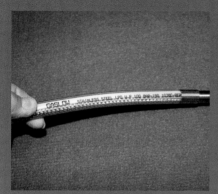

Regulators

A regulator is an essential component in a caravan's gas supply system. Its function is to ensure that gas is supplied to appliances at a consistent and appropriate pressure regardless of whether the supply cylinder is full or approaching empty. The pressure of gas in a cylinder is also affected by changing temperatures and that's another reason why a regulator is needed.

Inside its casing there's a diaphragm that stabilises the flow of gas and delivers it at the pressure required by the gas appliances. It's essential that a regulator is protected from the weather because its diaphragm relies on a tiny breather hole in the casing, which mustn't get blocked. If rain is able to enter this hole during cold spells in winter, it could freeze, thereby upsetting the diaphragm's operation.

Apart from the need to keep a breather hole clear, there is nothing in a caravan's regulator to service or adjust. Accordingly, its casing is sealed and a regulator normally gives unfailing service for several years.

Opinion is divided in respect of making a routine replacement. Some specialists stipulate every five years; others quote ten years – or at any time when it shows evidence of wear and damage.

Changes to systems

For many years it has been necessary for anyone buying a caravan to purchase a regulator to match the type of gas cylinder they want to use. It stands to reason that if a regulator is designed to be mounted on top of a cylinder, the respective couplings have to match. In addition, a different regulator is needed to fit a cylinder containing butane from the regulator needed to fit a propane cylinder.

Unfortunately for those caravanners who tour widely throughout Europe, the huge variety of cylinder connections means that an array of regulators or adaptors might have to be purchased.

▼ *The diaphragm in a regulator cannot operate properly if the tiny breather hole in its casing gets blocked with dust or frozen water.*

Technical tip

If you ever get a frightening tall flame on a stove burner, this is 'over-gassing', which is usually caused by a faulty regulator. The condition typically occurs when the breather hole on a regulator gets blocked.

It became increasingly clear that standardisation of products and practices was needed in European Union member states. New European Norms were therefore published in 2001 (BS EN 12864) and 2002 (BS EN 1949), and these made radical changes that affected both regulators and cylinder coupling arrangements. The new standards were implemented by UK manufacturers on 1 September 2003.

▼ *This butane regulator with its own gas control knob is purpose-designed to fit the connection on a Campingaz cylinder.*

Technical tip

Since the gas appliances fitted in a caravan have to be compatible with its installed gas supply system, gas specialists state categorically that anyone owning a caravan built before 1 September 2003 must not attempt to install the regulators and supply arrangements used for models built after that date.

Systems in caravans built before 1 September 2003

As mentioned already, mounting a regulator directly on top of a supply cylinder has been customary practice for many years. In addition, cylinder-mounted regulators have to match the type of gas and the style of coupling. To eliminate any chance of fitting an incorrect regulator, a propane cylinder always has a different coupling from a butane one.

On some butane cylinders there's a push-fit arrangement; on others there's a threaded coupling and you need to tighten this using a spanner.

Remember, too, that Calor Gas screw-type couplings have a reverse thread. So, forget the usual convention for threaded fixings. To carry out a coupling exercise you have to rotate the nut anti-clockwise to couple your regulator to a Calor Gas cylinder and vice versa if you want to remove it.

One of the implications of fitting a regulator directly to a cylinder is the fact that gas pressure is immediately reduced

▲ *Calor Gas sells an inexpensive spanner for tightening regulators that are attached using a threaded cap nut.*

Regulator spanner

Coupling a regulator to a Campingaz cylinder doesn't need a spanner; equally, a regulator to suit Calor's clip-on system doesn't require special tools either. However, all the Calor Gas propane cylinders, together with Calor's 4.5kg butane cylinders, require a spanner to tighten up the regulator connection. Accordingly, open-ended spanners are sold at caravan accessory shops.

But be warned. If someone else coupled your regulator using a plumber's wrench and unnecessary zeal, a Calor spanner isn't likely to be tough enough to loosen it when your cylinder needs changing. That's not something you want to discover when it's dark, cold, and pouring with rain.

and it can then be fed to a caravan's fixed copper pipes using a short length of approved *low-pressure* (LP) hose. This will be marked on the side, together with the date when it left the factory. It can also be coupled satisfactorily to the main supply pipe and the regulator using good-quality hose clips.

During an annual habitation service, the short length of low-pressure coupling hose will be replaced. Get this done even earlier if a hose shows premature wear or distortion, particularly near the clipping points.

This coupling system, which has been used for many years, has much to commend it – apart from the fact that regulators have to be cylinder-specific. However, regulators for cylinder mounting are not unduly expensive and (at the time of writing) are often sold for less than £10.

▼ *Low-pressure hose is only fitted when a regulator is directly coupled to a cylinder. This should be tightly secured to the regulator's ribbed nozzle using a hose clip.*

Technical Tip
Procedure when fitting and removing gas cylinders

NEVER COUPLE OR UNCOUPLE A GAS CYLINDER NEAR A SOURCE OF IGNITION LIKE A FLAME OR A LIT CIGARETTE.

1. Campingaz cylinders

Since there's a screw thread on top of a Campingaz cylinder, it means that when the regulator or adaptor finally loosens a small quantity of gas usually hisses out while the valve ball reseats itself. So, act promptly to complete the disconnection. The same thing occurs very briefly when connecting a new cylinder.

In view of this brief moment of leakage, you might prefer to lift a Campingaz cylinder out of the locker while making the connections. It also helps to hold the regulator and to rotate the cylinder itself, rather than the other way round which merely twists the connecting hose.

2. Screw-thread Calor cylinders

1. When connecting and disconnecting a cylinder, always make sure first that the cylinder's handwheel is OFF – *ie* turned fully clockwise (this has a conventional right-hand thread).

2. When a new Calor butane cylinder is supplied, it normally has a small black cap over the threaded outlet. Remove this by turning it CLOCKWISE when looking at its dome (the coupling has a left-hand thread). Keep it for when you return the empty cylinder.

3. When a new propane cylinder is supplied, it has a small black plug in the coupling. Remove this with a large slotted screwdriver, turning it CLOCKWISE when looking at the slot (the coupling has a left-hand thread).

4. Check the connection surfaces (whether it's a butane or propane cylinder) to confirm they're clean and unobstructed. Then offer-up the threaded coupling. Hand-tighten it first, turning it ANTI-CLOCKWISE, and complete the job using an open-ended spanner. Since they don't have a washer, propane couplings have to be tight.

5. Turn on the gas cylinder's hand-wheel, checking immediately for a hiss or smell. For a more thorough DIY test, apply a proprietary leak-detecting fluid or a prepared mix of soapy water to the coupling areas. Then look closely for bubbles, which signify an escape of gas.

6. When returning an empty cylinder to a supplier, the plastic cap (butane) or plastic plug (propane) should be refitted.

3. Clip-on Calor cylinders

No tools are needed to connect or disconnect this type of coupling. Furthermore, there isn't an ON/OFF turn-wheel; instead, the ON/OFF control is an integral part of a clip-on regulator or adaptor. On the regulator shown on pages 264 and 265, a retaining collar won't permit disconnection until the tap is turned OFF.

Preparing a new cylinder – Rotate the orange cap so that its arrow points towards the opening in the cylinder shroud. Remove the cap by pulling on the plastic strap and lifting as you do so.

◀ *Gas Leak Detector Sprays can identify a gas leak by producing a foam at the point of leakage.*

▼ **Attaching a clip-on regulator** – The retaining collar is lifted up with the thumb while the regulator is pushed down onto the cylinder connection.

▼ **Switching on the gas** – Once the regulator has seated properly and the retaining collar has been lowered you can rotate the operating tap to the vertical ON position.

▼ **Disconnecting a clip-on regulator** – The design of a clip-on regulator intentionally ensures that the release collar can only be pushed upwards when the turn-tap is in its OFF position.

▼ **When a cylinder is exhausted** – The orange cap is pushed back onto the coupling.

Systems in caravans built after 1 September 2003

The publication of new European Norms/British Standards prompted changes to gas regulators, and the type of hose used to couple-up to cylinders. Here are some of the main innovations:

» A new design of 'universal' regulator was developed that would operate using either butane or propane.

» A new standardised working pressure of 30mbar was introduced. Gas appliances now being installed are set to work at this pressure and are labelled accordingly.

▼ Wall-mounted 30mbar 'universal' regulators fitted in Bailey's gas lockers are from Clesse and are usually mounted high in the compartment as recommended.

» The new 30mbar regulators are almost always fixed on the wall or ceiling of gas cylinder lockers, thereby forming part of a caravan's factory-installed supply system. This practice means that regulators now receive manufacturers' soundness checks, together with the rest of the installation, before leaving the factory.

» The only component which a new owner has to purchase is a factory-made *high-pressure* coupling hose with crimp-fit connectors. These connectors are important and the types of hose clips hitherto used on low-pressure hoses must not be fitted.

» High-pressure hoses with different couplings are now manufactured. Whereas the connector for coupling to a wall-mounted regulator is standard, the connector on the other end has to suit the owner's choice of gas cylinder.

» Although there are coupling hoses to suit most types of cylinder connections used throughout Europe, a few systems require the owner to purchase an adaptor.

Changeover systems

A caravan's gas locker has space to accommodate *two* gas cylinders. Most owners ensure that two cylinders are duly fitted, and some caravanners have a manual or an automatic changeover device fitted as well.

When a supply cylinder runs out, this permits a hasty switchover because it eliminates the need to uncouple and reconnect hoses. Several products are manufactured and there are changeovers to suit a variety of combinations including:

>> Systems conforming to earlier British Standards with cylinder-mounted regulators.

>> Post-2003 supply systems with a 30mbar wall-mounted regulator.

>> Post-2003 supply systems with a wall-mounted regulator and supplied by a pair of Gaslow's refillable cylinders.

>> Post-2003 supply systems with a wall-mounted regulator and supplied by one Gaslow refillable cylinder paired with one normal propane cylinder.

▼ *Some caravanners have an automatic changeover device fitted so that a switchover from an emptied cylinder to its partner is carried out without owner intervention.*

As stated earlier, LPG is certainly a convenient product to use but it helps to have a good understanding of the many types of gas supply components. That, in turn, enables you to get the best from a caravan's system.

▼ *This caravan is fitted with a manual changeover system. High-pressure hoses from the two cylinders link with the regulator, and the hand-wheel valves on top of the cylinders determine which one supplies the gas.*

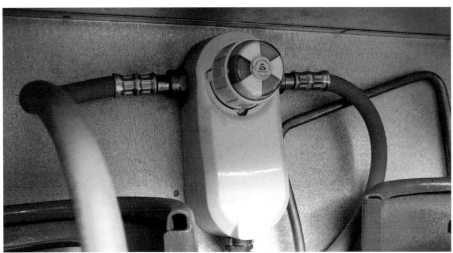

Chapter Thirteen

Cooking and heating appliances

▲ The array of kitchen appliances in this 2018 Swift Conqueror shows how well-equipped many modern caravans can be.

Following on from the earlier chapters which describe mains electricity and gas systems in caravans, this chapter looks at cooking and heating appliances. Many different products have been fitted in the last 30 years and it would be impossible to provide detailed operating instructions relating to individual appliances. However, there are some general issues to note that are discussed in the sections which follow.

▲ Like many high specification modern caravans, this Swift Conqueror has a three-burner and hotplate hob.

At one time, LPG was merely used to run a small hob and a couple of wall-mounted gas lights. With only two burners on many hobs, the preparation of a meal called for some forethought – but few caravanners complained. It would have been unthinkable in those days to envisage the level of provision that is commonplace today. Many modern caravans offer four-burner hobs and a few include an electrically-powered hotplate.

However, when the number of gas-operated appliances increased, caravan designers realised that the supply system had to adopt practices similar to those used for electrical wiring. In this arrangement, a main trunk route comes from the cylinder regulator, which then sub-divides into branches to provide separate supplies to individual appliances. There also has to be a control facility in order to isolate different gas appliances.

▼ These gas isolation valves are clearly labelled.

To achieve this, today's caravans have a series of gas isolation valves that control the flow serving each of the branches. These are usually well labelled and the information is normally reproduced in the caravan's owner's manual. If a manual is missing, you can often follow the route of the pipes, albeit on your knees, with a torch and maybe a mirror as well. Having established what each pipe seems to serve, you can verify your observations by igniting appliances individually and then closing off the valves. When you have identified the appliances being served by the different valves, it's then just a matter of marking them with adhesive labels.

Not that gas is the only fuel used for cooking and heating in caravans, mains electricity also plays an ever-increasing part. Now let's look at the all-important subject of safety.

Safety

When you buy a new caravan, its gas appliances will have been installed in accordance with the regulations applicable to LPG appliances in leisure vehicles. Documents provided with a purchase should verify their compliance, and certification papers are often signed by the LPG gas specialist who inspected the installation.

Things are seldom as straightforward when you purchase a second-hand caravan. Ideally, a pre-owned caravan will be supplied with a recently signed and dated certificate to confirm the integrity of the supply system and its appliances. A good service centre can arrange for this to be carried out prior to the sale and signed/dated documents will give a purchaser assurance that the gas system is in safe working order.

That's the 'ideal world'. In reality it's not unusual to find that this certification is missing and then it's up to you to have the checks carried out before putting your newly acquired caravan into commission. It only needs something like the gas/air mixture to be out of adjustment on a hob and there's a risk that carbon monoxide will be emitted. Since this can have disastrous consequences, always have your appliances checked and serviced regularly.

Bearing in mind the potential danger of carbon monoxide poisoning, some caravanners fit a battery-operated detection device. These are sold by specialists like Calor Gas and products can also be found on sale in many caravan accessory shops. It is recommended to select a carbon monoxide detector that is either National Caravan Council (NCC) approved or complies to the latest BSI testing standard (EN50291-2.2010).

When a caravan is built, its manufacturer also has to make provisions for possible gas leaks. These have to serve both the supply system and individual gas

▼ *This Fireangel Digital Carbon Monoxide alarm will provide an instant alert to dangerous levels of CO.*

appliances. This is why there are several low-level ventilators in caravans, often referred to as 'drop-out holes'. Since LPG is heavier than air, these ventilators allow leaking gas to escape to the outside.

Unfortunately, some owners find that 'drop-out' gas escape vents cause draughts so they cover them up, which is extremely unwise. If these vents do lead to uncomfortable draughts, it's usually possible to fit a deflector below the floor. This can shield a ventilator without affecting its function or reducing its dimensions.

Now let's look at some individual gas appliances.

Hobs and grills

Gas hobs have been a standard fitment in British caravans for a long time. As mentioned already, some models are fitted with two or three burners, others have a complete set of four.

In addition, many models offer automatic spark ignition which means that

▼ To prevent draughts from the drop-out holes inside the caravan, fit a draught shield on the underside of the floor.

▲ Never cover or restrict the opening of a low-level gas escape vent – which is often called a drop-out hole.

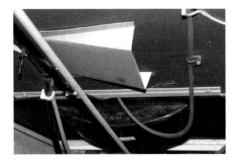

neither matches nor a hand-held igniter are needed. However, it is interesting that hobs installed in caravans imported from abroad are less likely to have a built-in spark igniter.

Whereas an igniter is a convenience item, a flame-failure device (FFD) is obligatory on recent models. Its function is to ensure that the gas supply to a hob's burners is automatically terminated if its

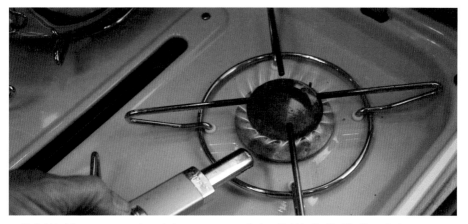

▲ *To light hob burners on many imported caravans you need a hand-held igniter like this Zippo device.*

▼ *British caravanners usually expect to find a grill installed under a hob or within an oven, whereas many imported caravans don't have one.*

flame gets blown out. To achieve this, a small probe is angled into the path of the flames and when this gets hot it automatically holds open the gas supply. However, its operation means that when you initially light a burner, you have to depress the control knob for several seconds to override the control mechanism, this gives the probe a chance to heat up.

As regards grills, these are normally only fitted to British caravans. Few Continental manufacturers fit a hob that embraces a grill in its design and it seems that caravanners from other European countries seldom use them. We can only presume they haven't discovered the pleasures of toast.

In recognition of our expectations, some importers of foreign models fit a separate grill unit as soon as every caravan is delivered to Britain. Other importers insist the manufacturer abroad makes special export models to suit British tastes.

Finally, please read the Safety Tip panel on page 274 on 'Hobs, heating and ovens'. It is most important.

Flame-failure device operation

So how does a flame-failure device (FFD) work? In simple terms, the metals used for its probe respond to heat, interact and create a small electrical current. This is conveyed to the gas control itself and the supply is powerful enough to open an electro-magnetic valve. Hence:

» When the probe is hot, gas flows to the burner.

» If a burner blows out, the probe becomes cold whereupon a spring shuts off the valve. At that point, gas can't get to the burner.

» Pushing in the control knob when you're lighting a burner merely overrides the electro-magnet and holds the valve open, thereby allowing the probe of the FFD to get hot.

If an FFD fails, get the appliance checked by a qualified specialist in LPG installations. Never prop open the control with a stick or peg.

▼ The small probe indicated here is part of the flame-failure device, not to be confused with the spark igniter.

Safety Tip
Hobs, heating and ovens

» Never use a hob (or an oven) to act as a space heater. There are some kitchen layouts where heat rising from a burner that hasn't been covered by a pan is sufficient to cause damage to the locker or shelf above.

» If the gas/air mix on a hob or oven is slightly out of adjustment, there's a possibility that small quantities of carbon monoxide are present in the products of combustion. If you find that the undersides of cooking implements become badly covered with soot, this indicates that the flame is incorrect. Get the hob checked by a qualified gas specialist at once.

» Never close the glass lid of a hob when its burners are still hot. Furthermore, if your hob is mounted close to a side wall, remember to lift up its safety heat shield.

◀ *A hob should never be used as a space heater for several safety reasons.*

▼ *Some hobs are mounted close to a plywood internal wall, so they have a heat shield that must be lifted before the burners are lit.*

Gas ovens

Although it's difficult to know if many owners use an oven regularly, modern caravans nearly always have one, whether it's wanted or not. Most full-size cookers are smart and efficient but they are also heavy, thereby taking up a significant part of a caravan's payload allowance.

Weight aside, if you bake cakes or like to cook a traditional Sunday lunch on holiday, a domestic-size 'cooker and oven' is obviously important. Whether it's worth having one just to heat a meat pie or to reheat fish and chips is debatable. With that in mind, some manufacturers fit lighter and less elaborate appliances.

The level of provision obviously differs, but whatever caravan you purchase please note the points mentioned already about safety and servicing.

Microwave ovens

Compact microwave ovens are fitted in many caravans. Once the cost of these appliances started falling, several caravan manufacturers decided to install them. It is patently clear that the inclusion of a microwave oven impresses many potential clients and acts as a purchasing incentive.

However, in practical terms these appliances only operate on 230V, and cooking times are normally longer than they are in the microwave ovens used in our homes. That's because site hook-ups only have a limited supply of current, and microwave ovens, especially during the initial start-up phase, consume a lot of power. Consequently, the models fitted

in caravans have lower wattages, thereby affecting their 'cooking time' performance.

As regards the installation, most manufacturers build an oven into a head-height locker. For some people the appliance can then be quite hard to reach, and if you are removing a mug of hot coffee, great care is needed to ensure that its contents aren't spilt.

Ventilation is important too. An appliance mustn't be allowed to overheat and generous ventilation is needed around its casing. If you compare different installations you will find that some caravan manufacturers fit more air escape outlets than others. It is certainly annoying when the safety mechanism of an appliance trips-out automatically because it is getting too hot.

Finally, there are many caravanners who prefer to use remote sites that don't offer hook-up facilities. To obtain a 230V supply,

▼ *To suit caravanners who don't want a full-size domestic cooker, this 2007 Avondale caravan is equipped with a smaller and lighter appliance.*

some then purchase a portable generator to run mains appliances like a microwave oven. Unfortunately, they subsequently find that their generator isn't powerful enough to operate this appliance.

The problem arises from a misunderstanding. Naturally, you'd imagine that a 1kW (ie 1,000-watt) generator ought to be able to run a 650W microwave oven. But it probably won't, for this reason: a microwave oven's rating of 650W refers to its *output* (or 'cooking power'), which is far less than the *input* it needs. As a rough rule of thumb, you have to double the quoted output and then subtract 10% to ascertain the required input needed from a supply source such as a generator. In other words, a 650W oven needs an input of around 1,170W – and that's more than the maximum output given by a 1,000W (1kW) portable generator.

There is no doubt that microwave ovens can be useful appliances, but operating them in a caravan is not always as straightforward as it might appear.

Space heaters

The term 'gas fire' has long been superseded for good reason. Moreover, the word heater is insufficient because modern caravans are fitted with two completely different heaters. One's a water heater, whereas the other heats the living space.

Gas fires

In the early 1970s, many owners had optional gas fires installed. Even in the 1980s, some caravans were equipped with a gas outlet mounted on the floor. Portable gas fires were sold for coupling up to these gas points using a flexible hose – this was simply pushed on to the ribbed nozzle of the outlet and clipped in place. That is no longer permitted.

In the past, many fires were lit using a match, and the problem of carbon monoxide emission – described above with regard to hobs – was potentially a source of danger; so these products are no longer fitted for safety reasons. Furthermore, if anyone purchases an older caravan and finds that an old-style open-burner fire is installed, they are strongly advised to have it removed by a gas specialist and replaced with a room-sealed space heater.

Room-sealed space heaters

Room-sealed heaters have the following features:

>> A modern space heater in caravans is permanently installed; it is never a free-standing, movable unit.

◀ *Microwave ovens tend to be positioned in a locker at head height, which can be dangerous when handling hot food.*

» Its gas burner is situated within a sealed enclosure which is referred to as a heat exchanger.

» A feed duct or specially constructed inlet draws oxygen into the enclosure from outside the caravan.

» All products of combustion are returned directly *outside* via a flue system.

» As the heat exchanger gets hot, it warms up the air around it.

▲ *Stray duvets often cover heating vents, which can lead to the heating cutting out in the middle of the night.*

» Provided it is regularly serviced, a room-sealed heater can usually be left in operation all night. However, you should confirm that this is the case by checking the owner's manual, or seeking advice from a dealer.

From this description you will note that the entire burning process is completely sealed off from the interior living area of your caravan. However, it stands to reason that a fully enclosed heating appliance needs an efficient and reliable ignition system. You cannot light the burner using a match because there's no point of access. On the other hand, as long as you have the heater serviced regularly, the electronic ignition system is unlikely to give you a problem.

Fan assistance

The idea of using a built-in electric fan to help distribute warm air from a space heater was developed in the 1980s. The air is usually sent along ducts and these enable you to heat a shower room and to control temperatures in other zones where heat is needed.

In most instances there are two main ducts emerging from the rear of heaters, which in turn serve the opposite ends of a caravan. However, on occasions you find that one end of a caravan stays rather cool whereas the other end seems to get hot.

After the introduction of ducted systems and the idea of mounting a 12V fan on the rear of space heaters, manufacturers then decided that they would increase an owner's options by fitting a 230V mains heating element *within* the fan casing as well.

Then another strategy was followed in which heating elements were fitted inside the heater cabinet and adjacent to the heat exchanger. This system was followed in the Carver 4000 Fanmaster heater and also in the Truma Ultraheat.

The Whale Space Heater offers 500W, 1,000W and 2,000W settings. An additional sophistication also allows it to be operated on gas or mains electricity and is positioned underneath the caravan for added space saving inside the caravan.

Wet heating systems

A few of the more expensive caravans are fitted with 'hydronic heating' or 'wet heating' that can use both electricity and LPG as energy sources. The self-convection technology pushes warm air upwards and when it reaches the ceiling it circulates back down to the floor and is reheated. Temperature is adjusted using the Alde touch screen control panel and there is the option to download the Alde App in order to control the heating from your mobile device. The efficient Alde Compact 3020 HE system, for example, is highly regarded and has been fitted in some of the models made by Bailey, Coachman and Swift. Buccaneer are now fitting the Alde Underfloor heating system, allowing you to step out of bed onto a warm floor on a cold day.

▼ The Swift Conqueror is fitted with a panel radiator in the washroom.

▲ The Whale Space Heater has three settings and can be run on gas or electric.

▼ The Whale Space Heater is mounted underneath the caravan, maximising space inside the caravan.

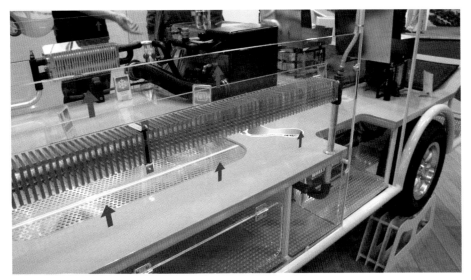

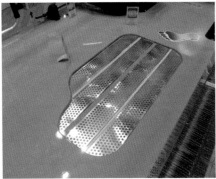

▲ *This display shows the Alde 3010 Compact heating system which uses convectors found behind the seats and beds.*

▲ *Some models of Buccaneer have Alde Underfloor heating, which works in synergy with the Alde Central Heating System, allowing you the pleasure of warm floors on a cold day.*

Water heaters

Developmental features

Not long ago, a water heater was regarded as a luxury item and few caravanners complained about the need to boil a kettle to provide washing-up water.

However, the arrival of caravan showers changed things for ever. Water heaters became commonplace and followed a similar evolutionary development to space heaters.

For example, heaters with exposed flames were deemed unacceptable more than a decade ago. In consequence, instantaneous water heaters like the Paloma or the Rinnai models are no longer fitted in British-built touring caravans. Instead, water-heating appliances that have a hot-water storage tank are the preferred choice. Since the stored water adds significant weight, some caravanning specialists advise that heaters are drained down before a 'van is towed. In practice, draining-down a tank that's full of hot water is rather wasteful so many owners disregard this suggestion.

Initially the water in an appliance's storage tanks was heated-up using a gas burner. Subsequent developments, however, saw tanks being fitted with a 230V immersion heater too. This meant that both gas and mains could be used – either as alternative fuels or together to speed-up the heating time when starting from cold.

Although some water heaters are integrated with a space-heating appliance, others are stand-alone products that include:

1. The Carver Cascade (several versions since its debut in the mid-1980s).

2. The Maxol Malaga (also made bearing the Belling badge).

3. The Truma water systems (in both 5 litre, 10 litre and 14 litre versions).

4. The Whale Expanse underfloor water heater (introduced in 2013).

Note: Fully integrated space and water heaters are usually quite heavy and tend to be fitted more often in motor caravans. However, some touring caravans have been equipped with products like the Alde 3020 and the Truma 'Combi'.

Storage water heaters

Many British caravans were fitted with a Carver Cascade water heater, and it has proved to be an excellent product. However, in 1999 Carver ceased manufacturing gas appliances for caravans.

Not that Carver's product was the only one on the market. For example, the Maxol Malaga and the Malaga E (with 230V heating element) have also been fitted into a number of caravans. Water heaters

▼ *Most water heaters are located in a bed box, like this Truma water heater.*

bearing the later name of the Belling Malaga were also fitted in the Bailey Hunter Lite range from 1997 onwards.

At present the Truma water system is the product most often fitted in UK caravans. Like the Cascade and Malaga units, Truma's water system is usually situated in a bed box with its intake and flue mounted on a side wall.

Then came the revolutionary Whale Expanse water heater in 2013, making it the first water heater to be fitted underneath the caravan, therefore saving precious storage space. It is a stand-alone dual-fuel (gas and/or electric) water heater. The outer casing is made from polypropylene, which is a lightweight and durable material, enabling it to cope with extremes in weather temperature, strong winds, corrosive road salt and water ingress. Thick insulation surrounding the tank protects it from sub-zero temperatures.

To operate these products correctly and safely you must check the manufacturer's instructions, which are usually repeated in the owner's user manual. Like any other gas appliance in a caravan, a water heater must also be serviced in accordance with its manufacturer's instructions.

Technical Tip
Draining down a
water heater

With the onset of frosty weather, it is absolutely essential that you drain off the water from a heater. This is explained in Chapter Fifteen. Apart from that, few caravanners drain-down their water heater before taking to the road, in spite of the fact that its heavy contents take up a significant part of the permitted payload. For instance, a Whale Expanse holds eight litres (1.76 gallons) thereby taking up approximately 5kg (11lb) of a caravan's payload potential. Draining the contents is undoubtedly a strategy to consider if a caravan is loaded perilously close to its payload limit.

▲ *The Whale Expanse water heater is fitted underneath the caravan, extending valuable storage space.*

▼ *When setting up, remember to remove the cover for the flue.*

Space and water heater servicing

The fact that caravan gas appliances are not used regularly throughout the year presents a problem. During storage periods it's possible that insects, moths and spiders may find their way into the air intakes or flues. In some instances, this can upset the delicate air/gas balance; it can also interfere with the ignition process. For example, it's not unusual for a pilot flame to ignite on a space heater whereas the main burner subsequently fails to fire up. This is usually caused by obstructions – even a spider's web spun around the cowl on a roof-mounted flue has been known to upset heater ignition.

This is one of several reasons why routine and regular servicing of these appliances is essential.

Barbecues

As a final comment, a few caravans have been manufactured with external gas connections mounted on a side wall. These are intended for gas-operated barbecues which are permitted on many, though not all, caravan sites. Here is another pleasure of the caravanning experience although, once again, the vigilance about individual appliances mentioned earlier should be noted.

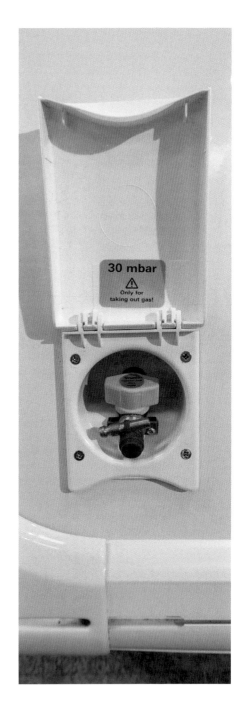

▶ *Many top-end models, like this Bailey Unicorn, have an external gas socket fitted as standard, making them ideal for barbecues.*

Chapter Fourteen

Servicing

For your peace of mind, always book in to an AWS workshop or mobile engineer to carry out your annual habitation service.

Although car owners recognise that vehicles need servicing on a regular basis, some caravan owners are surprised to learn that caravans need servicing too. For example, brake assemblies need to be periodically inspected, cleaned, and adjusted. Moreover, it is important to monitor the condition of a caravan's tyres; if they fail to meet the required standard, the owner is committing an offence. Then there's the importance of arranging routine checks of gas appliances, gas supply systems, and electrical components.

A caravan service involves several different areas of attention and the National Caravan Council advises that a standard operation would normally take four hours to carry out. The work helps ensure that a caravan is kept in good working order as a leisure home and that it's safe to use on the road. So how frequently should this operation be carried out?

Service intervals

With no mileometer in a caravan, there's no easy way of registering the distances it covers. Nor is it feasible to record the hours that a fridge or a cooker is in operation. As a rough guide, it is normally recommended that a caravan is serviced at least every 12 months, but more frequent inspections might be required if a caravan is used throughout the year. After all, the extremes of heat in summer and frost or snow in winter both take their toll.

It also seems that an increasing number of owners, especially those who have taken early retirement, are now spending several months of the year on touring trips – particularly in mainland Europe. With this pattern of frequent use, the recommendation of having a caravan serviced once a year is unlikely to be sufficient. All-important items like brakes are going to need checking and adjusting on a much more regular basis.

At the opposite extreme, the life of a caravan isn't helped if it stands unused for prolonged spells. For many mechanical components, remaining stationary is the worst thing possible. Even tyres deteriorate surprisingly quickly if the same part of the sidewalls remains flexed when a caravan is left parked and doesn't get moved. In reality, most caravans spend more time parked than being towed along the road.

Although it is generally recommended to have a caravan serviced annually, it is the owner who ultimately has to decide whether more regular attention is needed. However, don't presume that if it's seldom used, you could correspondingly extend the period between service work. Lack of use can lead to problems like brake seizure, and if body leaks develop these need identifying at once.

▼ *Some service jobs can be tackled by a practical and experienced owner but many operations call for the attention of a trained technician; specialist tools are sometimes needed too.*

Choosing a reliable service specialist

If you own a caravan that is still under warranty, its manufacturer will stipulate that it must be serviced in accordance with information given in the owner's manual and the warranty conditions.

Failure to do this is likely to invalidate the warranty. To be absolutely sure that your local caravan service specialist is authorised to carry out the work, a call to the customer helpline of a caravan manufacturer is strongly recommended. Get the manufacturer's advisers to give their approval of your chosen service provider before making a booking.

Recognising that there have been examples of poor servicing in the past, an initiative by The Camping and Caravanning Club, the Caravan & Motorhome Club and The National Caravan Council led to the establishment of a nationwide chain of Approved Service Workshops. This chain was instrumental in providing caravan owners with a list of reliable and accredited centres.

Training regimes at Approved Workshops have been improved, with the result that a customer is assured that the technician attending to their caravan has the necessary competence to carry out the work.

Before being accepted into the Approved Workshop Scheme (AWS), service centre applicants also have to undergo a lengthy and elaborate independent inspection. However, it doesn't end there, a re-examination inspection is also conducted annually. Although most workshops undertaking service work are situated at dealerships, there are accredited mobile workshops too.

At the time of writing, there are over 500

Approved Caravan Workshops

An Approved Caravan Workshop is required to:

1. Display a detailed list of prices and labour rates.

2. Provide an estimate for any additional servicing or repair work over £150.

3. Give a realistic estimated time for completion and collection.

4. Use genuine spare parts when available.

5. Always provide a checklist of work done.

6. Start work *only* when given an owner's express authority.

7. Contact a customer for authority to continue if additional work is identified.

8. Notify an owner in writing of faults that are not rectified, with an honest assessment of the urgency of the repairs.

Approved Workshops (to include both mobile and fixed base workshops) operating within the scheme and you can find your nearest centre by downloading the free Approved

Fixed workshop or mobile engineer?

Here are some considerations to take into account when deciding between a fixed workshop or mobile engineer. Before committing to either one, check that the engineer is authorised by the caravan manufacturer to carry out any warranty work.

Workshop

» The work is carried out under cover, therefore never hindered by the weather.

» There is space to keep items in stock.

» Annual service reminders help you to organise your time.

» It is your responsibility to deliver the caravan to the workshop and this may not necessarily be local.

Mobile technician

» Mobile technicians will come to where you store your caravan, whether on the driveway at home or a storage facility (check with your storage facility before making a booking).

» The technician will require 1 metre of clear space around the caravan.

» There is no need to tow your caravan to a workshop, which makes it convenient and saves on the cost of fuel.

» The process is time saving as there is no journey to and from a workshop.

Workshop Scheme App on your Android or iPhone device. Alternatively, there is both a postcode and town search facility on the website *www.approvedworkshops.co.uk*, which informs enquirers of the distance to their nearest fixed or mobile facility. Equally there are free leaflets describing Approved Workshops, which are available from the National Caravan Council. The address of the NCC is given in the Appendix.

It should be added that there are other servicing workshops which are not members of this scheme. In some instances, the standard of their workmanship is very good, in other cases it is open to conjecture.

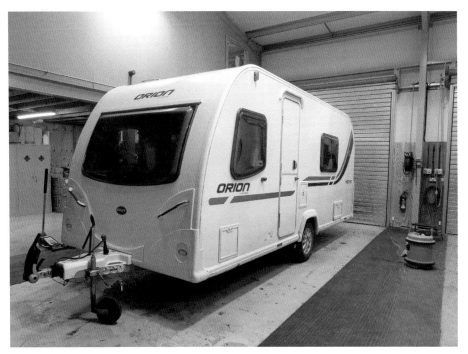

▲ Workshop services are carried out under cover, therefore protected from the elements.

▼ Mobile services are more convenient as the technicians come to you.

Servicing jobs

In a full service, around 50 jobs need to be carried out. Broadly speaking, these fall into the following areas of attention:

1. **The chassis and running gear** – which includes brake adjustment, wheel bearing checks, tyre checks, corner steady lubrication.

2. **Gas system and appliance checks** – this would include a check for leaks in the supply system. Appliances will also be switched into action and the flame pattern inspected. Depending on accessibility, the work might also include cleaning gas burners on space heaters, water heaters and so on. However, where this involves elaborate dismantling work, the servicing of individual appliances is usually treated as an 'optional extra' and priced accordingly.

3. **Electrical check** – to include road light operation, the safety of the mains supply system, operation of interior lights, etc.

4. **Water system check** – checking operation of the water pump, filter changing, and tasks like lubricating the valve seal on a toilet.

5. **Refrigerator operation check and service** – in a standard service a technician will check to see that a refrigerator is achieving cooling when running on each of its three sources of power. If you want the full refrigerator service that is recommended by its manufacturer, this will include tasks like replacing the gas jet, realigning the igniter, and cleaning the gas burner and flue. To carry this out, a fridge normally has to be taken out of a caravan and transferred to a workbench. That's why most dealers offer a full refrigerator service as an optional extra.

▼ *Lubricating the over-run assembly that moves with the coupling head can be done regularly by a competent DIY enthusiast.*

▼ *It is important to remove the brake drums in order to clean and lubricate moving parts in a brake mechanism.*

6. **Bodywork and general condition** – this important checking operation should include: a damp test, a visual inspection of sealant condition, a window operation check and so on.

7. **Fire warning system check** – to make certain that the smoke alarm and carbon monoxide alarms are working and that a fire extinguisher is within its stated date life.

▶ *The type of torque wrench needed to tighten the one-shot flanged nut holding a brake drum in place can be a costly bit of kit.*

▼ *Since the early 1990s, caravan brake drums have been held in place by a one-shot flanged nut; once it has been removed, a new one should then be fitted.*

▲ During a standard service, a new one-shot nut holding the drum in place is marked with a security paint to guard against tampering.

▼ A manometer measures gas pressure and is used to highlight any leaks in the gas supply system.

▼ All gas appliances are turned on to check that they are working properly.

▲ Many owners have a socket tester for checking a mains system; this is work included in a normal service.

▲ The Detectagas test kit enables safe and easy testing on a carbon monoxide detector to be carried out.

▼ To check for damp in a caravan, an electrical meter is used at various points around the interior. If the reading is 0-15% then there are no concerns.

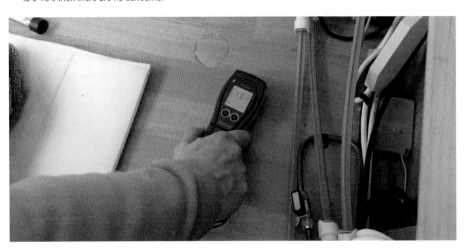

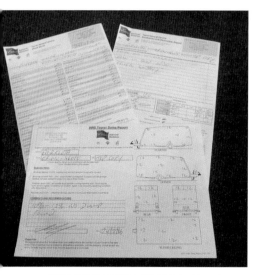

▲ *At the end of a service, it is important to get a copy of the service schedule and damp report signed, stamped and dated.*

Service schedule

As pointed out earlier, one of the aims of this book is to offer user guidance. It is not a DIY repair book, and readers who require more technical information about service operations are advised to consult *The Caravan Manual* - by John Wickersham.

Working to a strict job list is important, and when arranging to have your 'van serviced you should ask to see the centre's service schedule before confirming the booking. Equally, when the work has been completed you should be given a copy of the schedule duly signed, stamped and dated. This document should include guidance regarding the amount of wear on brake shoes, the tread left on the tyres and so on.

This point is emphasised because some so-called 'service specialists' provide customers with no documentation at all

about the work that they've carried out. Equally, there's no written advice on the condition of the brakes, tyres and so on; and no certification to verify the integrity of gas and electrical systems. Not only does this raise doubts about the thoroughness of an operation, but you also have no written evidence to state that servicing work has been carried out. Needless to say, this kind of documentation is useful when you want to sell your caravan. Look out for the AWS stickers to confirm that a caravan has been serviced by an approved workshop or mobile engineer.

Refrigerator service

It was pointed out earlier that where a refrigerator is concerned, a standard service is mainly only concerned with checking that it achieves cooling. However, manufacturers such as Dometic and Thetford recommend a more elaborate annual service as described in the earlier chapter on refrigerators. This is also covered in more depth in *The Caravan Manual* - by John Wickersham. Without doubt it is extremely inconvenient if a

▼ *The AWS sticker identifies that a caravan has been serviced in that year by an approved workshop or mobile engineer.*

Useful Tip

Having your caravan serviced regularly is strongly recommended. However, there's a problem caused by primroses, daffodils, and the delightful 'rustle of Spring'. As Easter approaches, many eager owners plan their first post-winter holiday break – only to find that the local service centre is fully booked for weeks and weeks. Be ever-mindful of the seasonal nature of this leisure pursuit and take steps to book the caravan for servicing well in advance of your first trip of the year. This is also particularly relevant if your caravan's warranty requires that a service is carried out by a particular deadline.

small items like this without a further labour charge – as long as there's time to do the job within the allotted period for carrying out the service. The cost of the component, however, has to be borne by the customer.

This raises another point to consider when arranging a service. It obviously wouldn't make sense to re-book and return your caravan to a workshop for later replacements of inexpensive components like fuses or light bulbs. However, what would be the position if a new water pump was needed? This is something to discuss when booking a service – most owners like to be consulted before a technician embarks on more costly repairs. With that in mind, you might want to agree a cost limit, so ask the service receptionist what procedure is followed if something serious emerges during the work.

fridge lets you down during an important break. So, a full refrigerator service makes good sense, even though many owners find their fridge works well for years and years without attention. However, that is no consolation if it eventually fails during a heat wave when you were enjoying a Mediterranean holiday.

Minor repairs and authorisations

When a service is carried out, it's not unusual for a technician to find items that are faulty. Perhaps one of the interior lights needs a new bulb or a fuse needs replacing. Many workshops will replace

▼ *To carry out a full service on a refrigerator, an appliance usually needs to be removed completely in order to get to the working parts.*

Chapter Fifteen

Winter lay-up and spring preparation

▲ *Autumn and winter in Britain can bring inclement weather, so protect your caravan with a breathable cover.*

Modern caravans are so well heated and insulated that they can be used at any time of the year. However, circumstances might necessitate that your caravan is laid-up for winter, in which case there will be some pre-storage tasks to carry out. Equally, when you want to recommence your travels the following spring, there are some pre-season matters to consider as well.

In Chapter Two, the subject of storage was discussed in detail. Here are some jobs that need to be carried out before you turn the key in the door, fit anti-theft devices, and possibly add a caravan cover.

Spare parts and servicing

>> **Spare parts:** Make a list of anything that was damaged during the season. If replacement items are needed, order them now. Anything from awning repairs to a light bulb should be arranged before the run-down to Christmas. Leave it until the spring and you may have to wait for weeks to receive delivery of the parts you need.

>> **Servicing:** Book a service for next spring – even if it's still only October. The 'silly season' at dealer workshops starts in earnest in February or March. Servicing 'slots' are soon filled and it's 'first come, first served'. So, think ahead and book in advance.

Pre-lay-up jobs

Indoor cleaning

>> Start with a good clean inside using a domestic vacuum cleaner that you'll probably run via your caravan's 230V supply system. Alternatively, some 12V car cleaners and rechargeable products are effective alternatives. If there's room in your house to store caravan cushions and mattresses in a dry place, so much the better. Finding a caravan with its upholstery missing is also a deterrent to thieves.

▼ *As an alternative to setting-up a 230V domestic vacuum cleaner, some owners clean their caravan with a 12V rechargeable compact appliance.*

>> Use proprietary cleaners on the stove-enamel or stainless-steel surfaces of your hob and oven. However, on plastic sinks and drainers, use the cleaning products recommended by the appliance manufacturer so that you don't abrade the surface.

>> Put plugs in the sink, the wash basin and the shower tray outlets to prevent smells infiltrating the living space from stagnant water that might be held in the waste pipe.

>> Clean out the inside of your refrigerator following the advice given in Chapter Nine. Then leave the door slightly ajar so that the interior is kept ventilated.

▲ *Some owners transfer their caravan upholstery to a warm room indoors. It also acts as a deterrent to thieves, who seldom steal caravans whose cushions are missing.*

▼ *Care needs to be taken when cleaning hobs and ovens. Use products recommended by manufacturers in the caravan industry, like Dometic.*

Failure to put plugs into the sink, basin, and shower tray means that odours from waste water pipes can get into the living area.

Outside cleaning

>> At the end of a season, it is always wise to give a caravan a good clean before putting it into store. However, busy owners and dark evenings often mean that it gets unceremoniously left. If possible, try to find time to remove the black streaks that form under external fittings. Products like Autoglym Caravan and Motorhome Cleaner are especially easy to use.

>> Dealers often use a high-pressure hose to clean caravans, and experienced operators recognise where a forceful blast of water is likely to cause damage. Unfortunately, there are inexperienced users who break plastic decals and introduce leaks – especially where sealants used under fittings and trim strips are starting to get brittle. Using a soft washer-brush on an extending pole is often considered a better way to clean a caravan.

>> As regards the parts which are hard to reach, it's often easier to apply a cleaning treatment with the help of a crank-handled brush. These products are normally used for painting the back of domestic radiators and are sold by paint merchants. You'll find that they're particularly useful for removing dead flies from the front of a caravan's roof panel.

>> Awning rail channels are notorious for attracting dirt and spiders. Use an awning rail brush to give it a really good clean.

It is very important to ventilate the fridge whilst in storage and this Thetford refrigerator has a clip to help keep the door ajar.

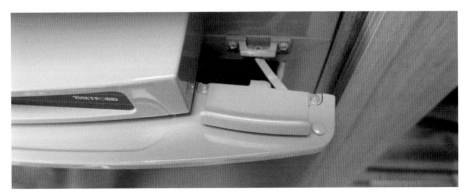

▲ Experienced users often clean a caravan with a high-pressure hose, but a powerful blast of water can sometimes introduce leaks, especially where body sealants are losing their flexibility.

▲ Always use cleaning products specifically made for caravans, like the Autoglym Caravan & Motorhome Cleaner.

▼ Many caravanners purchase a soft cleaning brush with an extending telescopic pole. These are often sold at caravan exhibitions and outdoor shows.

An awning rail brush is ideal for cleaning the awning rail channel.

>> If your water supply system is fitted with a taste filter, this is likely to retain some residual water. If that starts to freeze the expanding ice will often crack its casing. In Chapter Eight it was recommended that filters are removed before winter storage periods and that a replacement is purchased in readiness for your resumption of caravanning next season.

On lever-operated mixer-taps keep the lever central so that both hot and cold feeds are opened up.

Protecting a water system from frost damage

>> Before draining down a fresh water system, open all the taps and leave them open throughout the lay-up period.

>> On lever-operated mixer taps it's most important to keep the lever central so that both hot and cold feeds are opened up.

>> If your caravan is fitted with a Truma or Whale water heater, look for the yellow water release valve that drains off water from the unit.

>> Submersible-type water pumps sometimes retain a small quantity of water. It's recommended to shake this out as well.

▶ *If your caravan has a drain-down tap, open it to drain off water and leave it open.*

>> To avoid drain-down operations, many boat owners and American RV (Recreational Vehicle) owners prefer to add potable anti-freeze to their fresh water supply systems. This is poured into a container, pumped into the system, and left during the lay-up period. The product is not poisonous – although you wouldn't want to drink it. The water additive can also be used in stored caravans, although some water heater manufacturers, *eg* Truma, have not officially approved the use of anti-freeze in their appliances in case it reacts with seals and other components.

Avoiding frost damage

When water freezes in a pipe its volume increases by around 8.79%. If all the outlets are sealed – for instance, if none of the taps are left open – freezing water creates a serious pressure build-up in pipe sections that have not been completely emptied. Sometimes, flexible plastic hose can absorb this increase in volume without splitting, but couplings and water-operated devices often get damaged; so do some of the components in water heaters.

With the increasing popularity of lever mixer taps, it has been found that if the lever is left open in the hot-water supply position, the cold-water supply pipe may probably get damaged – and vice versa. So remember, if your caravan is fitted with this type of tap, make sure that its lever is lifted and left in its *midway* position. This precautionary measure means that both hot and cold feed pipes are then left open.

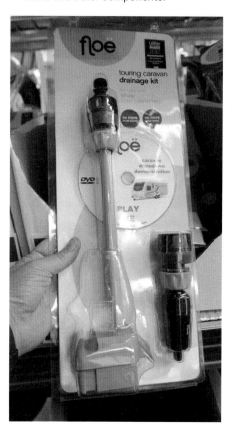

>> The Floë Water Drain-Down kit uses air to purge water from pumps, taps and pipes in order to prevent frost damage. It simply connects to a foot pump or 12/240-volt tyre compressor.

◁ *Floë uses a foot pump or 12V tyre compressor to purge water out of each tap and fitting.*

Toilet drain-down and preparation

A brief section on toilet lay-up procedures was given at the close of Chapter Eight. However, you should note these further points:

>> Leave the blade open when storing for long periods. This will prevent the blade seal from drying out.

>> Unscrew the pour out spout cap as this will ventilate the waste holding tank.

>> Ensure that the cassette tank has been emptied and cleaned before extended periods of inactivity in order to extend the product life and prevent nasty smells.

▲ *It is advisable to open the toilet blade to prevent the seal from drying out.*

▼ *Unscrew the spout cap on the toilet cassette to allow the waste holding tank to ventilate.*

▼ *Before storing for the winter, give the waste-holding tank a thorough clean using specialist products. Not only will it kill off any bugs, it will also smell better.*

▲ *Thetford Seal Lubricant is a silicone spray that protects and lubricates the rubber seal.*

>> Spray the rubber seal with either Thetford Seal Lubricant (which is a silicone spray) or rub in a little olive oil. This will prevent the rubber from drying out.

>> Empty the flush water tank by flushing the toilet until no water comes out. Alternatively, from the access locker to the toilet there should be a tube. Remove the cap, but remember to have a bucket ready to catch the water. Forgetting to do this could lead to frost damage and black grime could build up.

▼ *Forgetting to empty the flush water tank could lead to frost damage and black grime building up in the tank.*

▲ *Spiders will make their home in any nook or cranny, so close the caps on the waste water outlet and fresh water inlet.*

>> Put cap covers over both your caravan's fresh water inlet and waste outlet. Ignoring this means you are giving an open invitation to homeless spiders.

Plug and socket protection

>> The electrical coupling plug(s) on a caravan and the equivalent socket(s) on a tow car need spraying with a water-repellent product that cannot damage their plastic casing. Some sprays *do* cause damage. A particularly effective product is Tri-flow, which is designed to displace moisture, prevent rust and corrosion. It will keep brass pins/tubes clean and shiny for a long period after an application.

▲ *Spray the plugs and sockets with a water repellent product that doesn't damage their plastic casing.*

Gas cylinders

>> The wisdom of transferring gas cylinders to a safe, ventilated place was discussed in Chapter Twelve. It is also wise to tie a linen bag over the end of a coupling hose or a cylinder-mounted type of regulator to ensure that insects or spiders cannot get into the supply system.

▼ *It is often wise to remove gas cylinders from a caravan before a lay-up period, but refer to Chapter Twelve for advice about storage arrangements.*

Battery removal and charging

>> It is most important to keep a caravan's leisure battery charged throughout an extended lay-up period. The subject of charging is discussed in Chapter Eleven.

Tyres, suspension and brakes

>> Always be aware that the walls of a tyre get damaged through lack of use. To avoid storage damage, fastidious owners mount their caravan on robust axle stands and remove the wheels. This relieves the suspension as well.

>> Alternatively, you can use 'Winter wheels' which are angle-steel structures fitted in place of the normal wheels. Sometimes called 'square wheels', these stands also act as security devices; and the fact that you can then store your caravan's wheels in a garage means the tyres are rested and kept away from sunlight. However, 'Winter wheels' don't relieve the suspension – you need a pair of axle stands to achieve that objective.

>> As long as a caravan is parked on level ground, the wheels are chocked, and there is no risk at all of it running away, it's best to leave a hand-brake completely OFF. This means that any developing rust in the drum mechanisms won't leave the brakes well and truly ON.

▸ *If you can securely chock the wheels and there is no possibility of a caravan starting to move, it is beneficial to leave its handbrake off during a prolonged storage period.*

▼ *It is often best to transfer a battery to a bench for periodic charging during a long lay-up period, as described in Chapter Eleven.*

▼ *If a caravan is left unmoved for an extended spell, cracks and general weakening can seriously affect the sidewalls of tyres.*

Further measures

Other jobs may also be listed in your caravan owner's manual. Check this with care, because some of its appliances might be different from those discussed in this chapter. There is also a dilemma with regard to curtains and roller blinds. For example, it doesn't make sense to leave the interior of a stored caravan on view to passers-by, so many owners draw the curtains and close the roller blinds. This also helps prevent the interior fabrics from fading.

However, the manufacturers of roller blinds fitted with a recoil device point out that if they're left closed for extended periods, their recoil springs get weakened and lose their effectiveness. Although a 'tired' spring can be tightened, it is often difficult to reach its adjusting device. This might suggest that only the curtains should be drawn during a lay-up period – accepting that these might fade as well. All in all, owners have to make their own decision on the matter; some resolve the dilemma by

▲ *Damp traps are ideal for capturing any moisture in the air and preventing build-up of mould.*

▼ *During a long storage period it seems logical to close a caravan's roller blinds, but this often leads to a weakening of their recoil springs.*

▲ *If a leak is suspected a plastic cover might give short-term protection, but condensation will form on the underside of impervious materials.*

purchasing a caravan cover instead.

Placing a moisture trap inside the caravan during winter storage will help to prevent condensation, eliminate musty smells, mould, damp patches and wood rot. Simple damp traps that use absorbent crystals will help to capture any condensation.

Caravan covers

If you park a caravan for a long period, it is certainly going to get dirty, especially if left near trees. There are also owners who suspect that leaks might be developing and their response is to purchase a plastic cover sheet. This might offer a short-term solution pending proper repairs, but an impervious plastic 'tarpaulin' also seals in residual damp, and condensation

subsequently forms on the underside. This prompted the manufacture of tailor-made covers that are made from a 'breathable' fabric. Depending on the product, these are reasonably waterproof, but there's often the possibility of rainwater seeping through their stitched seams. Also be aware that covers are effective at keeping a caravan roof free of dirt, bird droppings and algae, although this might mean that a fabric's 'breathable pores' eventually get blocked with airborne dust.

Recognising that storing a caravan indoors is usually costly, a good quality, model-specific caravan cover is often a logical purchase. However, it should only be fitted to a dust-free, clean caravan otherwise the paintwork and windows will get abrasion damage as soon as there's a strong wind. Equally, any sharp projections need protecting before a cover is fitted. Secure straps are essential too. The accompanying illustrations draw attention to these issues.

Pre-season jobs

Before setting off after a winter lay-up, you need to get everything working again.

>> When parked near trees, caravans often get covered with green algae. Don't be too distressed if you go to collect a caravan from an outdoor storage compound and find it stained and dirty.

>> A good wash is usually needed and some owners do this using a high-pressure hose. However, as mentioned earlier, great care is needed. On its more powerful setting and used too close to a caravan, a pressure hose can blast away sealant from panel junctions, damage acrylic windows and decals.

▲ *Caravans usually have several sharp projections that can cause a cover to tear. Good products are supplied with protective buffers and materials.*

▼ *After parking a caravan near trees a coating of green algae looks dreadful, but it can usually be removed with careful cleaning.*

▼ *This is not a job to tackle in breezy weather and a helper is usually needed. On many caravans a broomstick handle helps as well.*

>> A soft hand brush is useful for removing spiders and their webs. There's also a purpose-made stiffened brush supplied by Towsure that cleans out awning channels too.

>> If the acrylic windows sustained scratches through windy weather and nearby branches, Fenwick's Windowize is a great product designed to reinstate their condition.

>> Products like Autoglym Polish will remove any dull patches on your caravan exterior. Polishing products have a cleaning action in them, which is used to correct the oxidisation that occurs as a result of UV damage. Realistically it only needs to be done once a year.

▲ *Spiders often take refuge in awning rail channels, so give them a good clean.*

>> Underfloor spare wheel carriers often get rusted up and it's regrettable that a carrier's telescopic tubing is seldom checked and lubricated during a caravan service.

▼ *It's good practice to clean your caravan prior to the start of a new caravanning season.*

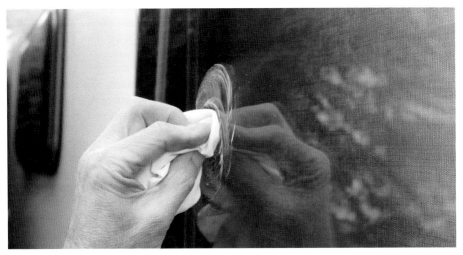

▲ *Fenwick's Windowize is very effective at removing scratches from acrylic windows.*

» Set up the water system and try it out before leaving home. It might be worth giving the fresh and waste water pipes a good clean.

» You'll also want to check fridge operation, the gas cooker and so on, especially if you couldn't get your caravan serviced because the local dealer was busy.

▼ *Oxidisation is a process where the sun's UV rays damage the paintwork and cause a bloom (dull patches). Giving your caravan a good polish will help maintain its shiny good looks.*

▼ *Using a steriliser and cleaner, prepare the cleaning solution and pour into the fresh water tank/ container. Open all the taps to draw the mixture through the pipes and allow to run down the waste pipes. Always check the product is safe to use in the fresh water tank/container.*

» Check the wheel fixings before departing on your travels using a torque wrench. Refer to your caravan manual for torque settings.

» Add to this a tyre-pressure check – not forgetting the spare – and you're well on the way.

As the summer season approaches once again, every best wish with your continuing caravanning adventures!

Photo courtesy of Bailey of Bristol

Appendix

A The national clubs for caravanners

The two principal caravan clubs have very large memberships and a long history. When they were formed around a hundred years ago, their activities and objectives were very different, but nowadays the services to members are much the same.

Membership benefits are wide-ranging and both clubs own and run some excellent sites. Some are for members only, whereas others admit non-members, albeit with an additional surcharge. In addition, both clubs provide excellent guidebooks which list privately owned sites of all sizes, including hundreds of small venues licensed to accept no more than 5 caravans at a time.

Insurance schemes, holiday booking services, monthly magazines, technical advice, and popular towing and caravan ownership courses are offered by both clubs. Equally there are regional groups whose committees arrange local functions to supplement the clubs' national events.

So, send for literature and decide if you'd prefer to join The Camping & Caravanning Club or the Caravan & Motorhome Club. Some owners cannot make up their mind so join both! The Clubs' addresses are given in the accompanying list.

B Owners' clubs

At the time of writing, there are around 50 clubs devoted to particular makes of caravan, together with specialist associations like the Historic Caravan Club and other formally constituted bodies catering for particular groups of people. If you would like to learn more about these organisations, the addresses of club secretaries are periodically listed in caravanning magazines.

Needless to say, clubs catering for owners of particular makes of caravan are extremely valuable if you want spare parts and your 'van is no longer being manufactured. Members show great brand loyalty and usually arrange a programme of social events. Moreover, it's not unusual to find representatives occupying small stands provided by existing manufacturers at major indoor caravan exhibitions such as the Caravan, Camping & Motorhome Show held every February at the National Exhibition Centre, Birmingham.

C The National Caravan Council

The NCC, to use its well-known acronym, was established as the UK trade body representing the four sectors of the UK industry, namely: Touring Caravans, Motor Caravans, Caravan Holiday-Homes and Residential Park Homes. Whilst its main reason for existence is to serve its fee-paying trade members, the NCC runs many schemes which help individual caravanners.

In particular the NCC Approval Badge displayed on most UK-manufactured caravans confirms that the product complies with the relevant British or European Standards or Industry Code of Practice, together with UK laws. Other initiatives include The Approved Workshop Scheme (AWS), Caravan Registration and Identification Scheme (CRiS), VIN Chip and TowCheck.

D Continental travel booking agencies

This handbook provides guidance about using a caravan, however there's no reason why you should restrict your touring to the UK. In fact, taking your caravan around Europe is not as daunting as many imagine. Nevertheless, many caravanners find that to reduce the amount of pre-holiday 'paper-work', it's worthwhile entrusting the booking arrangements to one of the specialist agencies. Both the national clubs run ferry and site booking services, as well as specialists like: Eurocamp Independent, and The Alan Rogers' Booking Service.

If you decide to travel in Europe during the low season, there are schemes whereby you can camp with a big discount on more than 3,000 campsites in Europe. You can save up to 60% per night with the CampingCard ACSI scheme.

E Address list of key accessory suppliers

Please note: *This address list was correct at the time of going to press. It includes specialist suppliers and manufacturers whose products and services have been mentioned in this book.*

ACSI
Geurdeland 9
Andelst 6673 DR
Netherlands
Tel: +31 (0)488 471434
www.campingcard.co.uk
(CampingCard ACSI)

Adria Concessionaires
Unit 2 Drury Drive
Woodhall Business Park
Sudbury
Suffolk CO10 1WH
Tel: 01787 888980
www.adria.co.uk
(Adria caravans)

Alan Rogers Travel Ltd
Spelmonden Old Oast
Goudhurst
Kent TN17 1HE
Tel: 01580 214051
www.alanrogers.com
(Guides listing inspected, high quality campsites)

Alde International (UK) Ltd
Huxley Close
Park Farm South
Wellingborough
Northamptonshire NN8 6AB
Tel: 01933 677765
www.alde.co.uk
(Central heating systems, Gas leak detector)

AL-KO Kober Ltd
South Warwickshire Business Park
Kineton Road
Southam
Warwickshire CV47 0AL
Tel: 01926 818500
www.alko-tech.com
(Chassis, running gear, security, stabilisers, wheel carriers)

Alpine Electronics (UK)
Earl Place Business Park
Alpine House
Fletchamstead Highway
Coventry CV4 9TW
Tel: 0345 313 1660
www.alpine.co.uk
(Rear-view cameras, mobile media products)

Approved Workshop Scheme
74-76 Catherine House
Victoria Road
Aldershot
Hampshire GU11 1SS
Tel: 01252 796055
www.approvedworkshops.co.uk
(Fixed and Mobile Workshop Finder)

Aten Lighting
Unit 14 North Street
Melton Mowbray
LE13 1NL
Tel: 01664 569457
www.atenlighting.co.uk
(LED lighting)

Aquaroll & Wastemaster
F L Hitchman Limited
46 The Trading Estate
Ditton Priors
Bridgnorth WV16 6SS
Tel: 01746 712242
www.aquaroll.com
(Aquaroll & Wastemaster retailer)

Autoglym
Works Road
Letchworth Garden City
Hertfordshire SG6 1NW
Tel: 01462 677766
www.autoglym.com
(Caravan and car interior/exterior cleaning products)

Avondale Coachcraft Ltd
(Ceased manufacturing caravans in 2008)

Bailey Caravans Ltd
South Liberty Lane
Bristol BS3 2SS
Tel: 0117 966 5967
www.baileyofbristol.co.uk
(Manufacturer of Bailey caravans)

Bags & Covers Direct Ltd
Thornes Lane Wharf
Wakefield
West Yorkshire WF1 5RF
Tel: 01924 565230
www.bagsandcoversdirect.co.uk
(Storage bags, tow hitch covers, padded TV bags, bike covers)

BCA Leisure Ltd
Unit H8
Premier Way
Lowfields Business Park
Elland
North Yorkshire HX5 9HF
Tel: 01422 376977
www.bcagroup.co.uk
(Trade supplier of Powerpart mains kits; see Pennine Leisure)

Belfield Furnishings Ltd
Furnace Road
Ilkeston
Derbyshire DE7 5EP
Tel: 0115 907 1791
www.belfielddirect.com
(Fixed and Mobile Workshop Finder)

Bessacarr Caravans – See The Swift Group

Blue Bio biological toilet fluid – See Sail and Trail

BPW Ltd
Centurion Way
Meridian Business Park
Leicester LE19 1WH
Tel: 0116 281 6100
www.bpw.co.uk
(BPW chassis)

Bolon Carpets for awnings – See Isabella International Camping

Brink UK Ltd
Nova Leisure
Century Park
Ballin Road
Nuneaton
Warwickshire CV10 9GA
www.brink.eu
(Towbars)

British Car Auctions
Tel: 0344 875 3480
www.bca.co.uk
(Caravan auctions)

Buccaneer Caravans - See Elddis

Bulldog Security Products Ltd
Units 1-4 Stretton Road,
Much Wenlock
Shropshire TF13 6DH
Tel: 01952 728171
www.bulldogsecure.com
(Bulldog stabilisers, SSK stabiliser importer, security devices)

C.A.K. Tanks - See Caravan Accessories

Cadac UK
Unit 14 Deanfield Court
Link 59 Business Park
Clitheroe
Lancashire BB7 1QS
Tel: 0333 200 0363
www.cadacinternational.com
(Quality barbecues)

Calor Gas Ltd
Athena Drive
Tachbrook Park
Warwick CV34 6RL
Tel: 0800 662 663
www.calor.co.uk
(Supplier of butane, propane and LPG appliances)

Calvers Caravan Storage
Woodlands Park
Bedford Road
Clapham
Bedford MK41 6EJ
Tel: 01234 359584
www.calverscaravanstorage-bedford.co.uk
(Indoor and outdoor caravan storage)

The Camping & Caravanning Club
Greenfields House
Westwood Way
Coventry CV4 8JH
Tel: 024 7647 5448
www.campingandcaravanningclub.co.uk

Campingaz
Coleman UK Inc.
The Courtyard
Wraxhall Hill
Wraxhall
Bristol BS48 1NA
Tel: 01275 845024
www.campingaz.com
(Supplier of Campingaz butane and LPG appliances)

Camping in the Forest
Greenfields House
Westwood Way
Coventry CV4 8JH
Tel: 024 7642 3008
www.campingintheforest.co.uk
(Campsites in the forest in partnership with The Camping and Caravanning Club and Forestry Locations)

Caravan Accessories (CAK Tanks) Ltd
Aqua House
Princes Drive Industrial Estate
Kenilworth
Warwickshire CV8 2FD
Tel: 0844 414 2324
www.caktanks.co.uk
(Water, gas, and electrical accessories)

Caravan Finder
11a Deben Mill Business Centre
Old Maltings Approach
Woodbridge
Suffolk IP12 1BL
Tel: 01394 610061
www.caravanfinder.co.uk
(Buy & Sell caravans)

Caravan & Motorhome Club
East Grinstead House
East Grinstead
West Sussex RH19 1UA
Tel: 01342 326944
www.caravanclub.co.uk

Caravan Panels Ltd
Unit 7 Willacy Yard
Bay Horse Lane
Catforth
Preston
Lancashire PR4 0JD
Tel: 01772 691929
www.caravanpanels.com
(Replica caravan panels in GRP)

The Caravan Repair Centre
Unit 3A Gilchrist Thomas Industrial Estate
Blaenavon
Torfaen NP4 9RL
Tel: 01495 792700
www.caravanrepaircentre.net
(Specialist breakers supplying caravan
products)

The Caravan and Boat Seat Cover Centre
Block 11 Cater Business Park
Cater Road
Bishopsworth
Bristol BS13 7TW
Tel: 0117 941 0222
www.cbscc.co.uk
(Re-upholsterer, loose covers, and foam
supplier)

Caravan Storage Site Owners' Association
(CaSSOA)
Market Square House
St James Street
Nottingham NG1 6FG
Tel: 0843 216 5802
www.cassoa.co.uk
(Register of approved caravan storage sites)

Carcoon Storage Systems Int. Ltd
Orchard Mill
2 Orchard Street
Salford
Manchester M6 6FL
Tel: 0161 737 9690
www.carcoon.com
(Trickle battery charger: Mail Order)

Carlight Caravans
(Ceased manufacturing caravans in 2004)

CEC Plug-In-Systems
(Contact your caravan dealer)

Clesse UK Ltd
Drakes Broughton Business Park
Worcester Road
Drakes Broughton
Pershore
Worcestershire WR10 2AG
Tel: 01905 842020
www.clesse.co.uk
(LP gas regulators and equipment)

Coachman Caravan Co Ltd
Amsterdam Road
Sutton Field Industrial Estate
Hull HU7 0XF
Tel: 01482 839737
www.coachman.co.uk
(Manufacturers of Coachman caravans)

Colapz
3 Ludgate Drive
East Bridgford
Nottingham NG13 8NW
Tel: 0115 727 0496
www.colapz.co.uk
(Buckets, watering cans, flexible pipes)

Compass Caravans Ltd – See Elddis

CRiS
PO Box 445
Aldershot GU11 9FS
Tel: 0203 282 1000
www.cris.co.uk
(Caravan Registration & Identification Scheme)

Dometic Group
Dometic House
The Brewery
Blandford St Mary
Dorset DT11 9LS
Tel: 0844 626 0133
www.dometic.com
(Formerly Electrolux Leisure, amalgamated with WAECO in 2007: Air conditioners, refrigerators, windows, cookers)

Dorema Awnings
Pioneer Way
Castleford
West Yorkshire WF10 5QU
Tel: 01977 555215
www.dorema.co.uk
(Caravan awnings and sun canopies)

Duvalay
Camtex House
Quarry Road
Gomersal
West Yorkshire BD19 4HX
Tel: 01274 877200
www.duvalay.co.uk
(Sleeping bags, pillows and mattress toppers)

Eberspächer UK
Climate House
Yeoman Road
Ringwood
Hampshire BH24 3FA
Tel: 01425 480151
www.eberspaecher.co.uk
(Diesel space heating systems for caravans)

EECO Caravan Windows Ltd
Exhaust Ejector Co Ltd
Wade House Road
Shelf
Nr. Halifax
West Yorkshire HX3 7PE
Tel: 01274 679524
www.eeco-ltd.co.uk
(Replacement acrylic windows made to order)

Elddis Caravans (Formerly the Explorer Group)
Erwin Hymer Group UK Ltd
Delves Lane
Consett
Co Durham DH8 7PE
Tel: 0371 964 2113
(Manufacturer of Buccaneer, Crown, Elddis, and Compass models)

Electrical Contractors Association (ECA)
Rotherwick House
3 Thomas More Street
London E1W 1YZ
Tel: 020 7313 4800
www.eca.co.uk
(Mains supply system inspection)

Electrolux Appliances – See Dometic Group

Elsan Ltd
Elsan House Bellbrook Park
Uckfield
East Sussex TN22 1QF
Tel: 01825 748200
www.elsan.co.uk
(Manufacturer of toilets and chemicals)

E&P Hydraulics
Unit 10 Elder Court
Lions Drive
Blackburn
Lancashire BB1 2EQ
Tel: 01254 297785
www.ep-hydraulics.co.uk
(Levelling system)

Explorer Caravans – See Elddis

Farécla Products Ltd
Broadmeads
Ware
Hertfordshire SG12 9HS
Tel: 01920 465041
www.farecla.com
(Caravan Pride acrylic window scratch remover and GRP surface renovator)

Fenwick's - available from most caravan accessory shops
(Caravan cleaning and care products)

Fiamma
Arleigh International Ltd
Units 1-5 Century Park
Ballin Road
Nuneaton
Warwickshire CV10 9GA
Tel: 02476 390129
www.fiamma.com
(Caravan accessories, bike racks, security and ventilation)

F.L. Hitchman
Unit 46 The Trading Estate
Ditton Priors
Bridgnorth
Shropshire WV16 6SS
Tel: 01746 712242
www.aquaroll.com
(Suppliers of portable water containers and cleaning chemicals)

Fleetwood Caravans
(Ceased manufacturing caravans in 2009)

FFC (Foam for Comfort) Ltd
Unit 2 Wyther Lane Industrial Estate
Wyther Lane
Kirkstall
Leeds LS5 3BT
Tel: 0113 274 8100
www.foamforcomfort.co.uk
(New foam supplier, composite bonded foam specialist)

Gaslow International
Unit 12 Castle Business Park
Pavilion Way
Loughborough
Leicestershire LE11 5GW
Tel: 01509 377377
www.gaslowdirect.com
(Refillable gas systems, Gaslow gauges, regulators, couplings and components)

Gas Safe Register™
PO Box 6804
Basingstoke RG24 4NB
Tel: 0800 408 5500
www.gassaferegister.co.uk
(The official industry stamp for gas safety, replacing CORGI)

General Ecology Europe
Worth Corner Business Centre
Turners Hill Road
Pound Hill
Crawley
Sussex RH10 7SL
Tel: 01293 400644
www.purewateronline.co.uk
(Nature Pure Ultrafine water purifier)

Grangers International Ltd
Enterprise Way
Duckmanton
Chesterfield
Derbyshire S44 5FD
Tel: 01773 521521
www.grangers.co.uk
(Awning proofing and cleaning products)

Grayston Engineering Ltd
115 Roebuck Road
Chessington
Surrey KT9 1EU
Tel: 020 8974 1122
www.grayston.biz
(Trade supplier of tow car spring assister kits)

Hawke House Ltd
Unit E1 Heritage Business Park
Heritage Way
Gosport
Hampshire PO12 4BG
Tel: 02392 588588
www.hawkehouse.co.uk
(Cut-from-roll Vent Air-Mat; mattress anti-condensation underlay)

Honda (UK)
Cain Road
Binfield
Bracknell
Berkshire RG12 1HL
Tel: 0345 200 8000
www.honda.co.uk
(Portable leisure generators)

Isabella Awnings
Isabella House
Drakes Farm
Drakes Drive
Long Crendon
Buckinghamshire HP18 9BA
Tel: 01844 202099
www.isabella.net
(Awnings, Isabella product alteration service and reproofing)

Jonic UK Ltd
Eastgate
White Lund Industrial Estate
Morecombe
Lancashire LA3 3DY
Tel: 01524 844106
www.jonic-uk.co.uk
(Memory foam, fitted sheets, mattress protectors, duvets)

Kenlowe Ltd
Burchetts Green Road
Burchetts Green
Maidenhead
Berkshire SL6 6QU
Tel: 01628 823303
www.kenlowe.com
(Radiator cooling fans and automatic transmission oil coolers)

Khyam Awnings
Unit 2c Chartwell Point
Wigston LE18 2FT
www.khyam.co.uk
(Quick-erect awnings)

Knott (UK) Ltd – See Miriad Products Ltd
Europa House
Second Avenue
Centrum 100
Burton upon Trent
Staffordshire DE14 2WF
Tel: 01283 531541
www.knottuk.com
(Trailer Components & Accessories)

Labcraft Ltd
Thunderley Barns
Thaxted Road
Wimbish
Saffron Walden
Essex CB10 2UT
Tel: 01799 513434
www.labcraft.co.uk
(Lighting and 12V products)

Lock 'n' Level
60 Knaves Hill
Linslade
Leighton Buzzard
Bedfordshire LU7 2UD
Tel: 01525 375271
www.locknlevel.co.uk
(Levelling system)

Lunar Caravans Ltd
East Bay
Channel Way Business Park
Channel Way
Preston
Lancashire PR2 2YA
Tel: 01772 337628
www.lunarcaravans.com
(Manufacturer of Lunar caravans)

Mark Caravan Medic
Tel: 07807 244 480
www.markcaravanmedic.co.uk
(Mobile caravan servicing and repair engineer)

Marlec Engineering Co Ltd
Rutland House
Trevithick Road
Corby
Northamptonshire NN17 5XY
Tel: 01536 201588
www.marlec.co.uk
(Wind and solar systems)

Magnum Motorhomes & Caravan Supplies
Unit 4 Cosalt Industrial Estate
Convamore Road
Grimsby DN32 9JL
Tel: 01472 353520
www.magnummotorhomes.co.uk
(Caravan surplus stock)

MA-VE
Unit 11 Aynsley Mill
Portland Works
Sutherland Road
Longton
Staffordshire ST3 1HH
Tel: 01782 330897
www.ma-ve.co.uk
(Levelling system)

Maypole Ltd,
Woodgate Business Park
162 Clapgate Lane
Birmingham
West Midlands B32 3DE
Tel: 0121 270 4301
www.maypoleltd.co.uk
(Towing accessories, electrical items)

Maxview Ltd
Grange Lane
Setchey
King's Lynn
Norfolk PE33 0AT
Tel: 01553 813300
www.maxview.co.uk
(Maxview TV dishes/aerials)

Mer Auto Shine Technologie
Broadmeads
Ware
Hertfordshire SG12 9HS
Tel: 01920 465041
www.merproducts.com
(Caravan cleaners and polish)

Milenco Outlet
Benedict Court
Southern Avenue
Leominster HR6 0QF
Tel: 01568 620444
www.milenco-outlet.co.uk
(Towing mirrors, ramps, steps, security locks)

Miriad Products Ltd
Park Lane
Dove Valley Park
Foston
South Derbyshire DE65 5BG
Tel: 01283 586060
www.miriad-products.com
(Accessories, UK distributor of Knott running gear & BPW chassis)

Morco Products Ltd
Morco House
Riverview Road
Beverley HU17 0LD
Tel: 01482 325456
www.morcoproducts.co.uk
(Instantaneous Water Heaters)

The National Caravan Council
Catherine House
Victoria Road
Aldershot
Hampshire GU11 1SS
Tel: 01252 318251
www.thencc.org.uk

**National Inspection Council for Electrical
Installation Contracting
(NICEIC)**
Warwick House
Houghton Hall Park
Houghton Regis
Dunstable LU5 5ZX
Tel: 0333 015 6625
www.niceic.com
*(Independent voluntary body for electrical
installation matters)*

National Trailer and Towing Association
PO Box 377
Worksop
Notts S80 9GN
Tel: 07498 311739
www.ntta.co.uk
*(Trade Association for all aspects of towing
and equipment)*

Nikwax
Unit F Durgates Industrial Estate
Wadhurst
East Sussex TN5 6DF
Tel: 01892 786410
www.nikwax.com
(Awning proofing products)

Paintseal Direct
38-40 Monsom Lane
Repton
Derbyshire DE65 6FX
Tel: 01283 703777
www.paintsealdirect.com
(Ceramic paint and fabric protection)

PCT Automotive Ltd
Holbrook Industrial Estate
Holbrook
Sheffield S20 3GH
Tel: 0114 251 1000
www.pctautomotive.com
*(Towbar manufacturers and towing
electrics)*

Pennine Leisure Supplies
Unit 2 Copley Valley Business Park
Copley Valley Road
Sowerby Bridge HX6 2WA
Tel: 01422 313455
www.plsgroup.co.uk
*(Wholesaler of Accessories and BCA
Powerpart products)*

Plug-In-Systems
(Contact your caravan dealer)

Powerpart electrical accessories – See
Pennine Leisure Supplies

Powrtouch Movers
Dove Valley Park
Foston
Derbyshire DE65 5BG
Tel: 01283 587900
www.powrtouch.com
(Caravan motorised movers)

Propex Heating and Leisure Ltd
Unit 10 Carvers Industrial Estate
Ringwood
Hampshire BH24 1JS
Tel: 0333 0110 488
www.propexheatsource.co.uk
(Space heaters and Malaga Water heaters)

Pro-Tec Covers,
Unit 3A, Marr Tree Business Park
Bowling Back Lane
Bradford BD4 8TP
Tel: 01274 780088
www.pro-teccovers.co.uk
(Breathable, model specific caravan covers)

Remis UK
(Caravan blinds – Order through dealer)

Regal Furnishings Ltd
Unit 3-4 18a Merlin Way
Quarry Hill Industrial Estate
Ilkeston
Derbyshire DE7 4RA
Tel: 0115 932 9988
www.regalfurnishings.co.uk
(Re-upholstery and re-foam service)

Reich UK
Unit 7 Miras Business Estate
Lower Keys
Hednesford
Staffordshire WS12 2FS
Tel: 01543 459243
www.reich-web.com
(Importer of motorised movers and accessories)

Right Connections UK Ltd
503 Queensway Business Park
Queensway
Hadley
Telford
Shropshire TF1 7UL
Tel: 01952 608750
www.rightconnections.co.uk
(Towbar vehicle-specific wiring kits)

RoadPro Ltd
3 Egerton Close
Drayton Fields Industrial Estate
Daventry
Northamptonshire NN11 8PE
Tel: 01327 312233
www.roadpro.co.uk
(Suppliers of chargers, inverters, satellite TV systems, electrical accessories)

Sail and Trail
The Old Barn
Newton House Farm
Main Street
Newton
Nottingham NG13 8HN
Tel: 0800 009 6944
www.sailandtrail.co.uk
(Mail Order: Blue BIO toilet fluids and leisure products)

Sargent Electrical Services Ltd
Unit 39 Tokenspire Business Park
Woodmansey
Beverley
Hull HU17 0TB
Tel: 01482 881655
www.sargentltd.co.uk
(Electrical control systems and low voltage panels)

Seaflo
Unit 10 Waterfall Trading Estate
Waterfall Lane
Cradley Heath
West Midlands B64 6PU
Tel: 0121 559 8580
www.seaflo-uk.com
(Evaporative Air Cooler)

Seitz products – See Dometic

Ship Shape Bedding
Ludham Road Business Park
Catfield
Norfolk NR29 5PY
Tel: 03704 464 233
www.shipshapebedding.co.uk
(Cut-from-roll DRY Mat™ Anti-condensation mattress underlay)

Shurflo Ltd
5 Sterling Park
Gatwick Road
Crawley
West Sussex RH10 9QT
Tel: 01293 424000
www.shurflo.com
(Shurflo diaphragm water pumps)

The Society of Motor Manufacturers and Traders
71 Great Peter Street
Westminster
London SW1P 2BN
Tel: 020 7235 7000
www.smmt.co.uk
(Publishers of SMMT booklet Towing and the Law)

Solar Solutions
Unit 46 Bailie Gate
Sturminster Marshall
Wimborne
Dorset BH21 4DB
Tel: 01258 268010
www.solarsolutionsltd.co.uk
(Solar panel accessories)

Sold Secure
1 Prospect Park
Valley Drive
Rugby
Warwickshire CV21 1TF
Tel: 01327 264687
www.soldsecure.com
(Test house conducting security device testing)

Specialised Accessories
Riverdale House
Dockfield Road
Shipley
West Yorkshire BD17 7AD
Tel: 01943 864646
www.specialisedcovers.com
(Breathable, model specific caravan covers)

Swift Group Ltd
Dunswell Road
Cottingham
Hull HU16 4JX
Tel: 01482 847332
www.swiftgroup.co.uk
(Manufacturer of Bessacarr, Sprite & Swift caravans)

The 12Volt Planet
Unit 22a Monument Business Park
Warpsgrove Lane
Oxford OX44 7RW
Tel: 01865 236446
www.12voltplanet.co.uk
(Mail order of twelve-volt electrical components)

Thetford (UK)
Unit 6 Brookfields Way
Manvers
Rotherham S63 5DL
Tel: 01709 766750
www.thetford-europe.com
(Refrigerators, toilets and treatments, cooking appliances)

Totalcool 12V Cooling System
1 Pond Barn Blackridge Farm
Twitter Lane
Clitheroe
Lancashire BB7 3LQ
Tel: 01200 423109
www.totalcool.co.uk
(Evaporative cooling system)

Towing Electrics Ltd
Unit 3L Moss Industrial Estate
Woodbine Street East
Rochdale
Lancashire OL16 5LB
Tel: 01706 638065
www.towingelectrics.co.uk
(Caravan and Towing relays)

Towsure Products Ltd
151-183 Holme Lane
Hillsborough
Sheffield S6 4JR
Tel: 0114 250 3045
www.towsure.com
(Accessory supplier and towbar manufacturer)

Towing Solutions Ltd
The Old Dyehouse
London Road Terrace
Macclesfield
Cheshire SK11 7RN
Tel: 01625 433251
www.towing-solutions.co.uk
(Complete towing installation service, Publisher of 'How to Pass the Towing Test: B+E explained')

Trav-L-Cool water-evaporative air conditioner – See CAK

Truma Ltd
Dove Valley Park
Foston
South Derbyshire DE65 5BG
Tel: 01283 587900
www.trumauk.com
(Space and water heating systems, gas components, water systems, air conditioning unit, caravan mover)

Tyron UK
Castle Business Park
Pavilion Way
Loughborough
Leicestershire LE11 5GW
Tel: 01509 377677
www.tyron.co.uk
(Tyron Safety Bands)

VanMaster Touring Homes Ltd
Rickath Farm
Ackhurst Lane
Orrell
Wigan WN5 0LW
Tel: 01942 212194
www.vanmastercaravans.co.uk
(VanMaster caravans)

Vanroyce Caravans
(No longer in manufacture)

Varta Automotive Batteries Ltd
Clarios UK Limited
Suite 5 Building 6
Croxley Green Business Park
Hatters Lane
Watford WD18 8YR
Tel: 01895 515650
www.varta-automotive.com
(Gel-type, non-spill leisure batteries)

Ventair mattress underlay – See Hawke House Marine

Ventura caravan awnings – See Isabella International Camping

V & G Caravans
107 Benwick Road
Whittlesey
Peterborough
Cambridgeshire PE7 2HD
Tel: 01733 350580
www.vandgcaravans.co.uk
(Replacement replica panels in GRP)

Vision Plus
Finch Close
Lenton Lane Industrial Estate
Nottingham NG7 2NN
Tel: 0115 986 7151
www.visionplus.co.uk
(Status TV aerials, Flat Screen TV and accessories)

W4 Ltd
Unit B Ford Lane Industrial Estate
Arundel
West Sussex BN18 0DF
Tel: 01243 553355
www.w4limited.com
(Suppliers of 230V kits, socket testers and ribbon sealants)

WAECO International - See Dometic
(Battery chargers, inverters and electrical accessories)

Watling Engineers Ltd
88 Park Street
Frogmore
St. Albans
Hertfordshire AL2 2LR
Tel: 01727 873661
www.watling-towbars.co.uk
(Designer/manufacturer/fitter of towing brackets)

Webasto Products UK
Webasto House
White Rose Way
Doncaster
Carr
South Yorkshire DN4 5JH
Tel: 01302 322232
www.webasto.com
(Water evaporative air conditioners)

Whale Pumps
Munster Simms Engineering Ltd
2/2A Enterprise Road
Bangor
Co Down BT19 7TA
Northern Ireland
Tel: 028 9127 0531
www.whalepumps.com
(Whale water pumps, water & space heating, plumbing, taps and showers)

Winterhoff coupling head stabilisers - See
Miriad Products Ltd and BPW Ltd

Witter Towbars
6-11 Drome Road
Deeside Industrial Park
Deeside CH5 2NY
Tel: 01244 459568
www.witter-towbars.co.uk
(Towbar systems and cycle carriers)

Zippo UK Ltd
The Barley Mow Centre
10 Barley Mow Passage
Chiswick
London W4 4PH
Tel: 020 8964 0666
www.zippo.co.uk
(General purpose large-size gas lighters)

Index

"Life is a journey of discovery."
Photo courtesy of Bailey of Bristol